DAY HIKING
Mount
Rainier

DAY HIKING

Mount Rainier

2nd edition

national park · crystal mountain
cayuse and chinook passes

Tami Asars

MOUNTAINEERS
BOOKS

MOUNTAINEERS BOOKS is the publishing division of The Mountaineers, an organization founded in 1906 and dedicated to the exploration, preservation, and enjoyment of outdoor and wilderness areas.

1001 SW Klickitat Way, Suite 201 • Seattle, WA 98134
800.553.4453 • www.mountaineersbooks.org

Printed in China
Distributed in the United Kingdom by Cordee, www.cordee.co.uk

Copyeditor: Margaret Cook
Design: Mountaineers Books
Layout: Kate Basart/Union Pageworks
Cartographer: Martha Bostwick
Cover photograph: *Mount Rainier pulls you forward like a magnet as you saunter through Grand Park (Hike 9).*
Frontispiece: *Whether you make it all the way to Indian Henrys Hunting Ground or simply do a shorter out and back, Kautz Creek Trail makes a fine respite in a busy world (Hike 66).*

The background maps for this book were produced using the online map viewer CalTopo. For more information, visit caltopo.com.

Library of Congress Cataloging-in-Publication Data
Names: Asars, Tami, author.
Title: Day hiking Mount Rainier National Park : Crystal Mountain, Cayuse and Chinook Pass / by Tami Asars.
Description: Second edition. | Seattle, Washington : Mountaineers Books, [2018] | Includes index.
Identifiers: LCCN 2017040145| ISBN 9781680510102 (paperback) | ISBN 9781680510119 (ebook)
Subjects: LCSH: Hiking—Washington (State)—Mount Rainier National Park—Guidebooks. | Trails—Washington (State)—Mount Rainier National Park—Guidebooks. | Hiking—Washington (State)—Guidebooks. | Mount Rainier National Park (Wash.)—Guidebooks. Washington (State)—Guidebooks.
Classification: LCC GV199.42.W22 M6425 2018 | DDC 796.5109797/782—dc23
LC record available at https://lccn.loc.gov/2017040145

Mountaineers Books titles may be purchased for corporate, educational, or other promotional sales, and our authors are available for a wide range of events. For information on special discounts or booking an author, contact our customer service at 800-553-4453 or mbooks@mountaineersbooks.org.

ISBN (paperback): 978-1-68051-010-2
ISBN (ebook): 978-1-68051-011-9

Table of Contents

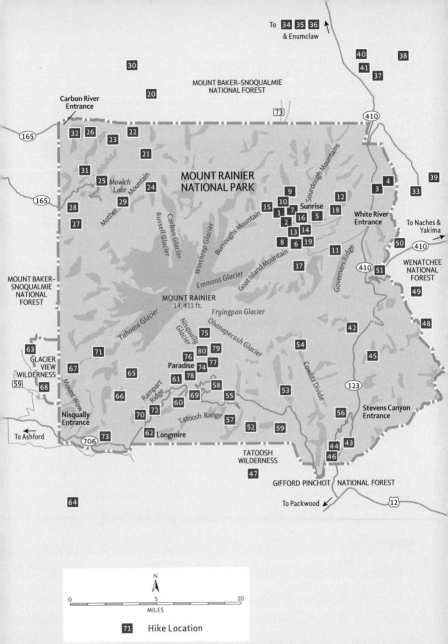

To 34 35 36
& Enumclaw

40
41
37
38

30

20

MOUNT BAKER–SNOQUALMIE
NATIONAL FOREST

73

Carbon River
Entrance

165

410

32 26
23
22

21

31

25 Mowich
Lake
29
24

Mother Mountain

Russell Glacier

Carbon Glacier

Winthrop Glacier

Burroughs Mountain

MOUNT RAINIER
NATIONAL PARK

Sourdough Mountains

9
10
15 1 7
2 16
13 14
8 6 19

Sunrise

5

12
18

3 4

33

39

White River
Entrance

To Naches &
Yakima

50

410

51

WENATCHEE
NATIONAL FOREST

49

165

28
27

Goat Island Mountain

17

11

Governors Ridge

410

MOUNT BAKER–
SNOQUALMIE
NATIONAL
FOREST

Emmons Glacier

MOUNT RAINIER
14,411 ft.

Tahoma Glacier

Fryingpan Glacier

Ohanapecosh Glacier

42

48

45

GLACIER
VIEW
WILDERNESS
59

63

67

71

68

65

66

Mount Wow

Nisqually
Entrance

To Ashford

706

73

75

80 79
76
77
74
78
61
69
58
60 72
70

Paradise

Nisqually Glacier

Rampart Ridge

Tatoosh Range

62 Longmire

55

57

53

54

Cowlitz Divide

56

Stevens Canyon
Entrance

123

52

59

44 43
46

TATOOSH
WILDERNESS

47

GIFFORD PINCHOT NATIONAL FOREST

To Packwood

12

64

N

0   5   10
MILES

71   Hike Location

Hikes at a Glance

HIKE	DISTANCE IN MILES (ROUNDTRIP)	DIFFICULTY	KID-FRIENDLY	DOG-FRIENDLY
WHITE RIVER/SUNRISE AREA				
1. Berkeley Park	7	3		
2. Burroughs Mountain Loop	9.1	3		
3. Crystal Peak	8.4	5		
4. Crystal Lakes	6	3		
5. Dege Peak	4.2	2	•	
6. Emmons Moraine Trail	3	2	•	
7. Forest Lake	4.6	3	•	
8. Glacier Basin	6.8	3		
9. Grand Park	12.4	4		
10. Mount Fremont Lookout	5.6	3		
11. Owyhigh Lakes	7.5	3		
12. Palisades Lake	7.2	3	•	
13. Shadow Lake and Sunrise Camp Loop	3.8	2	•	
14. Silver Forest and Emmons Vista	2	1	•	
15. Skyscraper Pass and Skyscraper Mountain	8	4		
16. Sourdough Ridge	4.7	2	•	
17. Summerland and Panhandle Gap	11.8	5		
18. Sunrise Lake	1.2	2	•	
19. White River Valley to Sunrise	6.7	4		
CARBON RIVER/MOWICH LAKE AREA				
20. Bearhead Mountain	6.2	4		•
21. Carbon Glacier	18	5		
22. Chenuis Falls	8.4	2		
23. Green Lake and Ranger Falls	10.4	3		
24. Ipsut Falls	10.8	4		
25. Ipsut Pass (easy way)	3	2	•	
25. Ipsut Pass (hard way)	18.4	3		
26. Mine Trail	3	3	•	
27. Mowich River	8.4	2		
28. Paul Peak Trail	7.8	4		
29. Spray Falls, Spray Park, and Seattle Park	7	3		
30. Summit Lake	5.2	3	•	•
31. Tolmie Peak and Eunice Lake	6.4	3	•	
32. West Boundary Trail	7.3	5		

WILDLIFE VIEWING	WILD-FLOWERS	WATER-FALL	EXCEP-TIONAL VIEWS	OLD-GROWTH	HISTORICAL	FIRE-LOOKOUT TOWER	GEO-LOGICAL FEATURES	SAVED TRAIL
•	•							
•			•					
	•		•		•			
•	•							
•	•		•					
			•					
•	•							
•	•		•		•			•
•	•		•					
•	•		•		•	•		
•	•				•			
•	•							
	•				•			
	•		•		•			
	•		•					
•	•		•					
•	•		•		•			
•								
•								
			•		•			
			•		•			
		•		•				
		•		•				
		•		•	•			
				•				
		•		•	•			
				•	•			
				•	•			
				•	•			
•	•	•	•					
	•		•					
	•	•	•		•	•		
		•						•

continued

HIKE	DISTANCE IN MILES (ROUNDTRIP)	DIFFICULTY	KID-FRIENDLY	DOG-FRIENDLY
GREENWATER/CRYSTAL MOUNTAIN				
33. Crystal Mountain Loop and Henskin, Miners, and Elizabeth Lakes	8.3	3		•
34. Federation Forest State Park	2.5	1	•	•
35. Greenwater River, Greenwater Lakes, and Echo Lake	13.2	3	•	•
36. Kelly Butte	3.6	2		•
37. Little Ranger Peak and Ranger Creek Shelter	10	4		•
38. Noble Knob and George Lake	5.1	3	•	•
39. Norse Peak Loop	11	4		•
40. Palisades Trail	8.4	4		•
41. Snoquera Falls Loop	3.8	3	•	•
CAYUSE PASS/SR 123/PACKWOOD				
42. Eastside Trail Waterfalls	7	3	•	
43. Laughingwater Creek and Three Lakes	12.2	4		
44. Ohanapecosh Hot Springs	0.6	1	•	
45. Shriner Peak	8.4	5	•	
46. Silver Falls Loop	3	2	•	
47. Tatoosh Lakes and Tatoosh Peak	11.7	5		•
CHINOOK PASS/SR 410				
48. Anderson and American Lakes	14	4		•
49. Dewey Lake	6.6	2	•	•
50. Sheep Lake and Sourdough Gap	6	3	•	•
51. Tipsoo Lake and Naches Peak Loop	3.7	2	•	
STEVENS CANYON ROAD				
52. Bench and Snow Lakes	2.8	2	•	
53. Box Canyon and Nickel Creek	2.2	2	•	
54. Cowlitz Divide and Indian Bar	14.6	5		
55. Faraway Rock and Lakes High Trail Loop	3	2	•	
56. Grove of the Patriarchs	1.3	1	•	
57. Pinnacle Peak	2.6	3		
58. Reflection Lakes and Paradise Loop	5.8	3		
59. Stevens Canyon Waterfalls	8	3		
ASHFORD/NISQUALLY ENTRANCE/WESTSIDE ROAD/LONGMIRE				
60. Carter and Madcap Falls	2.5	2	•	
61. Comet Falls	4	4		

WILDLIFE VIEWING	WILD-FLOWERS	WATER-FALL	EXCEP-TIONAL VIEWS	OLD-GROWTH	HISTORICAL	FIRE-LOOKOUT TOWER	GEO-LOGICAL FEATURES	SAVED TRAIL
•	•		•		•			
				•				
		•						
•			•		•	•		
					•			
	•		•		•			
•			•		•			
		•			•			
		•						
		•		•				
	•				•			
			•		•			
	•		•		•	•		
		•		•	•			
	•		•		•			
•	•							
	•							
•	•		•					
•	•		•					
•	•		•					
		•						
•	•	•	•		•			
•								
				•	•			•
	•		•					
•	•	•	•		•			
		•						
		•			•			
•	•	•	•					•

continued

HIKE	DISTANCE IN MILES (ROUNDTRIP)	DIFFICULTY	KID-FRIENDLY	DOG-FRIENDLY
ASHFORD/NISQUALLY ENTRANCE/WESTSIDE ROAD/LONGMIRE (CONTINUED)				
62. Eagle Peak Saddle	7.4	5		
63. Glacier View	4.2	3	•	•
64. High Rock Lookout	3.2	3	•	•
65. Indian Henrys Hunting Ground	14	5		
66. Kautz Creek	11.4	4		
67. Lake George and Gobblers Knob	12.6	4		
68. Mount Beljica (southern trailhead)	3	3	•	•
68. Mount Beljica (northern trailhead)	5.4	3	•	•
69. Narada Falls	0.4	1	•	
70. Rampart Ridge Loop	5.2	3		
71. South Puyallup Trail	12	4		
72. Trail of the Shadows Loop	0.8	1	•	
73. Twin Firs Loop	0.4	1	•	
PARADISE AREA				
74. Alta Vista Loop	1.4	3		
75. Camp Muir	9	5		
76. Deadhorse Creek, Moraine Trail, and Glacier Vista	3.8	4		
77. Myrtle Falls and Golden Gate Loop	4.1	4	•	
78. Nisqually Vista Loop	1.2	1	•	
79. Paradise Glacier	5.6	3	•	
80. Skyline Trail and Panorama Point	5.6	4		

WILDLIFE VIEWING	WILD-FLOWERS	WATER-FALL	EXCEP-TIONAL VIEWS	OLD-GROWTH	HISTORICAL	FIRE-LOOKOUT TOWER	GEO-LOGICAL FEATURES	SAVED TRAIL
•			•					
			•		•			
			•		•	•		
•	•		•		•			
•	•		•		•			
•			•		•	•		
			•		•			
			•		•			
		•						
				•				
					•		•	
•					•			
•				•				
•	•		•		•			
	•		•		•		•	
•	•		•					
	•	•	•		•			
•	•		•				•	
•	•		•		•			
•	•	•	•		•			

Acknowledgments

Mount Rainier has always been a very important place to me. As a third-generation Washingtonian, not only have I grown up visiting the park, but some of the significant spikes on the timeline of my life are marked by visits. On my way home from visiting the park in June 1999, my phone rang with the exciting news of my nephew's birth. In September 2003, while sitting on a rotting log in the open landscapes northwest of Mystic Lake, my future husband asked me to marry him. In 2010, while looping the Wonderland yet again, the idea of writing a guidebook sprang into my head and two years later, I was holding my book, *Hiking the Wonderland Trail*, in my hands. Later came a smartphone app for the Wonderland that I produced. Today, it's my privilege to share this book on day hiking in the park with you and give you information on the pathways that have meant so much to me. For all of those reasons and more, the first acknowledgment in this book is to Mount Rainier National Park itself, which has always been there for me whenever I needed it—it is an inspiration and my soul shampoo.

Special thanks to my husband, Vilnis, who supports me endlessly as I immerse myself in the hinterlands summer after summer and then sequester myself in the subsequent winters to pen what I've seen. Your love and support mean the world to me.

To my fur baby, Scout, thank you for understanding that dogs aren't allowed in national parks and allowing me to traipse off to go hiking, much to your disappointed protests. You joined me on hikes outside the park, and I loved having you bouncing along beside me.

To my friends and family, thank you for helping me get through some of the bumps of this career I've chosen, even when you may not know it. Thank you for being such great cheerleaders!

Thanks to Carl Fabiani, retired park trails foreman, who knows the park like the back of his hand. Your thoughtful answers to my questions helped give life to the historical details in this guide.

Special thanks to recently retired superintendent of Mount Rainier National Park, Randy King, for your prompt responses to my correspondence. I stood in awe of your leadership, your friendship, and your ever-present smile. You were the shining example of superior park management, and we were all very grateful for your service. May you continue to enjoy nature's bounty in retirement. Along those same lines, thank you, Daniel Keebler, Lindsey Kurnath, and all the other park personnel who passionately care for the park, ensuring it lasts for generations to come.

Lastly, thanks to you, my readers. If you picked up this book, it's likely because you are looking for a place to escape the constant mind-noise of daily life and rest safely in the restorative arms of the backcountry. You are why I write. May all our hearts find ease and our heads find clarity when we visit the places described in these pages. Happy trails!

A budding photographer works to captures the perfect macro flower shot.

Introduction

Standing at 14,411 feet, boasting 26 major glaciers and 2 craters, Mount Rainier is a vision and a legend. For years, folks have both revered and admired this massive volcanic giant, the highest mountain in the Cascade Range, for its grandeur, beauty, and power. The spectacular volcano is visible from Seattle and from many points in Washington State, but seeing it from a distance is simply not enough. To truly bond with the great peak and to appreciate its scale, you must visit Mount Rainier National Park and get up close and personal.

The park is one of the best places in the state to spend the day exploring. From old-growth mossy evergreens, some more than 1000 years old, to wildflower meadows bursting with sweet fragrances, your camera will be snapping nonstop. The giant volcano positions itself as the backdrop on trail after trail, forcing you to stop and marvel at in-your-face views of the giant ice flows, gaping crevasses, and crumbling, sheer rock walls.

This guide contains hikes where you can spend an entire day marinating in mountain magic from sunup to sundown as well as short hikes for kids and those with limited mobility. Keep in mind that for all the beauty and trail variety it offers, the mountain is an active volcano and deserves the utmost respect.

A stone and concrete monument bench stands at the spot (near Paradise Glacier Trail) where Sluiskin, a Native American guide, waited nervously for the first two men to reach the summit of Mount Rainier (Hikes 77, 79, 80).

AN ACTIVE VOLCANO

Mount Rainier has a dangerous reputation and is considered one of the most potentially hazardous volcanoes in the world, primarily due to its proximity to major cities and a past history of spitting out destructive volcanic tantrums of debris. Known as a *stratovolcano*, a conical volcano built up by layers (strata) of lava and ash, Mount Rainier first started its activity roughly 1 million years ago and had its last eruption about 500 years ago. Eruptions have ranged from small lava-producing episodes to much larger debris outbursts.

As frightening as the threat of a Mount Rainier eruption is, *lahars*, or volcanic mudflows, are much more common near Mount Rainier and are a more realistic risk. A lahar occurs when pressure builds in a glacial lake or when melting snow and ice rupture loose and head down the slopes of the volcano, generally toward the path of least resistance, which in the case of Mount Rainier, is almost always a river valley. The moving water, sediment, and debris become a fast-moving flow of a viscous, wet-concrete-like substance that destroys whatever is in its path. These thick, muddy debris flows can achieve speeds of 50-plus miles per hour, wreaking havoc for dozens of miles from their initial outburst and carrying with them boulders as big as cars and large uprooted evergreen trees. Because of the potential destruction, the US Geological Survey keeps a very watchful eye on Mount Rainier's moods and monitors it for signs of volcanic activity. There are seismic monitoring stations installed on Mount Rainier, and elsewhere in the Pacific Northwest, with geohazard warning sirens to help alert the public in the event of impending volcanic activity. It's vital to be alert when hiking or traveling in volcano country. If you feel prolonged shaking of the ground, notice a rapid rise in water levels near rivers or creeks, or hear a roar like a freight train, and especially if you hear a warning siren, move to higher ground immediately. Once you are at least 160 feet above a river level, you are out of the flood zone.

Thankfully, for those of us who enjoy the raw beauty of the volcano and its foothills, experts say the odds of a volcanic eruption in our lifetime is low. Folks who wander the backcountry shouldn't worry too much about the potential hazards, so enjoy the fragrant breezes, the eye-popping views, and the giant mountain framed by white puffy clouds—but remain aware and alert.

HISTORY

Before Mount Rainier became a national park, five Native American tribes—the Nisqually, Muckleshoot, Yakama, Puyallup, and Taidnapam (or Upper Cowlitz)—lived, hunted, and picked berries around the area. In fact, many of our present-day hiking trails were originally their paths to their harvesting grounds.

To the native tribes, Mount Rainier was one of the most feared volcanoes in the Pacific Northwest, and the legend was that an angry spirit lived in a lake of fire near the summit's crater. When the first party of white men wanted to summit the mountain, they hired a Native American guide named Sluiskin to lead them. He knew the mountain and its pathways very well but believed in the angry spirit in the lake of fire so he pleaded with them not to go. As the climbing party reached the base of the summit, he became extremely nervous and uneasy and refused to go any farther. Today, this spot is marked with a monument that you can visit (see Hikes 77, 79, and 80). When Hazard Stevens and P. B. (no, not peanut butter, but Philemon Beecher) Van Trump reached the summit in 1870, they stopped briefly to enjoy the warm steam vents, which Sluiskin had thought was the lake of fire. Sluiskin assumed the men were dead, so when he saw them returning from their summit bid, he hailed them, shouting "Skookum tillicum! Skookum tillicum!" meaning strong men with brave hearts.

In 1888, John Muir, legendary naturalist, author, and Sierra Club founder, climbed the mountain. While he enjoyed the views from the summit, he thought that the best view was from below. Day hikers will likely agree that the best views of Mount Rainier are not necessarily seen when standing on its summit, but rather from various angles as you hike near its base.

Eleven years after Muir's visit, in 1899 to be precise, Congress recognized the natural features of the landscape and the importance of preserving the area from development and officially deemed Mount Rainier the nation's fifth national park.

In the 1920s, the number of visitors skyrocketed as folks flocked to the park to see the mountain up close. For visitors who wanted to extend their stay and see more of the areas where there were no roads, the backcountry became a popular destination. The iconic Wonderland Trail, a 93-mile loop around the mountain's flanks, kicked off its recreational acclaim when members of the Seattle-based Mountaineers organization pioneered the first official expedition.

Today, Mount Rainier has become one of America's most iconic and well-loved parks, welcoming close to 2 million visitors a year. Some come for luxury visits at the historic inns and to dine in scenic restaurants, while others stay for a week or more, throwing down a tent in the park's backcountry or frontcountry camps, cooking on a camp-stove, and basking in the park's splendor. Others simply pack a sack lunch and visit the park for the day, finding pathways to hike and discovering treasures of wildflowers, wildlife, and views. Wherever you decide to stay and dine, you'll definitely want to choose the activity of hiking to truly immerse yourself in the majestic areas that aren't visible through a car window. Mount Rainier displays a spectacle of natural pageantry, so put on your trail shoes and experience its breathtaking trails.

FEES, PERMITS, AND REGULATIONS

As with most activities these days, we must pay to play. Mount Rainier National Park relies on park **entrance fees** to pay staff, maintain trails and roads, update campgrounds, and monitor the health of the park's flora and fauna as well as keep a close eye on volcanic geohazards.

Entrance fees are collected via staffed entrance booths at the main entrances (Nisqually, White River, and Stevens Canyon) during daylight hours and peak seasons. Self-service payment booths are available after hours at those locations and also at the Carbon River and Mowich Lake areas.

As of 2018, park fees break down as follows:

- A Mount Rainier National Park annual pass, good for the pass holder and the passengers in their vehicle: $50.00
- An Interagency Annual Pass, also known as the America the Beautiful pass, good for all national parks and other federal public lands: $80.00
- A single-vehicle entry fee, good for one noncommercial vehicle and its passengers (15 passengers or fewer) for seven consecutive days: $25.00

- Per-person fee, good for a walk-up or single bicycle for seven consecutive days: $10.00
- Motorcycle fee, good for one motorcycle and its passenger for seven consecutive days: $20.00

Several times a year the park also offers **free days**. Generally, free days celebrate holidays like Martin Luther King Jr. Day (January), National Park Week (April), National Public Lands Day (September), and Veterans Day (November). The dates for these holidays vary each year, and more dates are often added. For example, in 2016, the park celebrated its birthday weekend and provided free access at the end of August. For a list of all the free days, visit the website listed in the appendix.

Permits for day hiking within the park are not required. However, should you decide to turn one of your day hikes into an overnight backcountry adventure, you must secure a permit from a ranger station either the day before or the day of your visit, or make a reservation in advance.

For hikes on public lands outside the park, you may need a special parking pass. For areas managed by the state, such as Federation Forest State Park (hike 34), a Discovery Pass is necessary. Those managed by the Forest Service, often, but not always, require a Northwest (NW) Forest Pass. The notes

Vibrant colors abound along the shoreline of Sheep Lake when autumn comes to the high country (Hike 50).

section for each hike lists necessary passes. Both the Discover Pass and the NW Forest Passes are available at retailers and online (see appendix).

In addition, **wilderness permits** are required for wilderness areas outside the park. At most trailheads you'll find a wooden box filled with carbon-copy permits and a dull pencil (if you're lucky!). Once filled out, put one copy in the box and carry the other copy with you. These help the Forest Service track the number of people and stock (if applicable) using the trail, providing valuable data for funding and grants. The permits also help the Forest Service know the approximate whereabouts of hikers in case of a natural disaster, like a wildfire.

If you secure your wilderness camping permit the day before, or the day of your trip, it's considered a **first-come, first-served permit** and does not have a fee. Keep in mind the camp(s) you desire are subject to availability, so always have a Plan B. To obtain a first-come, first-serve permit, visit any ranger station in the park.

You may apply for a backcountry **wilderness permit reservation** in advance via the park's website. Wilderness permit reservation requests have a reservation fee of $20.00 but come with peace of mind since you know that your camping spot is reserved for you after a long day of hiking. The reservation-request period runs from March 15 to September 30. If your reservation request is accepted, an email from the National Park Service will confirm your dates. Remember that the email is simply a placeholder and is not your actual permit. All permits must be picked up in person the day of your trip.

Those with mountaineering and rope-team training and glacier-travel experience may want to take a crack at climbing Mount Rainier and standing on its snowy summit. Taking a class with The Mountaineers or other local, outdoor-focused organizations will help you achieve the education and skills you need for such a feat! Should you plan on climbing to the top, crossing a glacier, or simply climbing above 10,000 feet, you'll also need to secure a **climbing pass**. Those hiking/climbing only as far as Camp Muir or Camp Schurman on the main trails do not need the pass. The fee for the climbing pass as of 2017 is $46.00 per person if you are 25 years or older and $32.00 per person if you are 24 years or younger. The pass lasts for one calendar year. You may obtain a climbing pass in advance online on Mount Rainier's website, purchase the pass when you check in for your climb, or purchase the climbing pass at the same time you submit your reservation for a wilderness camping permit, should you plan to camp overnight high on the volcano. You'll also need to register with a valid photo ID in person the day before or the day of your climb. In summer you can register at one of the following locations: the Climbing Information Center in Paradise, the Henry M. Jackson Visitors Center in Paradise, the White River Wilderness Information Center at the White River Entrance, the Longmire Wilderness Information Center, or the Carbon River Ranger Station. In the winter, you can only register at the Longmire Information Center or on weekends and holidays at the Jackson Visitors Center in Paradise. From September 15 to May 15, climbers can also self-register for a climbing permit at the Old Ranger Station in Paradise, the Carbon River Ranger Station, or the White River Ranger Station.

When it comes to caring for the wilderness with so many park visitors, Mount Rainier National Park has some **regulations**. A few items and activities are prohibited on all trails and in all backcountry areas:

1. **Fires.** When campfires are prohibited, as they are in all park wilderness areas, it's for a good reason. Respect the rules and impress your friends by whipping up s'mores over a Jetboil flame. White-gas, canister, and alcohol stoves are okay, but biofuel stoves, such as those using twigs, sticks, pine cones, etc., are prohibited.

2. **Large group size.** Limit your group size to 12 people and stock. This includes people, pack and saddle animals, and humans who feel like pack and saddle animals!

3. **Pets and stock.** Yes, leave the pup (and all furry friends or pack animals) at home if you intend to hike on trails within park boundaries. The only exception to the pet rule is a short stretch of the Pacific Crest Trail (PCT) that pops in and out of the park's borders. The only stock-use exception is on the Laughingwater Creek Trail from Highway 123 to the PCT near Carlton Pass (Hike 43). If you have stock, feed them certified weed-free food to prevent the spread of invasive plants. Also, avoid letting livestock graze or tethering, hobbling, or hitching them within 200 feet of lakeshores.

4. **Motorized equipment and equipment used for mechanical transport.** This includes motor vehicles, motorboats, bicycles, hang gliders, wagons, carts, portage wheels, and aircraft (like landing a helicopter). In other words, you can't land your Learjet in a mountain meadow. The only exception is that bicycles are permitted on washed-out Carbon River and Westside roads but not on any connecting trails along them.

5. **Use of firearms.**

6. **Bow/arrows, slingshot, etc.**

7. **Destroying or disturbing natural, cultural, or archeological features.** Cutting standing green trees, snags, and boughs is prohibited, so don't channel your inner Paul Bunyan and hack away at an old-growth cedar. This also includes **respecting closed areas**. Natural vegetation in populated alpine areas needs a chance to recover during the short growing season so avoid walking, camping, or bustin' a move in posted restoration areas.

8. **Disturbing, hunting, or feeding wildlife.**

9. **Switchback cutting on any trail.** Cutting switchbacks and making new trails, no matter how small, damages soil and vegetation.

10. **Polluting or contaminating any water source.** This includes soaps, food scraps, and waste of any kind.

11. **Disposing of human waste within 100 feet of water or within sight of a trail.**

12. **Camping within 100 feet of water**, except in designated campsites.

13. **Leaving trash in toilets or elsewhere** in the wilderness.

14. **Possessing marijuana.** Even though Washington State law allows legal recreational marijuana use, federal laws still consider it illegal, so the possession of marijuana in any amount is still prohibited in the park and is punishable by fines and/or imprisonment.

15. **The use of drones.** Launching, landing, or operating an unmanned drone from or on lands and waters administered by the National Park Service within the boundaries of Mount Rainier National Park is prohibited.

IF YOU LOVE IT, HELP IT! VOLUNTEERING IN MOUNT RAINIER NATIONAL PARK
Few have walked the pine-needle-cushioned trails of Mount Rainier National Park without admiring the quality of the trails and the well-marked signs, and marveling at the tremendous work involved in keeping the trails open for all to enjoy by replacing washed-out backcountry bridges and removing debris and fallen trees.

Whether you can help with trail projects, volunteer ranger patrols, campground hosting, fundraising, or advocacy, a little of your time and/or your money goes a long way. Many volunteer opportunities with nonprofit organizations are available, so please join them in their efforts! For a full list of partnerships and current volunteer opportunities, please visit the park's website or see the list of nonprofits in the appendix.

16. **Backcountry camping without a permit.** All backcountry campers must possess a valid wilderness permit and must adhere to the stated itinerary and party size. Also note that leaving or storing equipment, personal property, or supplies is prohibited, as is leaving items unattended for more than 48 hours.

17. **Climbing above 10,000 feet without a climbing pass.** All climbers, except those day hiking to Camp Muir or Camp Schurman, must have a valid climbing pass and be registered with park authorities.

18. **Hitchhiking.** Bumming a ride either by the side of the road or in a parking lot is prohibited in Mount Rainier National Park.

WHEN TO VISIT

While Mount Rainier can be enjoyed year-round (with limited services in the winter months), day hikers flock to the park in the summer when trails are snow free, sunshine warms the landscape, and wildflowers are at their peak. Late summer and early fall are also great times to visit since trails are generally less crowded, park foliage pops in colorful shades of reds, oranges, and browns, and wildlife-viewing opportunities increase when berries ripen. After Labor Day, however, park visitors centers, such as the one at Sunrise, shut down most services, and seasonal volunteers and employees leave the park. That means fewer backcountry patrols and fewer cheeseburgers from snack bars, but hey, if you plan ahead and pack your own lunch . . . you'll be set!

Seasons

Lowland trails, such as those through forest groves or to rushing waterfalls, are usually snow free by early May and kick off the hiking season. Since the most popular areas of the park are at high elevations, the most optimal time to visit the high country and visitors centers, such as Paradise and Sunrise, is in the beating heart of the Northwest summer in mid-July through mid-September. Fall, when the weather turns cooler and the foliage turns colors, runs from mid-September through the end of October. Snow generally starts falling near the end of October and continues well into the spring months. Mount Rainier offers opportunities for visitors to play in the snow with ranger-guided snowshoe walks, winter camping, and sledding areas near the Henry M. Jackson Visitors Center. Since weather

Snow often lingers in the high country well into August along the Paradise Glacier Trail (Hike 79).

and snowpack vary greatly from year to year, it's best to check with the park's website or contact one of the wilderness information centers for up-to-date information on trail conditions (see appendix).

Visitors Centers

While Mount Rainier is open year-round, hours vary by season and can depend on snowpack and weather.

The **Sunrise** area, including a visitors center and day lodge (with a gift shop and concessions), is generally open daily from July through mid-September and is closed in the winter. The road to Sunrise is high, steep, and winding and is treacherous in snowy conditions, so even the road to Sunrise is closed and gated for the winter.

The **Paradise** area is open year-round, but services are limited in winter months. In summer it is open daily and boasts a large visitors center, the Climbing Information Center, a picnic area, the Paradise Inn, a snack bar, a deli, a full-service restaurant, and two gift shops. In winter, generally October to May, the visitors center and gift shop are open only on weekends. The snack bar at the visitors center usually closes after the holidays and remains closed until spring.

The **Longmire** area of the park houses the National Park Inn (which has a restaurant), a general store, a wilderness information center, and a museum. All the concessions are open daily during the busy summer season, generally May to October. The rest of the year, the National Park Inn (and its restaurant) and the general store remain open, but the wilderness information center is closed. Occasionally on busy winter weekends, a ranger will open and staff the wilderness information center even if it's officially closed. The museum stays open in the winter, but generally closes after the holidays for a short time. The museum does double duty as an information center and is

Moss blankets the trail near Rampart Ridge, while evergreens provide welcome shade in warm summer months (Hike 70).

staffed by rangers who can issue permits or help you with your questions during the winter.

The **Ohanapecosh** Visitors Center, located in Ohanapecosh Campground, is usually open from late May until late September, but closes in the winter months.

Campgrounds

Mount Rainier's three **frontcountry campgrounds**, Cougar Rock, Ohanapecosh, and White River, are usually open by late May and close by October. **Wilderness camping** within the park requires a permit year-round, which you can obtain at any open ranger station or the self-registration stations at the Carbon River Ranger Station, the Ohanapecosh Ranger Station, and at the State Route 410 entrance at the park's north boundary. During the winter months, you can usually find a ranger at the Longmire area who can issue you a permit.

Roads

There are roughly 12 roads leading in, out, and around Mount Rainier: Carbon River Road (to its washed-out entrance just beyond park boundaries), SR 410 (Cayuse Pass) north boundary to south boundary, SR 410 (Chinook Pass), Nisqually–Longmire Road, Longmire–Paradise Road, Mowich Lake Road, Paradise Valley Road, Ricksecker Point Road, Stevens Canyon Road, Sunrise Road, Westside Road (to the Dry Creek closure), and White River Road (to White River Campground). By late June and early July, most roads in the park are open and will stay open until September or October. Summer months bring lots of ongoing construction projects, so it's best to check the park's website before you go to find out the best course of travel (see appendix).

In winter the following roads are open: Nisqually–Longmire Road and Longmire–

Paradise Road. These roads provide access to the Paradise area for winter recreation.

Trail Conditions

Trails in the park range from wide, flat cruising lanes cushioned with pine needles to narrow, overgrown pathways that switchback down steep slopes. Mount Rainier is known for a deep snowpack that, in some years, can linger into August. Flooding in the off-season can create deluges that wash out log footbridges over fast-moving waterways or wash out hillsides in places. In the early season, trail crews work to repair the bridges and mend the trail tread, but it can take time.

Mount Rainier National Park's website has a link for current trail conditions and it's updated fairly frequently by backcountry patrols. You can also visit the Washington Trails Association website (see appendix) for current trip reports to see if any other hikers have posted trail conditions for the hike you hope to enjoy.

Road Conditions

Overall, park roads in the summer months are usually in good shape, save for construction projects on the main thoroughfares and a couple of loose gravel roads (such as Westside Road and Mowich Lake Road).

Westside Road has been washed out for several years and is now approachable by vehicle for only the first 3 gravel-laden miles. After that, there is a gate, and hikers must walk or bicycle, to get to the trails. There are rumors that it may reopen at some point, so be sure to check before you go. **Mowich Lake Road** has its own set of issues, as winter weather can leave potholes, muddy spots, and erosion along the roughly 17-mile stretch. However, when it opens in June or July, most passenger cars can get up it if driven cautiously.

The washed-out gravel stretch of **Carbon River Road** is no longer in service for vehicles between the park's entrance to Ipsut Creek Campground. This roughly 5-mile stretch of road washed out year after year until the Park Service finally threw in the towel and closed it permanently. Today, hikers can access it only on foot or by bicycle, and Ipsut Creek Campground is considered a wilderness camp. Thankfully, the road, which leads to the entrance, is paved.

The biggest dangers on park roads are due to **winter travel,** when roads can become snowy, foggy, and icy despite the park's best efforts to keep them plowed. For this reason, **all vehicles are required to carry tire chains when traveling through the park from November 1 to May 1**. This rule applies to all vehicles, including four-wheel drive ones, regardless of tire type or weather conditions.

Weather

On November 6 and 7, 2006, 18 inches of rain fell on Mount Rainier National Park in just 36 hours. The park has seen its share of weather challenges, but in its 107-year history, there has been nothing as devastating. The impact of rain on land can be hard to visualize, and when you think about 18 inches of rain, you might think of a yardstick or tape measure. But that amount of water came down not just into rivers and creeks but also onto snowy glaciers as high as 10,000 feet. The destructive storm centered itself in the middle of the park, bringing hurricane-force winds and warm temperatures, the perfect storm for utter destruction.

Water found the path of least resistance and quickly made its way down the mountain into creeks, rivers, and drainages, dislodging huge boulders and old-growth trees, causing logjams, and sending debris in all directions.

When the storm was over, the damage was catastrophic. The debris-laden water destroyed park roads, boardwalks, entire campgrounds, and bridges and undermined park structures and utilities, rendering many areas of the park unsafe and unstable. The park had no choice but to close for an unprecedented six months to allow staff to make repairs.

Thankfully, volunteers from all over the country stepped up to help repair the park. Private citizens donated countless hours and thousands of dollars to recovery efforts and before long, the park was back in action. You can still see scars from this huge storm in undercut riverbanks, log bridges knocked askew, and rebuilt portions of trails, such as the Wonderland.

Since then, whenever a big storm approaches, park lovers hold their collective breath and hope it passes quickly with few consequences.

LODGING AND TRANSPORTATION

Should you decide to spend a few days enjoying the park, you may want to secure a reservation at one of the park's hotels or a frontcountry campsite. If you need transportation to and from the park, your options are fairly limited, but a few suggestions listed in this section may help.

Hotels

Within the park's boundaries are two hotels, the National Park Inn at Longmire and the Paradise Inn at Paradise. The Paradise Inn is open only in the high season (usually May to October), whereas the National Park Inn is open year-round. Both hotels require reservations, which you can make online or by calling Mount Rainier Guest Services (see appendix).

The **National Park Inn** is an old, historic building with 25 guest rooms, a full-service restaurant, and a general store full of snacks and sundries as well as a post office. While clean and comfortable, the rooms are fairly primitive, lacking televisions or phones. Some even lack private bathrooms and rely on shared facilities. Some rooms have only bathtubs, while others have only showers. When booking, be sure to ask a lot of questions about your room so there are no surprises when you arrive. Also, check out the porch of the National Park Inn where you can catch a glimpse of Mount Rainier from the comfort of rocking chairs and cozy blankets while cerulean Steller's jays with their pointy heads hippity-hop all around you.

The **Paradise Inn**, built in 1916, is a rustic, historic lodge with 121 guest rooms, a dining room, a gift shop, and a snack bar. As with the National Park Inn, many of the rooms are small, primitive, and lack telephones and televisions. Some of the rooms in the main building have shared bathrooms and showers, but the annex area, built in 1920, offers private bathrooms and even suites with sitting areas.

Outside the park, there are some privately run quaint cabins and inns. If you approach the park from the Nisqually Entrance (near Paradise) in the park's southwest corner, you can find lodging in the towns of Ashford or Elbe. If you approach the park via the White River Canyon Entrance (near Sunrise), your best options are to check out the lodging near Crystal Mountain Resort and the towns of Greenwater and Enumclaw.

Camping

The park has three frontcountry camp-grounds (Cougar Rock, Ohanapecosh, and White River) which are open from roughly May to October. You can make advance reservations at Cougar Rock and Ohanapecosh (see appendix); White River is first-come, first-serve. There is also a walk-in front-country campground at Mowich Lake as well as wilderness camping.

Not far from Longmire is **Cougar Rock Campground**, near the Nisqually River, which has 173 campsites, drinking water, flush toilets, and picnic tables. This camp is a great base for visiting trails near Paradise, Long-mire, and the west side of Stevens Canyon. Although popular, the campground is heavily wooded and offers a fair amount of privacy.

At the southeastern park boundary, off State Route 123, lies **Ohanapecosh Campground**, with 188 sites, drinking water, picnic tables, a visitors center, flush toilets, an RV dump station, and an amphitheater. It is a good base for hiking near the eastern end of Stevens Canyon, SR 123, and near the town of Packwood. Adjacent to the Ohanapecosh River, this campground has spectacular old-growth trees that make you feel tiny as you explore the area.

In the park's northeast corner lies **White River Campground**. This camp is a good base for those wishing to hike near Sunrise, White River, SR 123, and near the town of Greenwater. There are 112 campsites, drinking water, flush toilets, and picnic tables. Its proximity to the White River means day

The placid shoreline of calm Anderson Lake is a treat for the eyes and a welcome opportunity for the camera (Hike 48).

CARPETS OF WONDERFUL WILDFLOWERS

Mount Rainier has some of the most beautiful meadows of wildflowers in the country, and seeing them, as well as smelling their subtle fragrances, is a summer rite of passage when visiting the park. Most folks simply enjoy the brilliant colors and whip out their cameras to snap the beautiful blossoms in the foreground of giant, snowy Mount Rainier, but if you take a little time to learn which one is which, you can impress your friends and become a wildflower whiz!

Lupine, pronounced "lou-pin," is a purplish flower found in almost every meadow in the park. Varieties vary in coloration and size, but all have tall, vertical, spiky clusters of flowers that bloom for several months. Lupine seeds and buds are important for the diets of migratory hummingbirds, small songbirds, game birds, bees, and butterflies.

Asters are other flowers of the purplish coloration that thrive in the park. They vary from subalpine meadows, where they are often found in a single stem, to those that boast multiple flowers on each stem. You can identify asters because they look very similar to purple daisies. They bloom all summer and are also favorites of birds, bees, and butterflies.

Sitka valerian flowers are common in subalpine wildflower meadows. This showy white flower often towers high above the others, and its sweet fragrance is usually worth stopping for a good, long sniff. Tiny clusters of white or pink-tinted flowers make up the main crown, giving it a similar appearance to plants in the mustard and carrot family. To find this one, just follow your nose!

Another white flower that is fun to find in summer is the kitten-ear-soft **American bistort**. This flower looks similar to a pussy willow and is one of the first to bloom in meadows near Paradise and Sunrise. Look for a single narrow white flower, usually less than an inch in length. Gently run your fingers up and down the flower and feel how wonderfully soft it is, then take a sniff and close your eyes. You're welcome!

For more wildflower ID fun, head to www.nps.gov/mora/learn/nature/wildflowers.htm to find a listing of the most common flowers in the park and where to find them.

Carpets of vibrant wildflowers provide a fun identification exercise for amateur botanists.

hikers and climbers walk from the parking lot through the campground to access the trails, but it's still a restful area to catch some z's after a long day on the trail.

Mowich Lake Campground, the smallest frontcountry campground, is located in the northwest corner of the park. It is a good base for hiking near Carbon River, Spray Park, Mowich Lake, and the Mowich River and Ipsut Creek areas. It has 10 primitive, walk-in, tent-only sites. Folks often use this campground when hiking the Wonderland Trail.

Wilderness campgrounds are located in 41 different locations throughout the backcountry of Mount Rainier. All wilderness camps have privies, flat tent sites, and are fairly close to creeks or rivers for water sources. You must make arrangements in advance to camp at a backcountry wilderness camp, either through the reservation system or the first-come, first-serve system.

When it comes to getting to the mountain, there are no easy means of transportation. Mount Rainier is in the beautiful, remote boonies and the only true attraction in the area is the park. That said, there are a few options for those who don't want to drive. A handful of outfitters offer customized sightseeing tours that have designated stops in the park and offer a set schedule for hiking and mountain viewing (see appendix for more information).

Aside from taking a tour from an outfitter or talking a friend into driving, your other options for getting to the park on your own are taxis, rental cars, or public buses. Taxis can cost roughly $2.50 per mile, plus tip. Count on it being about 90 miles from Seattle to the park, so roughly $450 or more for the roundtrip fare. Costly, right? A rental car for a whole week might run anywhere from $175 to $400, a better deal if you need

wheels. There are no public buses that run close to the park. To get somewhat close, you can take a Pierce Transit bus from Tacoma to Sumner (roughly $2.50) and then take a taxi the remaining 60 or so miles. Or you can use L.E.W.I.S. Mountain Highway Transit, which runs from Centralia to Packwood. Packwood is still about 11 miles from the Stevens Canyon Entrance of the park, however, and there are no taxis, so you have to either walk or sweet-talk someone into driving you. If possible, find a friend with a car who likes hiking and will drive you to the mountain in exchange for gas and/or food.

TRAIL ETIQUETTE

They say a little kindness goes a long way, and no place is this truer than on the trail, especially a crowded one. In the summer months, particularly around visitors centers on weekends, using good etiquette with people, wildlife, and the backcountry is always appreciated. Most of the following are obvious, commonsense rules (aka Leave-No-Trace principles), but reviewing them is always a good idea.

Leave what you find behind. While it might be tempting to pick a flower in a meadow or bring a small rock back as a souvenir, removing them means there are fewer for others to enjoy. Take a picture as a souvenir instead. However, picking up any litter you see is strongly encouraged!

Plan ahead and know before you go. Make sure you have the proper attire and gear for your day on the trail (see What to Bring later in this chapter) so that you don't suffer a mishap and end up a statistic. Study the weather forecast, leave the dog at home if pets are prohibited, and know how to use the map and compass you'll bring with you. Follow park rules and don't forget toilet paper and some baggies to pack it out, just in

A survey marker marks the spot where a former lookout tower used to stand on the summit of Tatoosh Peak (Hike 47).

case! If you do bring the pup on trails where dogs are allowed, keep him or her under control and don't allow your animal to disturb wildlife or other trail users. Keep your dog on a leash or under voice control at all times.

Respect wildlife. Duh, right? Seriously, though, keep your distance from anything with horns or claws, and whatever you do, don't feed them. This includes the sweet faces of gray jays as well as golden-mantled ground squirrels or hoary marmots that shamelessly beg as you open your pack for lunch. When you're done, pick up any crumbs or wrappers. Also, observe and photograph wildlife from a distance, and allow even more space if the animal is with young.

Dispose of waste properly. If you brought it in and didn't eat it, pack it out. If you find yourself with a potty emergency and no potty in sight, dig a cathole 6 to 8 inches deep at least 200 feet (100 big steps) away from water, camps, and trails. When done, cover the

cathole completely and pack out your toilet paper. If you smoke, pack out your cigarette butts. Use only biodegradable soap, if any, and keep all suds and any other chemicals you might wash off yourself, such as sunscreen or bug spray, 200 feet from creeks, lakes, and rivers. Pollutants in bug spray and other products can jeopardize the health of salamanders, frogs, and other water-dependent creatures (including you). In subalpine areas, if you have to tinkle, the rule is "piddle on pumice." Mountain goats and deer seek out urine because it contains lots of salt, and unfortunately, they will dig at the ground to get at it, which disturbs fragile plants. A better option is sprinkling the rocks so the animals can do what they do without harming the landscape.

Stay on the trail. Don't cut switchbacks, make new trails, or walk in fragile areas.

Stay to the right when on the trail. When coming up behind another person, be sure to announce your presence so you don't scare the liver out of them, then pass them on the left if your pace is faster.

Give ascending hikers the right-of-way. We've all been there! Huffing and puffing up big hills is tough, so if you are on the downhill stretch, step aside and give the right-of-way to those working the hardest!

Select durable surfaces for your pack and your hiney when you stop for a break. In other words, avoid flopping down in an alpine meadow filled with wildflowers. Instead, find a rock or a log to perch on. Also, be aware of where you are seated so that other hikers can comfortably get by you and your pack without having to go off the trail.

Keep noise to a minimum. Laughing and talking loudly might all be part of your fun, but keep in mind that others are there to enjoy the solitude and perhaps even listen to bird calls. As a courtesy, keep your voices low and enjoy the experience without too much boisterous hobnobbing. Also, while Bluetooth speakers are convenient for listening to tunes, leave them off when hiking.

Hike single file in groups and allow others to pass you. Remember, everyone has their own speed, their own goals, and their own ways of enjoying the park. Let them go by, and do things your way!

Follow the Golden Rule. There may be situations that call for you to lend a hand, share your gorp, or even give a grin to those who have lost theirs. Do your best to be a good steward of the land and a good citizen to your fellow trail users.

H₂O FOR THOSE IN THE KNOW

Where there is water, there is life, and you'll find plenty of both around the park. Plants and animals, including those of the human variety, enjoy the bounty of the park's water features, from rushing canyons to drippy creeks. With a few tips, your experience with this life-sustaining liquid will remain a pleasant one.

Drinking It

Water is responsible for carving all of Mount Rainier's huge valleys and for constantly changing the landscape of Mount Rainier National Park. Knowing that, it should come as no surprise that water is found on many of the trails described in this guidebook. As always, treat water before drinking it to limit your chances of ingesting bacteria such as *Cryptosporidium*, *Giardia*, and *Leptosporidium*, names that seem straight out of science-fiction movies. Nothing says "bad day" like having a protozoa do the backstroke in your tummy. Keep your gut happy by treating water either with chemical tablets such as iodine or chlorine or by running it through a portable water filter.

Crossing It

The Park Service does its best to ensure footbridges are securely in place over waterways. However, there may be cases where heavy rains or melting snow have taken bridges away and you'll have to decide whether or not to cross the creek. If you are unsure about getting across because of either the rushing water or your own abilities, don't risk it. If you decide it's safe to cross a rushing waterway, use extreme caution and follow these tips:

- **Locate the best spot** to cross. Don't assume that crossing the creek right where the trail spits you out is the best place. Walk up and down the riverbank to find a spot that looks shallower, has less current, or even better, has a downed log that can serve as a makeshift bridge.

- Before crossing, **unbuckle your pack's waist belt** for an easy exit strategy if you accidentally go for a swim.
- When crossing, **focus your gaze on the log or the opposite bank** instead of looking down at the cranking current, and **use trekking poles or a long stick for balance**, especially if the water is silty and you can't see the bottom.

Doing these few simple things can be the difference between a fun day on the trail and a catastrophic adventure.

WILDLIFE

One of the joys of national parks is seeing wildlife. Watching a ground squirrel or a marmot go about its busy life can give folks almost as much joy as seeing the grand scenery of the park itself. Mount Rainier is home to 65 species of mammals, 14 species of amphibians, 5 species of reptiles, 182 species of birds, and 14 species of native fish. These numbers are constantly changing as global weather patterns shift and new species are discovered. The most common animals you may see (or hear) in the park are golden-mantled ground squirrels, hoary marmots, mountain goats, elk, deer, black bears, Cascades frogs, Cascade red foxes, gray jays, Steller's jays, blue grouse, Clark's nutcrackers, common ravens, American crows, and garter snakes.

Bear Smarts

Black bears are the only bears located in Mount Rainier National Park, as far as biologists have found, and the park is lucky to have a healthy population. The descriptions for several hikes in this book include notes about areas where you are likely to encounter bears if you are hoping for a photo or a glimpse of one of the forest's most majestic creatures. Avoiding a bear-human

A golden-mantled ground squirrel flexes his wee-bitty arm muscles as he intimidates hikers along Golden Gate Trail in the Paradise region of the park.

confrontation is straightforward, and with a little know-how, seeing a black bear can be an enjoyable experience with pictures to show and excitement to share.

Make some noise on blind corners or in thick forest. Do your best not to startle a bear by suddenly coming face-to-face with one. Bears are solitary creatures and prefer to be left alone, most times keeping to themselves as they carry on with munching greens or berries. Talk frequently and give a few claps, especially on blind corners, to let bears know that you are entering their turf. Doing so gives them a chance to make themselves scarce or at least move off the trail into meadows or thickets. Oh, and don't fall for those fancy-dancy bear bells every outdoor retailer sells. Studies have shown they aren't as effective as voices, and voices are cheaper!

Watch for evidence of bears being close by, such as scat laden with berries, tree bark that has been clawed by hungry bears looking for grubs, and pawprints on riverbanks or in muddy spots. Bears will also turn over logs looking for tasty bugs and will occasionally shred the log in the process. Also keep your eyes out for huckleberry bush branches broken downward; when feeding, bears often use their dexterous paws to pummel the bushes.

Use caution with food and scents. Bears have an incredible sense of smell and have been known to smell odors from more than half a mile away. Wearing floral perfumes, coconut sunscreen, or cherry lip balms may be fine in the city, but in bear habitat, leave them behind. If you happen to find an animal carcass of any kind, leave the area immediately and report it to park authorities as it will likely attract predators and scavengers. When camping, always use bear poles and bear boxes to store your food, never cook in your tent, and never sleep in the same clothes you wore while cooking.

Bear Encounters

Bears become agitated if they are disturbed while guarding a food source, protecting their young, or if they simply feel threatened. If you've practiced good bear smarts but still encounter one, you can do a few things to help avoid an unfortunate incident.

Avoid eye contact. This is extremely hard to do if you come into close contact, but if you can, look at the bear's paws or somewhere else on its body instead of directly into its eyes. Bears perceive eye contact as a direct threat, especially for prolonged periods.

Give them room. If you feel like you are too close to a bear, you probably are. If the bear has not exhibited signs of aggression, give it plenty of space and slowly back away while talking softly so the bear can identify you as a human. Getting out of its way and respecting

its personal space may be all it really wants you to do. Do everything you can to defuse the situation. If you are in a group, stick together to appear larger and more intimidating.

Never turn your back on the bear, and avoid running. Keep your eye on the bear to watch its behavior and determine its reaction. Most times, the bear will walk or run away, but sometimes, especially on trails where bears are used to seeing people, they will carry on feeding on berries or going about their routine. If this happens, you have the opportunity to watch from a safe distance and maybe even snap a few photos. Just don't get greedy with the snapping camera no matter how comfortable the bear may seem. Bears are wicked fast and can turn on a dime. Losing a limb can really mess up an otherwise great day.

Mountain Lions

Mountain lions, also known as cougars or pumas, pass through the park occasionally but are rarely seen due to their stealthy behavior. In general, mountain lions want nothing more than to be left alone to live, hunt, and raise kittens in quiet privacy. Attacks on humans are extremely rare, but since you are hiking in areas where they may also be roaming, here are a few tips:

Keep your eyes out for tracks. Mountain lion tracks are usually very large, have no claw marks, and have an unusual heel pattern of three distinct ridges near the bottom.

Listen for loud birds. Birds, such as Steller's jays and pileated woodpeckers often sound alarms if they see or hear a predator nearby.

Never let small children or dogs run in front of you or get out of view.

Leave the area immediately if you come across a carcass or fresh kill, as it's likely to draw predators.

Cougar Smarts

If you encounter a mountain lion, these tips may help you avoid escalating the situation.

Make eye contact. Looking them directly in the eye tells them that you see them and that you are a formidable opponent. This is the opposite of bears!

Make yourself look larger. Put your coat or your trekking poles over your head to make yourself appear larger than you really are. They may decide it's not worth their time to mess with you.

Pick up small children or place them up high on boulders or stumps where they appear larger.

If safe to do so, **back away slowly and do not run or turn your back**. Remember Tom and Jerry, the cartoon cat and mouse? Cougars, like house cats, instinctively give chase if they see something suddenly take off running. Avoid triggering their predatory response and do your best to defuse the situation by remaining calm.

If all efforts fail and the cougar attacks, **fight back with gusto**. Use every move you know: punch, kick, throw rocks, poke eyes, rip ears, and use bear spray. Those who have survived cougar attacks have done so by being extremely aggressive.

APPAREL AND GEAR

Having the right stuff with you when you set out into the hinterlands is key to having a warm, safe, and enjoyable outing. Whether you are new to hiking or an experienced trail traipser, a review of what to wear and what to bring is always a good idea.

What to Wear

Northwest climates are anything but consistent. In summer months, warm weather when you set out can turn to a cold mist in a matter of hours, ending your day in a hurry if you aren't prepared. Most Northwest hikers have a routine of dressing in layers so they can peel off the outer shells when they get too warm and easily throw on extra layers if a squall sets in.

Wear layers of non-cotton clothing since cotton retains moisture and takes a long time to dry. Wet clothes can easily lead to hypothermia, so stay dry and keep warm. **Choose synthetic or wool fabrics that dry** quickly and help retain warmth, sometimes even when wet. Don't forget about keeping your underwear, including sports bras, non-cotton too. Start off your layers with a short-sleeve, quick-dry shirt or tank top. Next, choose an insulation layer that will keep you warm and protect you against the elements, such as a fleece or puffy jacket. Finish the ensemble with a waterproof, breathable jacket with a good hood. You may not need to wear all of this on warm summer days, but having them in your pack is a good idea. A good pair of waterproof rain pants is usually enough protection to slide on over shorts or hiking pants if you encounter showers.

Over the years, **hiking footwear** has transitioned from stiff leather boots to more forgiving lightweight footwear. You'll need to know your body to determine whether you are comfortable with less ankle support in exchange for a lighter shoe, but most folks find a good compromise once they start their shopping. Footwear known as mid-hiking boots come up a little above the ankle and are more forgiving and less stiff than traditional hiking boots. Some hikers prefer very lightweight footwear known as trail-running shoes, which look like sneakers but have a deep, thick tread designed for uneven surfaces and a strong framework to prevent the sole from twisting and turning. Whatever you choose, break them in correctly so you can give yourself the best chance of avoiding blisters.

Blisters happen when you combine moisture, friction, and heat. If you eliminate any one of those elements, you'll increase your chances of avoiding blisters. If you are prone to sweaty feet or if your trail plans will take you through snow, mud, or puddles, bring an extra pair of socks and change them if they get damp. If you suffer from friction blisters, consider wearing sock liners, which act as a barrier, or second skin, and help prevent rubbing. If your feet are hotter than two embers in a pepper patch, try stopping once an hour and taking off your shoes and socks to help your feet cool down.

What to Bring

Most hikers have an assortment of items from various companies that they insist are the best. And it's probably true—for them. Since gear is so subjective and there are so many options, what works for one person may not work for another. The best strategy when you go outside to play is to make sure you have the ten essentials (developed by The Mountaineers) so that the unforeseen doesn't turn into misfortune. I stash mine in a lightweight stuff sack that keeps it organized and allows me to easily transfer it from my summer day hiking pack to my winter ski pack.

Mount Rainier's waterways are a powerful sight to behold (Hike 61).

1. **Navigation** (map and compass): No matter how good smartphone apps are today, phones can be unreliable and batteries can fail. Always bring a physical copy of a map in a waterproof case as well as a good compass. Equally important is knowing how to use them so you can find the car if you get turned around.

2. **Headlamp or flashlight**: Search-and-rescue personnel will tell you that leaving just one thing behind can be the difference between a good day and a bad day. Even though you may not intend to be out after dark, always pack a good flashlight or headlamp with a strong battery just in case the unforeseen happens. Again, don't rely on that smartphone light as it can chew up the battery you may need if you have to make an emergency call.

3. **Sun protection** (sunglasses, hats, and sunscreen): There is nothing quite like a warm summer day in the Pacific Northwest, but hot sun can spell bad news if you are unprepared. To avoid sunburn, snow blindness, heat exhaustion, or heatstroke, be sure you toss in some essential items, such as sunscreen, sunglasses, hats, and bandanas. For a quick cooldown, soak your hat or bandana in a creek or lake.

4. **First-aid**: Experienced hikers never leave home without basic first-aid gear, such as bandages, Ace wraps, moleskin, and pain reliever. You never know when you might have to stop for a quick fix of a hot spot.

5. A **knife** should be part of your repair kit: A few good "what-if" items are the key to success if you break a pack strap or have a backcountry mishap. Safety pins, a small roll of duct tape, a shoelace, a knife, and a multitool are all helpful things to tuck in your pack in case you need them.

6. **Fire** (firestarter and matches): While fires are prohibited in the Mount Rainier backcountry, emergency situations may require you build one to survive. Always carry reliable firestarting materials (available at outdoor retailers) as well as waterproof matches to get your spark ignited, even in damp weather.

7. **Extra clothes**: You can never be sure what kind of weather you may encounter; even the most beautiful day can turn cold, damp, or downright wet. Being exposed to weather without the proper gear can be miserable and even dangerous, leading to hypothermia. Throw an extra layer of insulation into your pack, such as a fleece or down jacket, as well as a waterproof rain jacket, to ensure you are covered if you get stuck in the cold. On extra-long day hikes in the shoulder seasons, I often throw in a very lightweight sleeping bag. Even if I don't need it for an emergency, it's nice to toss over my legs as I sit and enjoy a vista.

8. **Shelter**: Carry something that can serve as an emergency shelter if you need to hunker down. A small tarp, a waterproof backpack cover, a large garbage bag, a bivy sack, or an emergency space blanket can all serve this purpose.

9. **Extra food**: Should the unplanned happen, always have enough food to keep you sustained for a couple of extra days. I have several energy gel packets and a couple of granola bars that live in my ten essentials kit for just-in-case situations. Being prepared is all about planning for the best but being prepared for the worst.

10. **Extra water**: Water is on almost every trail in Mount Rainier National Park, but in very hot summers, creeks may dry up. Plan on bringing more than you'll need for the entire hike, and as a backup, throw in a water filter or purification tablets.

TRAIL SAFETY

Most folks find that national parks are generally fairly free from criminal activity. I mean, let's face it, who would pay money to get into a park only to create malicious mischief? But since it does occasionally happen, prevention is key to keeping you and your possessions safe and sound during your outing. Here are a few tips to help you avoid an unfortunate situation:

1. **Tell someone where you are going.** Include details of your hike and when you plan to return. Leave a phone number for them to call, such as the land management agency, at a specific time if you don't return as planned. Remember to give yourself enough buffer time if the hike takes longer than expected or if something small like a broken shoelace causes a delay. If possible, purchase or print two topographical maps and mark both with your planned route. Take one with you and leave one with

The rock garden of the Burroughs Mountain Trail feels a world away from the hustle and bustle below (Hike 2).

a trusted friend. You may also want to note important things like the number in your party and any health issues they may have. It might seem like overkill for just a day hike, but the few extra minutes you spend might save a life!

2. **If solo, never tell those you meet on the trail you are alone**. Use words like *we* and *us* to cause some confusion about how many are in your party. If you get an uneasy feeling, shout off into the bushes "Are you almost done?" or "Hurry up, let's keep moving" to cause a creep to have even more hesitation should he or she have bad intentions. Also, don't tell them where you are going, even if the end of the hike is obvious, such as a lake or a summit. If they ask, use vague terms like "We're planning on hiking until we are tired," or "We aren't sure yet." **Don't ignore those red-flag feelings**. You've lived on this earth long enough to know when something doesn't feel right, so follow your gut and be rude if necessary to get

away from an uncomfortable situation or people who seem "off."

3. **Don't leave valuables in plain sight in your vehicle**. In fact, don't leave valuables in your vehicle at all. A pair of sunglasses left out or even a glasses case can be all it takes for a thief to decide your car is a good target. I have a plastic laminated sign that I leave in my car when I hike that says "No Valuables in Vehicle." The goal, of course, is to let criminals know that you've already done a once-over and ensured it's not worth their time. I haven't asked any would-be robbers if this sign is a deal-breaker, but so far, knock on wood, my car has yet to get hit. Before you leave home, pull out what you really need from your wallet: national park pass, a credit card, your medical card, your ID, and a few dollars. Slide those essentials, along with your phone and any medications, into a plastic baggie and tuck it into your pack. Not only does this lighten the load on your back, it also alleviates

any worry. If your car gets burglarized, the thieves get nothing.

4. **When parking at trailheads, look around before you park and get out of your car**. In particular, look for anything that strikes you as odd, such as someone sitting in their car eyeballing you or your vehicle. If anything seems amiss, leave the trailhead and find a different hike. That hike will always be there for another day, and it's better to be safe than sorry.

5. **Don't hike with headphones**. Rocking uphill with headphones in volcano and bear country is simply not the smartest idea. Keep your wits about you as you wander along trails and save the tunes for the before-and-after drive.

6. **Don't get lost or injured**. Sure, no one tries to do this, but it happens. A few tips can help you avoid some unfortunate consequences if you find yourself in a bad situation. If you are injured, stay put! Search and Rescue teams will be out looking for you, and it's easier for them to find a fixed target than a moving one. Be patient and wait calmly. While Search and Rescue does move quickly, it can seem like an eternity when you are feeling stressed. Use your waiting time to gather firewood, filter water, and assess your food situation. With any luck, you'll be in your warm bed by nightfall. Additionally, consider investing in a **personal locator beacon** (PLB) or a backcountry communication device such as a satellite phone, Spot Satellite Messenger, or a Garmin inReach. Cell phone coverage in the backcounty is often spotty and unreliable, and forking over a little extra cash can be a lifesaving move or simply give you some peace of mind should you shake the hand of "Miss Fortune."

ENJOY THE TRAIL

Every one of us who steps into the beautiful, beloved backcountry of Mount Rainier is blessed with the opportunity to see spectacular scenery. The park is for the people and the people help preserve the park. It's a simple symbiotic relationship that works through the magic of realizing how special these landscapes are, treasuring the opportunity to hike through them, and preserving them for future generations.

If you love and enjoy these trails, get involved in volunteering! Various nonprofits work year-round to help fund trail projects and assist in keeping the pathways open for all to enjoy. For more information on how you can help, please see the sidebar on volunteering in this chapter.

Above all else, enjoy the trails! Take your time to stop and smell the wildflowers, note the tree growth patterns, ID the birds and shrubs, listen for the roar of avalanches high on Rainier, close your eyes on the shoreline of a purring river and enjoy the purity of the white noise, and lastly, let your soul find a quiet place among the evergreens to be refreshed and renewed. Happy trails, friends!

How to Use This Book

Over my lifetime, I've spent many summers on trails in Mount Rainier National Park. I know them like the back of my hand, but in order to ensure that you, my hiking friends, have the most accurate information, I rehiked every single trail in this guide carrying my GPS unit. My GPS gave me readings about elevation gain and distance, which I then compared to various maps for accuracy. When you set out into the hinterlands, rest assured that this guide is here to give you everything you need for an enjoyable adventure. Here are a few tips to help decipher the ratings in this guide.

What the Ratings Mean

At the beginning of each hike is an information block with detailed hike information. This gives you guidelines to help you choose the best possible hike for you and your hiking partners' enjoyment, abilities, and time limits. I also include recommendations for the best time to take your hike based on my knowledge of trail conditions. I hope you'll enjoy the variety of both simple and challenging hikes in this guide and find something that fills the soul each time you set foot into the backcountry.

The sun tries to steal the show as it peeks through the trees along the Silver Forest Trail (Hike 14).

Each trail in this guide has a **rating** of 1 to 5 stars based on landscape, views, wildlife, unique trail features, and popularity. This number is subjective; I'm giving you my opinion on each trail, hoping you'll agree. Some may find beauty in quiet forest valleys and think they are a solid 5 stars, while others may believe that 5 stars should be reserved for subalpine meadows. Whatever your preference, I tried my best to give each hike the most accurate rating I believe the majority of you would choose. Here is a rough guide to how I chose my ratings:

★★★★★ Spectacular scenery, a unique trail experience, photographer's dream, worthy of driving a long distance to enjoy, and one of the best hikes in the book

★★★★ Great trail experience, enjoyable scenery, potential for wildlife viewing

★★★ Trail offers a worthy experience and enjoyable scenery

★★ Good landscape to explore, an opportunity to practice macro-photography and focus on details, a good place to get exercise

★ Decent opportunity to find some solitude, but trail may not be in optimal shape or may be frequented by other trail users such as horses or mountain bikers

The **difficulty** scores range from 1 to 5, with 1 being the easiest and 5 being the most difficult. Again, this number is subjective; folks who hike often and are conditioned may find a very steep, challenging trail rated a 4 or 5 to be an easy walk, while those new to hiking or out of practice might find a hike rated a 1 or 2 a taxing undertaking. I've done my very best to make the most accurate assessment of the hikes in this guide, taking into consideration steepness, trail obstacles, distances, and elevation gain and loss. The guidelines I used are as follows:

5 Very strenuous and steep/long, with challenging sections

4 Steep, possibly with obstacles, poorly maintained tread, and/or grueling sections

3 A moderate workout and average physical challenge

2 A decent grade with straightforward routefinding

1 Easy, peasy! A walk in the park

The **roundtrip mileage** includes out-and-back or loop mileage based on GPS and map calculations. Mileages can be very difficult to determine because both paper and online maps vary greatly. In fact, if you take two GPS units down the same trail, you'll get different results because nothing, it seems, is an exact science. I've compared the data from my GPS to the data on several maps to ensure that I've done my due diligence to provide you with the best accuracy possible. At the end of the day, the true feather in your cap isn't the exact 0.1 mile reading, but rather the fact that your legs carried you to grand wilderness landscapes.

Elevation gain is the total feet you'll gain in both directions for the whole trip. For example, if the trail ends with a steep descent to a lake basin, the elevation gain includes the climb back out of the lake basin and any other ascents the trip contains. Elevation gain is also difficult to measure. Many GPS units use barometric altimeters, which depend on consistency in weather systems (an impossibility) so the barometer doesn't affect the altimeter's accuracy. Other units use satellite-based coordinates and math equations to calculate the height above sea level. With these units, base readings can vary or be incorrect from the get-go and accuracy can be challenging. Obstructions such as dense tree cover, deep river valleys, or mountainous terrain can create inexact measurements in both types, and you can go crazy seeking perfection. Trust me, as a guidebook author who works with data, I've wanted to toss my GPS units over a cliff at times while wondering why I bought the high-tech toys in the first place. The bottom line is that nothing related to GPS units is an exact science, but for the sake of making this guidebook as accurate as possible, I've used GPS technology as well as other map sources to ensure my data is as precise as possible.

The **high point** is the highest point you'll encounter along the trail. This helps you know the tippy-top elevation on the hike and is a good guide if you are planning a journey in early summer when you may find snow along high ridges or on mountaintops. Keep in mind the high point may be encountered anywhere along the trail, not necessarily at the hike's final destination.

The **season** is meant to reflect the most optimal time to hike, taking into consideration the time when the trail is in the best shape with respect to mud, snowpack, and/or trail maintenance from the Park Service. Northwest weather is fickle and snowpack

varies from year to year. Some years, snow may cover a trail well into August, while others it's gone by June. A rainy, wet spring may make trails sloppy and muddy one year, while a hot, dry spring may make for dusty journeys another. Since every year is different, the best season to hike the trail is based on an average year and an average snow-pack. To find trail conditions, it's always a good idea to check Mount Rainier National Park's website or contact one of the wilderness information centers. (See appendix.)

Next is more information designed to make it easier to enjoy the trails. For **maps**, I rely on Green Trails maps. They are updated regularly and have "boots on the ground" hikers and runners who track trails with GPS units to ensure the best accuracy. Green Trails is a Pacific Northwest company and offers a range of colorful, detailed, and user-friendly maps specific to Mount Rainier National Park!

Each hike also tells you what ranger station or agency to **contact** for up-to-date information. You'll generally find the folks staffing the information centers to be quite knowledgeable about trail and road conditions, trail maintenance projects, overnight permits, and not-to-miss trail features. Since Mount Rainier is an active volcano, park

LEGEND

⟨410⟩	State Highway	①1	Hike Number	) (	Pass/Saddle
	Secondary Road	🅣	Trailhead	▲	Summit
	Unpaved Road	Ⓣ	Alternate Trailhead		River/Lake
== 24 ==	Forest Road	----------	Hiking Route	⛰	Campground
■ ▬ ■ ▬	Park Boundary	----------	Other Trail	△	Backcountry Campsite
▰	Ranger Station	⌐⌐⌐	Bridge	🄰	Picnic Area
■	Feature	🗼	Fire Tower		

personnel can also give you updates on any recent geological events or special concerns.

The **permit** section tells you what passes you'll need to use the various trails, while **notes** offer various important tidbits of information relevant to your hike selection. For example, forest roads on trails just outside the park may require high-clearance vehicles or four-wheel drive. You'll also find information about which trails allow dogs, so you'll know whether or not to leave Fido at home.

The **GPS coordinates** (based on the WGS 84 system) for the trailheads will help you find the trail, or find your car if you make a wrong turn during your adventure.

The **icons** give you a good idea of what each trail has to offer and help you determine if it's what you seek.

 Kid-friendly

 Dog-friendly

 Exceptional wildlife viewing

 Exceptional wildflowers in season

 Exceptional waterfalls

 Exceptional views

 Exceptional old growth

 Historical relevance

 Fire-lookout tower site

 Exceptional geological feature

 Saved trail (rescued from permanent loss)

Getting there guides you to the trailhead with turn-by-turn driving directions and **on the trail** gives you detailed descriptions of each hike.

A NOTE ABOUT SAFETY

Safety is an important concern in all outdoor activities. No guidebook can alert you to every hazard or anticipate the limitations of every reader. Therefore, the descriptions of roads, trails, routes, and natural features in this book are not representations that a particular place or excursion will be safe for your party. When you follow any of the routes described in this book, you assume responsibility for your own safety. Under normal conditions, such excursions require the usual attention to traffic, road and trail conditions, weather, terrain, the capabilities of your party, and other factors. Keeping informed on current conditions and exercising common sense are the keys to a safe, enjoyable outing.

—Mountaineers Books

Sunrise is a subalpine playground as seen from Dege Peak (Hike 5).

white river/sunrise area

Visitors have been flocking to the White River Valley and the Sunrise area for years to take in the splendor of the rushing, glaciated waters and riparian landscapes as well as the high subalpine meadows teeming with wildflowers. The area, originally known as Yakima Park, opened to visitors in the early 1930s and has been popular ever since. Today, you'll find the White River area offers a car campground and a plethora of hiking options, while Sunrise has a visitors center complete with exhibits, a gift shop, a snack bar, and immensely beautiful views of Rainier, even from the parking lot. Trails leaving from Sunrise are some of the most scenic in the park and offer expansive vistas, impressive flower meadows, and wildlife such as mountain goats and marmots. The area is so divine that when you head off into the hinterlands, you can feel the effulgence of such grandiosity seeping into your pores with each shuffle of your boots! Get there!

1 Berkeley Park

RATING/ DIFFICULTY	ROUNDTRIP	ELEV GAIN/ HIGH POINT	SEASON
★★★★/3	7 miles	1520 feet/ 6800 feet	mid-July –Oct

Maps: Green Trails Mount Rainier East No. 270, Mount Rainier Wonderland No. 269SX; **Contact:** Mount Rainier National Park or Sunrise or White River Ranger Station; **Permit:** Mount Rainier National Park Pass or America the Beautiful Pass; **Notes:** Sunrise/ White River Road is open seasonally most years from late June to mid-Oct. Concession area and visitors center are open for limited

The vastness of Berkeley Park spreads out over the greater Sunrise area, creating a breathtaking playground for visitors.

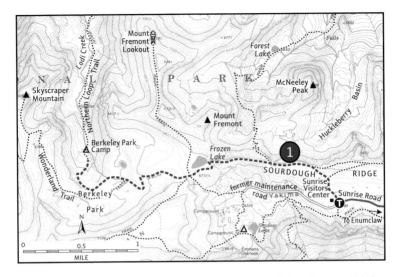

daily hours and close for the season soon after Labor Day. Check with the park before you go for road and trail conditions. Trails open to hikers only. Pets prohibited; **GPS:** N 46 54.884 W 121 38.542

Lose yourself in the beauty of both grand high country and a forested valley. Enjoy showy meadows, a large, open cirque, and a forested paradise where bears are frequently seen grazing on berries in late fall; the ice-cream cone you'll eat at the snack bar afterward just puts the metaphoric cherry on the sundae of a perfect day!

GETTING THERE

From Enumclaw, follow State Route 410 eastbound for just shy of 38 miles to a junction with the White River Entrance of Mount Rainier National Park. Turn right onto Sunrise/White River Road and continue for 15.5 miles, passing the entrance booth, the ranger station, and White River Campground,

to the Sunrise Visitors Center, which has ample parking. Restrooms available.

ON THE TRAIL

From the parking lot, locate the trailhead by following the wide paved pathway to the west of the store/snack bar and east of the restrooms. Follow the trail as it heads north for roughly 200 feet, taking you off the pavement and onto a wide gravel cruising lane. Climb north for 0.2 mile to a fork in the trail. Stay left and continue for another 0.2 mile to Sourdough Ridge. Getting to Sourdough Ridge is a good, short warm-up for the quads and really gets the heart pumping. You'll be escorted through the meadows by a phalanx of wildflowers during the summer months; with Mount Rainier as a backdrop, it's fit for a photo stop! Snap your fill, then turn left (west) on the ridgeline and continue with gentle ups and downs as you walk the Sourdough Ridge Trail high above the Sunrise area. Continue straight past the Huckleberry

Creek Trail junction and the viewpoint for Frozen Lake until you reach a five-way signed trail junction, located 1.1 miles before the ridgeline. Follow the sign for the Wonderland Trail to the right (west).

Head 0.8 mile west on the Wonderland Trail to reach a junction with the signed Northern Loop Trail and for Berkeley Park Camp. Follow the Northern Loop Trail as it descends through wide meadows bursting with seasonal, low-growing huckleberries and colorful wildflowers in hues of violet, magenta, and white—a rainbow carpet! To the west, the peak of Skyscraper Mountain towers above as you sink lower, eventually entering sparse trees that thicken up as you drop deeper into the backcountry.

Look for signs of bears that frequently scratch the trees in this area looking for tasty insects under thick bark. Lodi Creek playfully babbles along the trail as you approach Berkeley Park Camp, a good

turnaround spot. Here, 1.2 miles from where you turned off the Wonderland, you'll find a primitive privy as well as a couple of flat spots to spread out a picnic if you haven't stopped to nibble already. Enjoy the deep forest with all the senses awakened, then put the leg motors in gear to climb out of the basin and back to a well-earned ice-cream cone at Sunrise.

2 Burroughs Mountain Loop

RATING/ DIFFICULTY	ROUNDTRIP	ELEV GAIN/ HIGH POINT	SEASON
★★★★★/3	9.1 miles	1730 feet/ 7830 feet	July–Oct

Maps: Green Trails Mount Rainier East No. 270, Mount Rainier Wonderland No. 269SX; **Contact:** Mount Rainier National Park or Sunrise or White River Ranger Station; **Permit:** Mount Rainier Park Pass or America

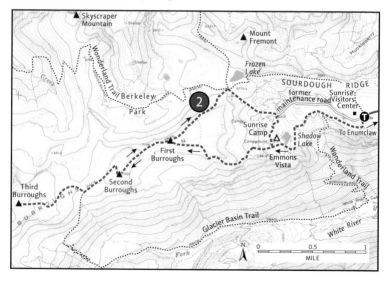

the Beautiful Pass; **Notes:** Sunrise/White River Road is open seasonally most years from late June to mid-Oct. Concession area and visitors center are open for limited daily hours and close for the season soon after Labor Day. This hike is very high in elevation and subject to hazardous snow crossings even into warm summer months, so check with the park before you go for road and trail conditions. Trails open to hikers only. Pets prohibited; **GPS:** N 46 54.884 W 121 38.542

Experience Mount Rainier through some of the highest country attainable by day hiking in the park. Three peaks, named the First, Second, and Third Burroughs, are woven into the loop hike and can be reached from either direction at the trailhead. Whichever way you go, you'll spend the day in absolute alpine bliss!

GETTING THERE

From Enumclaw, follow State Route 410 eastbound for just shy of 38 miles to a junction with the White River Entrance of Mount Rainier National Park. Turn right onto Sunrise/White River Road and continue for 15.5 miles, passing the entrance booths and ranger stations, to the Sunrise Visitors Center, which has ample parking. Restrooms available.

ON THE TRAIL

The Burroughs Mountain Trail is a loop accessible from several connecting trails that you can hike either clockwise or counterclockwise from Sunrise. I prefer to start the adventure on the south side of the Sunrise parking area along the Sunrise Rim Trail, where the grade gently eases you into the start of your day.

Wander to your heart's content along one of three lofty vistas on Burroughs Mountain Loop.

Burroughs Mountain was named in tribute to American naturalist and nature writer John Burroughs, whose eloquent essays include his observations of birds, fish, and landscapes. The high points along this trail are now referred to as "Burroughs," such as "First Burroughs," to match his name, although the three together are called Burroughs Mountain. Confusing, right? Whatever you call it, you'll love what's ahead!

To locate the trailhead, head to the southern side of the parking lot and follow the wide gravel, well-traveled trail signed with a "no pets" reminder and little fanfare. In roughly 425 feet, you reach a signed junction for the Silver Forest Trail, Emmons Vista, the Sunrise Rim Trail, the Wonderland Trail, and Sunrise Camp. It's a lot of arrows and names, especially if you aren't familiar with the area, but just head right (southwest) toward Sunrise Camp and your feet will be on the correct path.

In 0.5 mile, arrive at a junction with the Wonderland Trail. Stay westbound, simply continuing the same way you've been going. The sign here now says Burroughs Mountain Trail and has an arrow pointing the way—reassuring if you feel discombobulated.

From here, and all the way to First Burroughs, watch for bears. Black bears are frequent visitors to these areas, especially around Sunrise Camp during late summer months when sweet, low-growing huckleberries ripen in the meadows. Bears here may be used to seeing and hearing people; as always, keep a safe distance and don't jeopardize your safety or theirs in the name of Instagram. Remember, they are at a food source and may be defensive.

The path bobs and weaves through forest and meadows with peekaboo Rainier views until it passes the shoreline of Shadow Lake to the right (north), followed by a trail junction near Sunrise Camp, 1.3 miles from where you started. Sunrise Camp is a wilderness camp set along the Wonderland Trail and requires a permit to stay overnight. As luck would have it, it has an outhouse near the trail junction, which anyone can use if nature is calling. Because it gets so much use, however, it can be atrociously pungent and might wilt the nearby flowers if you leave the door open too long. Use it if you must and suppress the memory.

The trail junction at Sunrise Camp is signed with a variety of trails and arrows. Your hike continues westbound; the sign now points to First Burroughs. The trail ahead is visible from the junction and you'll notice it starts to ascend, so give your quads a persuasive "you can do it" pep talk and grab a snack if you need a little extra energy.

Reward yourself as you climb higher with grand views of Mount Rainier and Emmons Glacier as well as the White River Valley. Note the signs remind you that you are entering a fragile tundra-like environment and to stay on the trail. At 2.6 miles, arrive at First Burroughs, a flat plateau, and another trail junction with another arrow-filled sign. If you are happy seeing only First Burroughs and want to head back, this is where you'll loop back to Sunrise. If you have more steam, continue to wander and follow the arrow toward Second Burroughs to the left (west).

Crank another 0.6 mile up the well-worn trail to Second Burroughs. The trail now begins a gentle descent toward the Glacier Basin Trail, but just before it does, an unsigned, boot-beaten path leads toward Third Burroughs, 0.8 mile farther. Climb again until you are standing on the top of the wonderfully weird landscape. You can see all the way to the west, including the

Mystic Lake basin, from this vista. This is the perfect place to stop for lunch and exhaust your camera battery—what a spectacular view!

With your camera battery kaput but your spirits refreshed, backtrack the signed junction near First Burroughs, and this time follow the arrows pointing toward Frozen Lake and Sunrise. Down, down, down you go until you reach a five-way trail junction, just under a mile northeast of the signed junction. Turn right (southeast) and follow the arrows pointing toward the Wonderland Trail. Watch your footing as you walk since this is the land of large rocks that can make you perform an unplanned interpretive dance.

In 0.6 mile from the five-way intersection, arrive at a signed junction with a maintenance road that will get you back to the Sunrise Visitors Center more quickly. The arrow here points to Sunrise, which is 0.9 mile east, making the total distance for this trip 7.7 miles. If you continue along the Wonderland the way you came, you'll reach Sunrise in 2.3 miles from this point, making the total distance for this trip 9.1 miles.

Views of the White River Valley and Mount Rainier await on the Crystal Peak Trail.

3 Crystal Peak

RATING/ DIFFICULTY	ROUNDTRIP	ELEV GAIN/ HIGH POINT	SEASON
★★★★/5	8.4 miles	3052 feet/ 6595 feet	July–Oct

Maps: Green Trails Mount Rainier East No. 270, Mount Rainier Wonderland No. 269SX; **Contact:** Mount Rainier National Park or Sunrise or White River Ranger Station; **Permit:** Mount Rainier Park Pass or America the Beautiful Pass; **Notes:** This trail is accessible without passing through national park pay stations but is still in the park and technically requires a park pass, although nothing is required to be displayed on your windshield. Overnight camping requires a permit from the Park Service. Pets and stock prohibited; **GPS:** N 46 55.352 W 121 32.020

When you think of sitting on top of a peak with sweeping views of Mount Rainier and the White River Valley, think Crystal Peak! The mountain views are amazing and the flower-filled meadows you cross are equally impressive. Take a lunch, take a picture, take a snooze—it's all fair game . . . just get there!

GETTING THERE

From the last stoplight in Enumclaw on State Route 410 eastbound (284th Avenue SE/Farman and Roosevelt), proceed for 32.2 miles, passing the town of Greenwater, to enter Mount Rainier National Park under a large wooden sign. Continue for another 4 miles to the large parking area/pullout on the right (west). More parking and the trailhead are across the road to the east.

ON THE TRAIL

The trail begins on the east side of the road and is hard to spot until you walk toward the forest and see a little log bridge that takes you over rushing Crystal Creek. Just beyond is the official trailhead sign with the classic "you are here" red-dotted map. Suddenly you are under an evergreen canopy so thick, little light penetrates the understory. The climb takes your mind off your surroundings as you start to huff and puff your way up the trail. Foliage, such as pipsissewa, moss, saplings, salal, and Oregon grape, competes for light on the trail edges. Log stairs help prevent erosion and escort you higher into your switchbacking climb. Crystal Creek runs nearby and tempts you with trail pullouts to see its banks, even though the view isn't great.

In 1.3 miles, arrive at a trail junction with sign arrows pointing straight ahead to Crystal Lakes (Hike 4) and to the right for Crystal Peak. If time and stamina permit, visit both. If not, turn right (south) and head toward Crystal Peak. As with most park signs, the mileage noted here, 2.5 miles, is incorrect.

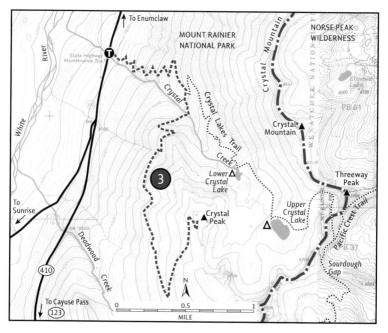

The actual distance to the top of the peak is 2.9 miles, so if those quads scream you'll know why. If you visit in early summer, you might find yourself surrounded by so-green-it-hurts vanilla leaf, which graces the trail's edges. Combined with the brown trail, it almost looks like a fairytale forest as you descend slightly to reach a crossing of Crystal Creek, 0.2 mile from the junction. This log bridge washes out from time to time, but the Park Service does its best to ensure it's there for you. Cross the log, using the handrail if necessary. You may want to wrap your arms around the impressive Douglas fir on the other side for a great photo or just to receive some good juju.

The trail continues under the conifers, then crosses a scree field and dips back into the woods heading south. The trees become spindly as you continue your ascent. At roughly 0.7 mile from crossing the creek, you can glimpse Mount Rainier to the right (west) and start anticipating the views ahead. Shortly thereafter, the trail crosses a couple of avalanche chutes that bear the scars of harsh winters. In summer, however, the sunlit hillsides produce colorful flowers, including pearly everlasting, penstemon, and lupine. Up, up, up you go, getting into more open country with eye-popping views. The long switchbacks through the meadows are a wonderful reward for all your hard work.

Back and forth you hike, surrounded by views of Mount Rainier, the White River Valley, the Sunrise area, and even Burroughs Mountain. Several silver snags draw your attention just before the summit push. At 2.7 miles from the signed junction, arrive at a rocky outcropping that used to have a fire-lookout tower. Built in 1934, the tower stood watch over the vast views until it was removed, like so many, in the 1970s. Remnants of the fire-lookout tower remain, including some cement posts and a few rusty nails. The view from here is good, but the view just 0.2 mile beyond at the true summit is even better. Follow the rocky trail up the ridge and perch yourself on the rocks near the top of the peak. Be sure to catch the views of Crystal Lakes and Sourdough Gap to the east in the basin below. With views like this, you might just want to stay forever.

When you've gazed your fill, head back the way you came.

4 Crystal Lakes

RATING/ DIFFICULTY	ROUNDTRIP	ELEV GAIN/ HIGH POINT	SEASON
★★★★★/3	6 miles	2310 feet/ 5830 feet	July–Oct

Maps: Green Trails Mount Rainier East No. 270, Mount Rainier Wonderland No. 269SX; **Contact:** Mount Rainier National Park or Sunrise or White River Ranger Station; **Permit:** Mount Rainier Park Pass or America the Beautiful Pass; **Notes:** This trail is accessible without passing through National Park pay stations but it is still in the park and technically requires a park pass, although nothing is required to be displayed on your windshield. Overnight camping requires a permit from the Park Service. Pets and stock prohibited; **GPS:** N 46 55.352 W 121 32.020

If you are looking for sensational grandeur, look no further than this hike! A decent workout leads to a pair of sparkling lakes set in a splendid subalpine basin. If it's a Rainier view you seek, put in a little extra effort to hike just beyond the lakes and discover a photographer's dream.

GETTING THERE

From the last stoplight in Enumclaw on State Route 410 eastbound (284th Avenue SE/Farman and Roosevelt), proceed for 32.2 miles, passing the town of Greenwater, to enter Mount Rainier National Park under a large wooden sign. Continue for another 4 miles to the large parking area/pullout on the right (west). More parking and the trailhead are across the road to the east.

ON THE TRAIL

The trail immediately crosses Crystal Creek on a sturdy bridge and begins climbing to the soundtrack of the playful water. For 1.3 miles, the trail ascends on relatively tight switchbacks, climbing through native forest foliage, such as vanilla leaf, pipsissewa, and towering conifers, until it reaches a signed junction for Crystal Peak heading off to the right (south).

If gumption and time permit, you may want to take this side trip (Hike 3). For now, continue ascending and enjoy the treat of a peekaboo view of Mount Rainier to the southwest.

In 2 miles, the landscape gives way to a more open subalpine feeling with seasonal wildflowers; finally you feel like you're getting somewhere. At 2.4 miles, reach a signed junction with a short spur delivering you to Lower Crystal Lake. Be sure to check it out, but save your picnic lunch and climb just 0.6 mile more to the more scenic upper lake. Wilderness camps at both the lower and upper lakes offer primitive backcountry privies for those who need a rustic bio-break.

Scan the meadows for the elk, bear, and marmots that call this area home. The upper lake, set in a bowl below craggy peaks, is home to frogs and other aquatic life that thrive in this healthy ecosystem and hop

Plants thrive in the wet environment at Upper Crystal Lake.

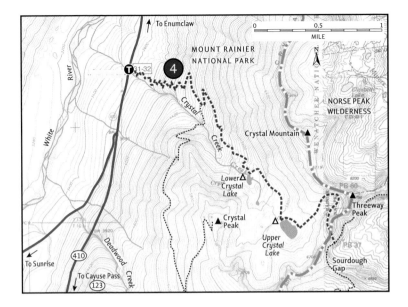

about the shoreline, showing you their beautiful living rooms.

During dry season, those who still have some energy to spare may want to keep hiking eastbound, following a well-blazed trail around the lake's northern side. During wet seasons or in late spring and early summer, this trail is impassable due to runoff that submerges the trail. Ramble roughly 0.9 mile as the trail winds its way up to an unnamed ridgeline with views of Mount Rainier and the Crystal Lakes basin. Turn back once you've gawked enough, or continue wandering to your delight. You can make a two-car shuttle/thru-hike by leaving one car at the Sheep Lake Trailhead (Hike 50) and following this trail down the other side of the ridgeline, connecting with the Pacific Crest Trail, and heading southbound past Sourdough Gap and Sheep Lake.

5 Dege Peak

RATING/ DIFFICULTY	ROUNDTRIP	ELEV GAIN/ HIGH POINT	SEASON
★★★★/2	4.2 miles	785 feet/ 7006 feet	July–Oct

Maps: Green Trails Mount Rainier East No. 270, Mount Rainier Wonderland No. 269SX; **Contact:** Mount Rainier National Park or Sunrise or White River Ranger Station; **Permit:** Mount Rainier Park Pass or America the Beautiful Pass; **Notes:** Sunrise/White River Road is open seasonally most years from late June to mid-Oct. Concession area and visitors center are open for limited daily hours and close for the season soon after Labor Day. Check with the park before you go for road and trail conditions. Pets and stock prohibited; **GPS:** N 46 54.884 W 121 38.542

The eye-popping views of the Sunrise area might knock you, or at least your socks, off the top of Dege Peak.

 Want sweeping panoramic views of Mount Rainier and the Sunrise area? This hike will have you grinning and fill up your camera! Dege Peak is a rocky knoll that sits high above the Sourdough Ridge Trail and gives you an excellent perch for gawking in all directions.

GETTING THERE

From Enumclaw, follow State Route 410 eastbound for just shy of 38 miles to a junction with the White River Entrance of Mount Rainier National Park. Turn right onto Sunrise/White River Road and continue for 15.5 miles, passing the entrance booths and ranger stations, to the Sunrise Visitors Center, which has ample parking. Restrooms available.

ON THE TRAIL

Dege Peak can be hiked either as an out-and-back or a thru-hike, if you have two cars. You can also reach it in a shorter distance by hiking west from Sunrise Point. Hiking to it from the Sunrise Visitors Center is, in my opinion, the best way to experience every drop of sweetness the area has to offer.

If you decide to thru-hike, leave one car at the Sunrise Point parking area, located on a hairpin turn roughly 12 miles from the junction of SR 410 and the White River Entrance. Otherwise, you can do an out-and-back from Sunrise Point or from the Sunrise Visitors Center, as described here.

From the parking lot, locate the trailhead by following the wide paved pathway to the west of the store/snack bar and east of the restrooms. The trail heads north in roughly 200 feet, taking you off the pavement onto a wide gravel path. As you climb, notice the beautiful seasonal wildflowers at your feet, which beg you to stop and snap a picture or two.

At 0.2 mile, reach a fork and bear right, continuing your ascent through open grassy slopes until you reach the ridgeline and the Sourdough Ridge Trail, 0.6 mile from where you started. The Sourdough Ridge Trail is a wonderful walk whether you wander east or west. Today, follow it to the right (east) and meander along gentle ups and downs under the broad shoulders of Antler Peak. Whistling hoary marmots scurry around collecting wildflowers for snacks while Clark's nutcrackers chatter in the firs around the meadows.

In 1.2 miles from the ridgeline, arrive at a small, signed spur trail to the left (northeast) toward the top of Dege Peak. Watch your footing on the rocky ground as you climb a couple of switchbacks to the summit and your grandiose perch, 0.3 mile from the spur. Take a deep breath of that fresh air and look

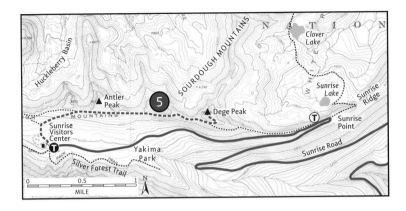

around. To the east, you can see Sunrise Lake in the protected basin below the peak, while farther out, busy SR 410 is in view as it climbs toward Cayuse Pass. Mount Rainier and the Sunrise area are visions to the southwest. Everywhere you look it's a feast for the eyes and a balm for the soul. When you've gazed your fill, head back the way you came or continue heading east along Sourdough Ridge if you are thru-hiking to Sunrise Point.

6 Emmons Moraine Trail

RATING/ DIFFICULTY	ROUNDTRIP	ELEV GAIN/ HIGH POINT	SEASON
★★★/2	3 miles	880 feet/ 5100 feet	July–Oct

Maps: Green Trails Mount Rainier East No. 270, Mount Rainier Wonderland No. 269SX; **Contact:** Mount Rainier National Park or Sunrise or White River Ranger Station; **Permit:** Mount Rainier Park Pass or America the Beautiful Pass; **Notes:** Sunrise/White River Road is open seasonally most years from late June to mid-Oct. Concession area and visitors center are open for limited daily hours and close for the season soon after Labor Day. Check with the park before you go for road and trail conditions. Trails open to hikers only. Pets and stock prohibited; **GPS:** N 46 54.103 W 121 38.755

When crowds are at a maximum during the summer months, you can usually count on the Emmons Moraine Trail to be less busy. While sweeping views of Mount Rainier are limited, this trail offers the opportunity to get up close and personal with the toe of Emmons Glacier, touted as the largest glacier (in surface area) in the contiguous United States.

GETTING THERE
From Enumclaw, follow State Route 410 eastbound for just shy of 38 miles to a junction with the White River Entrance of Mount Rainier National Park. Turn right onto Sunrise/White River Road and continue for 5.3 miles, passing the entrance booth, restrooms, and ranger station. Turn left into White River Campground and look for the day-use parking area to the left. Restrooms and picnic areas available.

Sediment and stone deposited by the Emmons Glacier is under your feet along the Emmons Moraine Trail, but it's the view that will capture your attention.

ON THE TRAIL

Locate the Glacier Basin Trail at the west end of White River Campground and follow the wide path, which gradually narrows. The White River sings a gentle lullaby to the trail's south as you wander through the forested path on a gentle climbing grade. Seasonal wildflowers, such as Lewis's monkeyflower, penstemon, and tall bluebells, thrive in the damp soil, while small saplings in the forested pockets look up to their very large parents.

In just shy of 1 mile, arrive at a trail junction with the Emmons Moraine Trail, noted by a sign. Turn left (south) here and almost immediately drop to cross a small branch of the silted White River on a sturdy log bridge. Once across, the trail ascends the moraine on a ridgeline and wanders in and out of mixed pine and fir trees until it pops out at

several viewpoints. Watch your footing when you stop to look since the ground is a sandy, rocky mixture and can be loosey-goosey beneath your feet.

Emmons Glacier is named after American geologist Samuel Franklin Emmons, a Harvard graduate who surveyed Mount Rainier in the 1860s. He traveled extensively in the United States, earning himself several namesakes besides Emmons Glacier; Colorado and Utah both have peaks named Mount Emmons.

The White River wanders through the valley to your left (southeast), looking small compared to the large glacier just above it. But don't let it fool you; the river and the glacier feeding it are powerful tools that Mount Rainier has often used to rearrange the scenery. An unnamed lake, formed by glacial

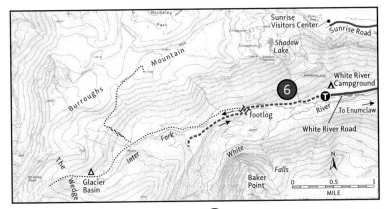

meltwater, is visible from several vantage points and is a vision of brilliant turquoise thanks to the sunlight reflecting against the lightweight, suspended glacial flour.

Nearly 5600 years ago, a landmark event known as the Osceola Mudflow occurred. During a very active volcanic period, volcanic material slid away from the volcano's summit and northeast slopes, collapsing into the White River Valley and flowing almost all the way to Puget Sound. The mountain was built up after the flow by subsequent eruptions and now looks like the Rainier we know. Today, geologists keep a close eye on the area for signs of volcanic tantrums. The most recent lava flow happened roughly 2200 years ago, so don't worry too much as you enjoy the volcanic hinterlands. The communities of Orting, Buckley, Puyallup, Enumclaw, and Auburn are primarily located on top of Osceola Mudflow deposits.

With history buzzing about in your head, enjoy this area and turn back when you've wandered to your heart's content. Either return the way you came or, when you reach the Glacier Basin Trail, continue hiking west for more adventure (see Hike 8).

7 Forest Lake

RATING/ DIFFICULTY	ROUNDTRIP	ELEV GAIN/ HIGH POINT	SEASON
★★★★/3	4.6 miles	1620 feet/ 6800 feet	July–Oct

Maps: Green Trails Mount Rainier East No. 270, Mount Rainier Wonderland No. 269SX; **Contact:** Mount Rainier National Park or Sunrise or White River Ranger Station; **Permit:** Mount Rainier Park Pass or America the Beautiful Pass; **Notes:** Sunrise/White River Road is open seasonally most years from late June to mid-Oct. Concession area and visitors center are open for limited daily hours and close for the season soon after Labor Day. Check with the park before you go for road and trail conditions. Pets and stock prohibited; **GPS:** N 46 54.884 W 121 38.542

If you love the idea of getting away from it all but think it's not possible anywhere near the bustling visitors center of Sunrise, think again! Forest Lake is a lovely mountain lake set in conifers, with a soundtrack of a

Tranquility abounds in the quiet backcountry near Forest Lake.

nearby dribbling creek and the fragrance of sun-warmed firs. So few people visit that some who have lived near the park for years look bewildered when the lake is mentioned. While this hike doesn't highlight grand views of Mount Rainier, you'll enjoy them on the way to and from the lake as you make your way up to Sourdough Ridge. Because of the tranquility and the change of scenery, this little lake has become one of my absolute favorite places to visit when I need to refresh my soul.

GETTING THERE

From Enumclaw, follow State Route 410 eastbound for just shy of 38 miles to a junction with the White River Entrance of Mount Rainier National Park. Turn right onto Sunrise/White River Road and continue for 15.5 miles, passing the entrance booths and ranger stations, to the Sunrise Visitors Center, which has ample parking. Restrooms available.

ON THE TRAIL

At the visitors center, find the trailhead by following the wide paved pathway to the west of the store/snack bar and east of the restrooms. In roughly 200 feet, the official trailhead cruises north, taking you off the pavement and onto gravel, staying wide at first. Up, up, up you go on wide wooden, erosion-preventing stairs, waking up your muscles and challenging your lungs to suck in some fresh mountain air. Be sure to stop and snap a few photos because from here to Sourdough Ridge just ahead, the views—especially as the wildflowers bloom—are spectacular.

In 0.2 mile, arrive at a fork in the trail and stay left, following the pathway as it begins to climb toward the northwest ridgeline. The anticipation of what's ahead makes your legs go faster as you near the top. In 0.2 mile from the fork, reach Sourdough Ridge. Stop, look, and catch your breath. The view in front of

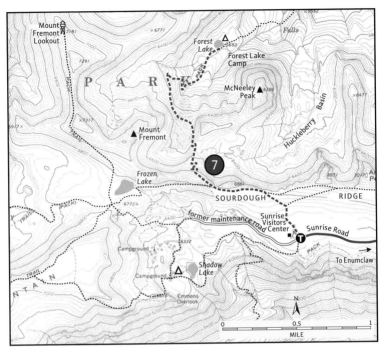

you to the north is Huckleberry Basin, not too far from where you are going, although Forest Lake isn't visible at this point. Keep your eyes peeled for black bears as they are frequently seen nibbling berries in the true-to-its-name basin; they'll look like little ants down in the valley below. Because you're so close to the basin on this hike, practice good bear etiquette and make some noise as you walk, especially on blind corners.

Follow Sourdough Ridge to the left (west) and ascend the ridgeline until you arrive at the signed junction noting "Huckleberry Crk. Tr., Forest Lk. Camp, Park Boundary and USFS 73 Road" located 0.3 mile from where you first reached Sourdough Ridge. Turn right here (northwest) and begin a rocky

descent toward the open, grassy, wildflower meadows near the edge of Huckleberry Basin. Watch for herds of mountain goats on the shoulders of nearby peaks.

The trail continues gradually dropping, crossing a rocky saddle surrounded by meadows and sparse trees. From here it intermingles with conifer thickets, grassy meadows, and creek crossings until in 1.8 miles you can see spectacular emerald-colored Forest Lake through the firs. Mosquitoes dance around your bare arms in early summer, so tango with your bug goo if you brought it, otherwise keep rolling for another 0.1 mile to find Forest Lake Camp, a privy, and a few logs for perching to take in the view. When you've enjoyed the lake, warm up the quads again for the hike back out.

8 Glacier Basin

RATING/ DIFFICULTY	ROUNDTRIP	ELEV GAIN/ HIGH POINT	SEASON
★★★★★/3	6.8 miles	1650 feet/ 5975 feet	July–Oct

Maps: Green Trails Mount Rainier East No. 270, Mount Rainier Wonderland No. 269SX; **Contact:** Mount Rainier National Park or Sunrise or White River Ranger Station; **Permit:** Mount Rainier Park Pass or America the Beautiful Pass; **Notes:** Snow travel beyond Glacier Basin is not recommended unless you have mountaineering gear and know how to use it. Pets and stock prohibited; **GPS:** N 46 54.103 W 121 38.755

 *One of the reasons I am smitten with Mount Rainier is the combination of subalpine scenery, river valleys,* wildflower meadows, and conifer forest. The hike to Glacier Basin contains all of these and is also one of the most easily accessed hikes in the park. The floods of 2006 seriously damaged the trail but in 2010 and 2011, the nonprofit Washington Trails Association worked tirelessly to reroute the Glacier Basin Trail, putting it higher on the hillside and exposing even more peekaboo mountain views. Kudos to them! The many small bridges over creeks and wetlands and the trail's gentle grade provide fantastic places for young and old to enjoy the splendor of the high country without too much elevation gain.

GETTING THERE

From Enumclaw, follow State Route 410 east for roughly 38 miles to Sunrise/White River Road and the White River Entrance of Mount Rainier National Park. Turn right on Sunrise/White River Road and continue for 5.3 miles, passing the entrance booth, restrooms, and

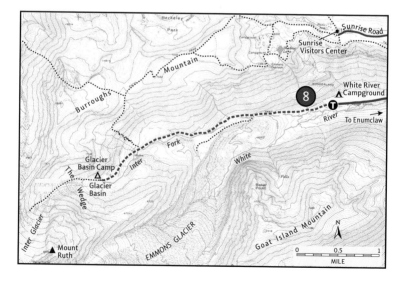

ranger station. Turn left into White River Campground and look for the day-use parking area to the left. Restrooms and picnic areas available.

ON THE TRAIL

The trail begins to the west of White River Campground and follows the White River, gently climbing above its banks and offering views of Goat Island Mountain to the south. The forested climb skirts creek banks where Lewis's monkeyflower, penstemon, and tall bluebells, among others, thrive in the damp soil. Beyond, Mount Rainier shines like a beacon through the trees and welcomes you as you stroll.

In roughly 1 mile, reach a junction with the Emmons Moraine Trail to the left (southwest). If time permits, the additional 3-mile roundtrip (Hike 6) is well worth the effort to view Emmons Glacier—a mass of ice, deep crevasses, and boulders—up close and personal. If not, save it for another time and continue your gradual climb toward Glacier Basin until you arrive at another junction 2.6 miles from the trailhead. This junction points toward Sunrise to the right (north) and connects to the Burroughs Loop (Hike 2) as it climbs. Make a mental note to come back and hit this trail as well, but for now continue onward, climbing a bit more steeply for another 0.8 mile until you reach the official wilderness camp of Glacier Basin, popular with climbers beginning their summit bids. Thankfully, a backcountry privy awaits if your bladder is dancing. You might be tempted to turn around here, but beyond the camp is where the scenery really starts blowing your mind.

The subalpine grandeur of Glacier Basin is a feast for the eyes and a workout for the camera.

The unmaintained trail ascends around several subalpine meadows and makes a perfect place for a picnic and a final destination. You could extend your hike by continuing up a barren spine toward an area called the Wedge and Saint Elmo Pass, but don't venture too far. Just beyond them, mountaineering and glacier-travel skills are required. Inter Glacier becomes the jumping-off point for the snowy ascent to Camp Schurman base camp, which provides climbers a place to throw down their four-season tents before the early-morning start to the summit.

Glacier Basin has a rich mining history, and rusty relics from the late 1800s and early 1900s are still strewn about. In those days, this basin contained two mining tunnels, a barn, two cabins, a sawmill, a power plant, a plank flume, and a 13-room hotel. The main trail you just hiked up was originally the road to the mining operation. Unfortunately for Peter Storbo, the claim holder, who along with his uncle bought 41 claims on these 800 acres, the mine yielded more rocks than ore and eventually closed down.

Mountain goats and bears are popular visitors to these areas, so keep your eyes open on the surrounding hillsides. Unlike the miners, please follow the Leave-No-Trace ethos closely here, as elsewhere in the park, especially in the meadows where flowers such as western anemone and glacier lilies tempt you to wander in for a photo. The short growing season must be protected and preserved by reducing bootprints, so step or sit only on impermeable surfaces, such as dirt, ice, or rocks. There are umpteen places to pull off the trail, sit on rocks, and nibble on gorp, so take your pick. Your eyes will be full of grandeur and your soul will be refreshed by the time you start back.

9   Grand Park

RATING/ DIFFICULTY	ROUNDTRIP	ELEV GAIN/ HIGH POINT	SEASON
★★★★/4	12.4 miles	1970 feet/ 6800 feet	mid-July– Oct

Maps: Green Trails Mount Rainier East No. 270, Mount Rainier Wonderland No. 269SX; **Contact:** Mount Rainier National Park or Sunrise or White River Ranger Station; **Permit:** Mount Rainier Park Pass or America the Beautiful Pass; **Notes:** Sunrise/White River Road is open seasonally most years from late June to mid-Oct. Concession area and visitors center are open for limited daily hours and close for the season soon after Labor Day. Check with the park before you go for road and trail conditions. Pets and stock prohibited; **GPS:** N 46 54.884 W 121 38.542

Grand Park is one of the few places in the park where, thanks to a geological abnormality, you can wander through flat meadows on a tabletop landscape amid a background of many peaks, including Rainier itself. Getting there requires some ups and downs, but once in Grand Park, meandering through terrain without huffing and puffing is a fine respite for the soul.

GETTING THERE

From Enumclaw, follow State Route 410 eastbound for just shy of 38 miles to a junction with the White River Entrance of Mount Rainier National Park. Turn right onto Sunrise/White River Road and continue for 15.5 miles, passing the entrance booths and ranger stations, to the Sunrise Visitors Center, which has ample parking. Restrooms available.

ON THE TRAIL

At the visitors center, find the trailhead by following the wide paved pathway to the west of the store/snack bar and east of the restrooms. In roughly 200 feet, the official trailhead cruises north, taking you off the pavement and onto gravel, staying wide at first. Climb northbound for 0.2 mile to reach a fork in the trail. Stay left and continue for another 0.2 mile to reach Sourdough Ridge. Once there, turn left (west) and continue with gentle ups and downs as you walk the Sourdough Ridge Trail high above the Sunrise area.

Pass the Huckleberry Creek Trail junction and the viewpoint for Frozen Lake until you reach a five-way signed trail junction, located 1.5 miles from the visitors center. Trails scoot off in almost every direction. Make a note to come back and check out more of these when time permits, but

for now, take the Wonderland Trail to the west, signed "Wonderland Trail, Granite Crk. Camp, Mystic Lake, Northern Loop Tr, Berkeley Pk. Camp, Lk. Eleanor Jct (Grand Pk)." The sign also lists distances to the various camps and landmarks, but, as with almost all the signs in the park, the mileages aren't exact.

Head west on the Wonderland Trail and in 0.8 mile, arrive at a junction with the signed Northern Loop Trail. Follow the Northern Loop Trail as it descends through open country toward Berkeley Park Camp in an area known as, you guessed it, Berkeley Park. Keep your eyes open for bears! This is sweet, low-growing huckleberry heaven in late summer and bears hang out here for the abundant grazing it provides. If you don't see one, look for evidence by the scratch marks on trees where they've ripped down

While getting there and back requires some effort, the mostly level playground of Grand Park invites you to catch your breath and enjoy the peacefulness of a vast, serene setting.

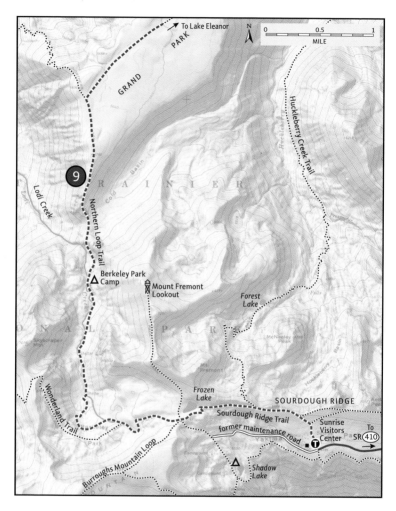

bark in a hunt for tasty bugs. In 2.6 miles from the visitors center, arrive at Berkeley Park Camp, located in a sparsely forested grove of conifers. Nearby Lodi Creek provides water for campers and anyone who needs to dip a filter.

Onward you go, making your way closer and closer to Grand Park. The trail stays in forested groves and mixed huckleberry thickets, then crests a small rise before descending and delivering you to the Lake Eleanor Trail, 5.4 miles from the Sunrise Visitors Center.

Follow the Lake Eleanor Trail to the northeast and immediately notice the huge grassy meadows and spectacular in-your-face views of Mount Rainier. You've arrived in Grand Park! Keep your eyes out for the elk, deer, bear, and mountain goats that frequent the area. Seasonal wildflowers such as aster, paintbrush, and lupine make a fine foreground for your photos as you gawk to the southwest, where Rainier shows its white snowcap. Also visible to the south is the historic lookout tower sitting proudly on Mount Fremont. After roughly a mile, the trail begins a gentle descent toward Lake Eleanor, which makes a fine place to turn back. Then again, your heart might beckon you to stay a little longer.

10 Mount Fremont Lookout

RATING/ DIFFICULTY	ROUNDTRIP	ELEV GAIN/ HIGH POINT	SEASON
★★★★★/3	5.6 miles	800 feet/ 7200 feet	July–Oct

Maps: Green Trails Mount Rainier East No. 270, Mount Rainier Wonderland No. 269SX; **Contact:** Mount Rainier National Park or Sunrise or White River Ranger Station; **Permit:** Mount Rainier Park Pass or America the Beautiful Pass; **Notes:** Sunrise/White River Road is open seasonally most years from late June to mid-Oct. Concession area and visitors center are open for limited daily hours and close for the season soon after Labor Day. Check with the park before you go for road and trail conditions. Pets and stock prohibited; **GPS:** N 46 54.884 W 121 38.542

 *When a sunny day offers a gentle breeze in the summer months, there might be no hike more interesting and pic-* turesque *than Mount Fremont. The views of Grand Park and its vast meadows from the lofty perch of the old fire tower make you want to stay all day. Then again the hike does start off at "Sunrise," so you could arrive just as the sun comes up and make a full day of it, immersing yourself in gorgeous vistas.*

GETTING THERE

From Enumclaw, follow State Route 410 eastbound for just shy of 38 miles to a junction with the White River Entrance of Mount Rainier National Park. Turn right onto Sunrise/White River Road and continue for 15.5 miles, passing the entrance booths and ranger stations, to the Sunrise Visitors Center, which has ample parking. Restrooms available.

ON THE TRAIL

From the visitors center, locate the trailhead by following the wide paved pathway (and the throngs of hikers) to the west of the store/snack bar and east of the restrooms. In roughly 200 feet, the trail heads north, taking you off the pavement and onto gravel, staying wide at first. Wide stairs guide you through meadows of seasonal wildflowers with grand views of Mount Rainier. You might be tempted to just stop here and enjoy the beauty all day, but more eye candy awaits!

In 0.2 mile, arrive at a fork in the trail and stay left, following the path as it begins to climb toward the northwest ridgeline. Your legs feel the burn as they get warmed up along this gradual incline. In 0.2 mile from the fork, arrive at Sourdough Ridge, offering a viewpoint and a chance to catch your breath and look for bears far below in Huckleberry Basin. During summer months, sitting here for a few minutes might allow the keen eye an opportunity to find one munching delicious dwarf huckleberries.

Follow Sourdough Ridge to the left (west) and continue on gentle ups and downs, passing an intersection for the Huckleberry Creek Trail and Forest Lake. Wandering westward, the trail passes several rocky hillsides and sparse conifers, offering occasional glimpses of hoary-marmot burrows and their occupants. Watch your footing carefully as in places the soil is rocky and you can twist an ankle.

In 0.9 mile from gaining the ridgeline, note the signs for the unusual body of water to the right, Frozen Lake, which true to its name stays iced over into the summer months. This lake provides water for the Sunrise Visitors Center as well as for park staff housing. It's off-limits to visitors but lovely all the same.

In 0.2 mile beyond Frozen Lake (1.5 miles from the trailhead), find yourself at a five-way trail junction. Follow the signs toward Mount Fremont, turning right (north)

along the wide-open, tundra-like slopes leading to the beautiful old lookout. As you ramble, look for the herds of mountain goats that are frequently seen on these hillsides chowing down on greens. Don't forget to look behind you occasionally—Mount Rainier is playing peekaboo and getting bigger and bigger as you continue onward. In 1.3 miles, reach the lookout tower and take a gander all around at the sweeping views. To the north are the meadows of Grand Park sprawling out like a savanna. To the southwest, Mount Rainier looms large over the Burroughs Mountain Trail.

The tower was built in 1934, but soon after, a freak wind gust ripped off the whole second story and blew it over the cliff into Huckleberry Creek. The following day, a group of carpenters showed up to attach the metal cables, but when they saw the giant mess,

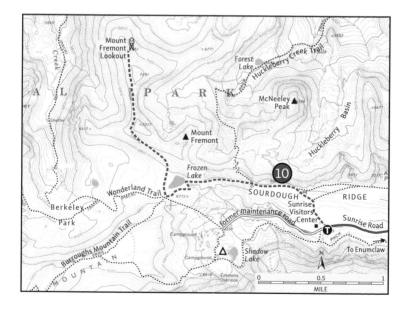

Built in 1934, the Mount Fremont Lookout has seen a lot of visitors, yet it still welcomes newcomers with its spectacular views.

they literally walked off the job and never came back. Thankfully, repairs were made by others who were up for the challenge, and today, the lookout stands tall and proud, staffed occasionally by park personnel who mostly use it as a base camp for backcountry patrols or for chatting with visitors.

11 Owyhigh Lakes

RATING/ DIFFICULTY	ROUNDTRIP	ELEV GAIN/ HIGH POINT	SEASON
★★★/3	7.5 miles	1650 feet/ 5400 feet	mid-July– Oct

Maps: Green Trails Mount Rainier East No. 270, Mount Rainier Wonderland No. 269SX; **Contact:** Mount Rainier National Park or Sunrise or White River Ranger Station; **Permit:** Mount Rainier Park Pass or America the Beautiful Pass; **Notes:** Pets and stock prohibited; **GPS:** N 46 53.450 W 121 35.823

This place has grandeur of its own, even without a Mount Rainier view. Two shallow lakes are set in a lovely grass-filled basin underneath rocky Governors Ridge, making this a great place to visit in the summer months, when pockets of wildflowers pop up from the damp soil or in the fall, when the grasses and the basin turn shades of orange and red.

GETTING THERE

From Enumclaw, follow State Route 410 eastbound for just shy of 38 miles to a junction with the White River Entrance of Mount Rainier National Park. Turn right onto Sunrise/White River Road and follow the road past the entrance booths and official entrance. In 2.1 miles, locate the parking area to the right (north). The signed trail is across the road (south). Restrooms and the White River Wilderness Information Center are just after the entrance booths. No facilities at trailhead.

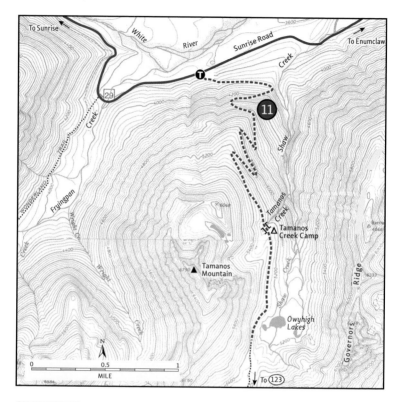

ON THE TRAIL

The trail starts off with a gradual climb through conifers mixed with patches of huckleberries and other acid-loving shrubs, switchbacking as it goes. Shaw Creek trickles nearby as you continue, climbing steeply at times, making your way to the east, then the west, and eventually to the south. Above you, gray jays and Clark's nutcrackers flit from tree to tree, squawking and carrying on as if to show you the way.

In 2.9 miles from the trailhead, cross a footbridge over Tamanos Creek and arrive at Tamanos Creek Camp. If you need a potty break, there is a privy here, along with several flat tent sites to drop a pack for a break and a snack. If you need water, you can filter some from the creek and enjoy deliciously cold sips.

After passing Tamanos Creek Camp, you are rewarded with fairly level travel along the shoulders of Tamanos Mountain far above you. The word *tamanos* means "spirit" in Chinook, a Native American trading language. Perhaps someone found this place hauntingly beautiful, or simply found a place to rest the soul.

The trail bobs and weaves through evergreens and pocket meadows before delivering

In the fall, the Owyhigh Lakes basin displays a variety of seasonal colors.

you to a vast open meadow with views of the Owyhigh Lakes basin, Governors Ridge, and Barrier Peak, all to the left (east). The Owyhigh Lakes are very shallow and their shorelines are swampy in most seasons. Most folks prefer the views from the trail, but those who are determined to see them up close will find a boot-beaten path, far from official, at the southern end of the lakes. Keep the rangers happy and practice solid Leave-No-Trace principles as you wander.

This area has some interesting history. Legend has it these lakes were named for the Yakama Indian Chief Owhi after he loaned his horses and guiding services to Theodore Winthrop (for whom Winthrop Glacier is named) for exploration of this area in 1853. Theodore Winthrop was a Yale graduate, a writer, lawyer, and explorer who wrote about his experiences in his book *Canoe and Saddle*, which became a best seller in its day and created buzz about the beauty of the West Coast. Mr. Winthrop never saw his book rise to fame as it was published after he was killed during the Civil War in 1861, just eight years after his expedition to what is now Mount Rainier National Park.

Walking in the footsteps of history is always a good way to get lost in thought as you explore and ramble along these open meadows. When you've seen enough, head back the way you came.

12 Palisades Lake

RATING/ DIFFICULTY	ROUNDTRIP	ELEV GAIN/ HIGH POINT	SEASON
★★★★/3	7.2 miles	1720 feet/ 6155 feet	mid-July– Oct

Maps: Green Trails Mount Rainier East No. 270, Mount Rainier Wonderland No. 269SX; **Contact:** Mount Rainier National Park or Sunrise or White River Ranger Station; **Permit:** Mount Rainier Park Pass or America the Beautiful Pass; **Notes:** Sunrise/White River Road is open seasonally most years from late June to mid-Oct. Concession area and visitors center are open for limited daily hours and close for the season soon after Labor

Day. Check with the park before you go for road and trail conditions. There are two trails in this book with the name Palisades; this one is inside the park and leads to lakes while the other (Hike 40) is a forested hike outside park boundaries and leads to various vistas. Pets and stock prohibited; **GPS:** N 46 55.063 W 121 35.254

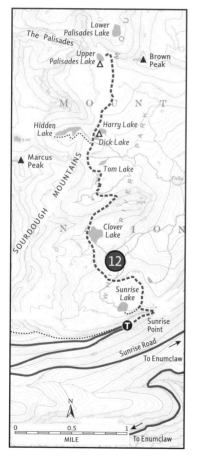

There is something magical about this hike, which ranks as one of my all-time favorites in Mount Rainier National Park. It doesn't have giant views of Mount Rainier, but it has a little bit of everything, including a trail that is gentle enough for most hikers as well as landscape features that make this hike very photo-worthy. The open meadows, frequent wildlife encounters, quiet lakes tucked into subalpine landscapes, babbling brooks, and views of craggy peaks along the way will make this hike stand out in your mind when you think back on places you'd like to visit again and again.

GETTING THERE

From Enumclaw, follow State Route 410 east for roughly 38 miles to Sunrise/White River Road and the White River Entrance of Mount Rainier National Park. Turn right (southwest) and continue for roughly 12 miles, passing the entrance booths and White River Campground, until you reach a hairpin turn with a parking area and viewpoint known as Sunrise Point. Park here and cross the road to the northeast to locate the trailhead. Sunrise Lake is visible from above.

ON THE TRAIL

The trail starts off with a gradual descent to Sunrise Lake, the first of four or five (depending on your stamina) lakes you'll see today. The rocky-at-times hillside is a reminder to keep watching your feet despite the urge to look around you at the subalpine hillsides. When you do stop, keep your eyes out for herds of mountain goats in the green meadows above you.

At 0.5 mile, reach a hairpin turn to the right (northeast). If you want to visit Sunrise Lake, stay straight (west) here and follow the unmaintained pathway a hop, skip, and a

The cerulean color of Palisades Lake is framed by lofty mountain heights making this area a true treasure.

jump to a great little spot on the lake's shoreline to snap a few pics. If you choose to skip Sunrise Lake, or after you've visited, continue on the main trail, following the hairpin turn until the trail wanders in gentle straightaways and sweeping turns all pointing, eventually, northbound.

Meadows bursting with green grasses and wildflowers play peekaboo with evergreen groves. Look for wildlife as you wander through these hills, as this area is a favorite for the elk and black bears that enjoy the bountiful, lush nibbles. In just 0.6 mile from the unmaintained turnoff for Sunrise Lake, cross a small footbridge over dribbling Sunrise Creek and swat a mosquito or two if you are here during early summer. Those bitty biters can be a nuisance!

Onward you go through pocket meadows and tree thickets, so engrossed in the scenery that you almost stumble upon Clover Lake before you realize you are there. The shallow lake, located 1.5 miles from the trailhead, has several boot-beaten pathways leading to its shoreline where folks enjoy a splish-splash in the hot summer months. Those with smaller kids, mobility challenges, or not much time may want to call this their final destination. Gentle green meadows dotted with magenta paintbrush and the brilliant azure waters make this a place you'll want to stay all day, but wait, there's more!

After Clover Lake, the trail climbs to a forest ridgeline. It's a rather gradual climb, but until now the trail has been very gentle so it feels more challenging than it really is. After the ridgeline, the path drops down the other side and passes by a couple of creeklets and tarns, then wanders gently up and down before reaching a turnoff with the signed "Hidden Lake Trail" to the left (west), 2.7 miles from the trailhead. If time permits,

large, sparkling Hidden Lake is definitely worth seeing! The roundtrip detour will add an extra mile (roundtrip) and climb roughly an extra 350 feet, but trust me, you'll ooh and aah.

Just 0.1 mile beyond the Hidden Lake junction, pass by Dick Lake to the trail's right (east). If you want to see every Tom, Dick, and Harry, you are in luck, since they all have lakes tucked into the forest near here, although Dick is the largest and the most obvious from the trail. Tom and Harry require a bushwhack and aren't really worth the effort. Dick Lake is really nothing to write home about either, since it's less impressive than those you've already seen, but I'm sure if you are a mallard, it's perfect. Dick Lake Camp, one of the park's many wilderness camps, is located on the lake's northern side and provides a rustic privy if nature is calling, along with a couple of campsites that, if not occupied, offer a flat place to stop for a break.

Another gradual climb leads to a series of wildflower-laden meadows under the spectacular rugged, craggy peaks of a mountain ridge known as The Palisades for the majestic barrier it provides around this basin. In 3.5 miles from the trailhead (0.6 mile from Dick Lake Camp), your eyes finally feast on the brilliant cobalt lake known as Upper Palisades Lake. Here a sign points the way to the lake's southern edge where a wilderness camp, Upper Palisades Lake Camp, provides another privy and a couple more campsites to plop down and spread out a picnic, provided they aren't occupied. Suck in the fresh air and let your eyes enjoy the spectacular scenery of these lofty heights and the sublime lake.

The main trail keeps going north after the camp sign and provides unmaintained access to Lower Palisades Lake, which isn't visited often, so it's best to have good navigation skills if you continue curiously rambling.

Migrate back the way you came after you've enjoyed the area.

13 Shadow Lake and Sunrise Camp Loop

RATING/ DIFFICULTY	LOOP	ELEV GAIN/ HIGH POINT	SEASON
★★★★/2	3.8 miles	650 feet/ 6800 feet	July–Oct

Maps: Green Trails Mount Rainier East No. 270, Mount Rainier Wonderland No. 269SX; **Contact:** Mount Rainier National Park or Sunrise or White River Ranger Station; **Permit:** Mount Rainier Park Pass or America the Beautiful Pass; **Notes:** Sunrise/White River Road is open seasonally most years from late June to mid-Oct. Concession area and visitors center are open for limited daily hours

and close for the season soon after Labor Day. Check with the park before you go for road and trail conditions. Pets and stock prohibited; **GPS:** N 46 54.884 W 121 38.542

 Those who want to explore the Sunrise area but may not have time to spend the whole day roaming trails will appreciate the simplicity and gentle grade of this loop, which shows off some of Sunrise's best landscape features. A quiet lake, flowering meadows, a wilderness camp, and the possibilities of seeing a bear grazing on huckleberries in late summer are just some of the reasons to lace up the boots and take a stroll!

GETTING THERE

From Enumclaw, follow State Route 410 eastbound for just shy of 38 miles to a junction with the White River Entrance of Mount Rainier National Park. Turn right onto Sunrise/

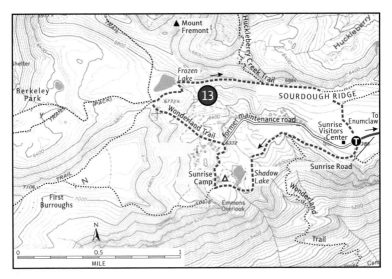

White River Road and continue for 15.5 miles, passing the entrance booths and ranger stations, to the Sunrise Visitors Center, which has ample parking. Restrooms available.

ON THE TRAIL

From Sunrise, locate the trailhead by walking to the southern side of the parking lot and then following the wide gravel trail heading south and marked by a "no pets" sign. In roughly 425 feet, arrive at a signed trail junction. Arrows here seem to point in every direction and may have your head spinning if you don't bring a good map or a quality guidebook (wink, wink).

Turn right at this junction (west) and find yourself in the midst of a sparse forest interspersed with grassy meadows and wildflowers. Look for hummingbirds flitting around the colorful, seasonal posies as you amble along taking in the sights.

In 0.5 mile, arrive at a junction for the Wonderland Trail. Continue going west, the direction you have been going, and keep your eyes open. From here all the way back to Sunrise along this loop, low-growing sweet huckleberries provide a tasty snack for hungry bears. In the late summer, it's not uncommon to see one munching in a meadow, completely indifferent to the fact that there are people nearby. Be sure to tap into common sense and steer clear of getting too close; the big bruins are completely wild and may be slightly more aggressive when protecting a food source.

The gently rolling landscapes near Shadow Lake make this hike an enjoyable outing for the whole family.

In 1.2 miles from where you started, pass the tranquil shoreline of Shadow Lake to the trail's right (north). Fishing and swimming are prohibited, so if you intended to lure a minnow into your swimsuit, think again. Luckily, the shoreline provides an excellent place for a photo or two before continuing your romp.

In 0.1 mile beyond Shadow Lake, arrive at a trail junction and turn right (north). You are now near Sunrise Camp, a wilderness camp along the Wonderland Trail reserved for those with prearranged permits. If your bladder is peeved, you are in luck! Well, sort of. A traditional wooden outhouse stands tall, proud, and offensively ripe for your piddling pleasure. Hold your nose because its stench can melt plastic, but hey, it beats the alternative. Behind the outhouse are the remains of a historic comfort station, which is locked and no longer in use but still interesting to observe.

Travel north along the Wonderland Trail and note the brilliant meadows bursting with colorful flowers and the occasional whistling hoary marmot. Hoary marmots are true hibernators that sleep away the winter months and work like crazy to eat their fill during the summer. Purple lupine seem to be among their favorite meadow snacks, and they often balance on their hind legs to grab the highest blooms because fresh is best!

In 0.4 mile from Sunrise Camp, arrive at a signed trail junction pointing the way back to Sunrise. Those who have little ones in tow, physical challenges, or time limitations will want to go right (east) at this junction and make their way back toward the visitors center via this maintenance road turned trail. Walking a maintenance road is not nearly as bad as it sounds. The 0.9 mile goes very quickly due to the views of the meadows and occasional vistas of the mountain when you turn around.

Those with more gumption and time will want to keep rolling, turning left at the trail junction to stay on the Wonderland Trail as it climbs up and over rocky terrain to arrive at a five-way trail junction, 1 mile north of Sunrise Camp (0.6 mile beyond the signed junction to Sunrise via the maintenance road). Turn right (northeast) at this junction and follow signs toward the Sourdough Ridge Trail and Sunrise.

To the left (north), just after the junction, note an unusual body of water known as Frozen Lake, often true to its name into midsummer. This lake is off-limits to visitors as it provides water for the entire Sunrise area.

Meandering onward, pass signs for the Huckleberry Creek Trail and Forest Lake. Make a mental note to come back and visit those another day (Hike 7), but for now, keep wandering the ridgeline until you arrive at an unsigned trail that heads downhill to the very visible Sunrise Visitors Center. Trust me, you won't miss it unless you are blindfolded.

In 1.5 miles from the five-way trail junction, arrive at Sunrise back where you started. Hit the snack bar for a cold drink, pop into the gift shop for a trinket, or simply flop down on the seat of your car and reflect on your enjoyable day.

14 Silver Forest and Emmons Vista

RATING/ DIFFICULTY	ROUNDTRIP	ELEV GAIN/ HIGH POINT	SEASON
★★★/1	2 miles	250 feet/ 6385 feet	July–Oct

Maps: Green Trails Mount Rainier East No. 270, Mount Rainier Wonderland No. 269SX; **Contact:** Mount Rainier National Park or Sunrise or White River Ranger Station; **Permit:**

Mount Rainier Park Pass or America the Beautiful Pass; **Notes:** Sunrise/White River Road is open seasonally most years from late June to mid-Oct. Concession area and visitors center are open for limited daily hours and close for the season soon after Labor Day. Check with the park before you go for road and trail conditions. Pets and stock prohibited; **GPS:** N 46 54.884 W 121 38.542

Years ago, this hike led to a silver forest of standing burned trees, but as time went on and the winds blew, the silver trunks eventually rotted and fell down. Today, despite the name, just a few silver trees remain. Instead, the rich soil provided by their decomposition is the perfect nursery for an abundance of wildflowers and grassy meadows! What's more, this hike offers a trail grade that is much more forgiving than most in this area and highlights overlooks of mighty Emmons Glacier and the deep White River valley.

GETTING THERE
From Enumclaw, follow State Route 410 eastbound for just shy of 38 miles to a junction with the White River Entrance of Mount Rainier National Park. Turn right onto Sunrise/White River Road and continue for 15.5 miles, passing the entrance booths and ranger stations, to the Sunrise Visitors Center, which has ample parking. Restrooms available.

ON THE TRAIL
From the Sunrise parking area, locate the trailhead by walking to the southern side of the parking lot and then following the wide gravel trail heading south and marked by a "no pets" sign. In 425 feet, arrive at a signed trail junction. Head left (east) and follow the arrows toward the Silver Forest Trail.

In roughly 100 feet more, a small vista pullout juts off to the trail's right (south) and allows for an impressive overlook of Emmons Glacier and the White River valley far below. The deep valley in front of you was carved by moving ice that continues to melt and form the headwaters of the White River. Steamboat Prow, the mountaineers' approach to the Emmons Glacier climbing route, is in full view, and often, in summer months, the well-worn bootpath looks like a ribbon heading directly up the slopes. Linger and enjoy; what a place!

Cruise eastbound until you reach Emmons Vista, 0.2 mile from where you started. The view from this exhibit is slightly better than the first, with a rocky retaining wall to help

The Silver Forest Trail offers a good path for meandering while gawking at Mount Rainier's ice-cream-cone-like summit.

you avoid going hiney over teakettle into the steep vegetation below. A modern sign explains the Osceola Mudflow, a massive landslide that occurred 5600 years ago; volcanoes are awesome!

An old wooden structure that presumably used to hold a primitive interpretive sign stands tall and weathered, sadly wondering what its purpose is. I made it feel better by using its lower log as a seat as I fished my jacket out of my pack. Considering its smoothness, I'm guessing I wasn't the first Einstein to have this idea!

Next up, you wander! The trail is gentle, so much so that you hardly realize you are gradually losing elevation until you have to turn around and schlep your carcass back to Sunrise. Evidence of the silver forest can still be found in a few rotting silver logs that provide rich compost for the soil and a palace full of hiding places for insects. These days, beautiful green subalpine fir trees have taken over the landscape and claimed the trail's identity for their own.

To the trail's right, roughly 0.5 mile from the trailhead, note a curious concrete structure

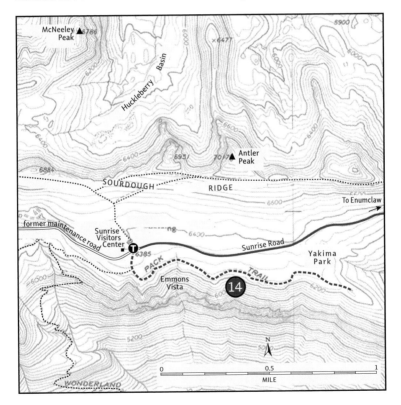

on the side of a steep hill below the trail. You might be tempted to trek off-trail to go check it out before you learn that this concrete structure was a holding tank for a very antiquated Sunrise sewage system back in the day. Rumor has it that they actually drained the tank off the side of the hill at the end of the summer, and theoretically, the waste would be gone before the beginning of the next summer. It's anybody's guess how that theory stood up, but there *are* some large, healthy trees on the other side of the tank.

On a much more pleasant olfactory note, if you brought your wildflower guide or app, see how many you can identify! Popular in this area are mountain daisy, western anemone, magenta paintbrush, subalpine lupine, spreading phlox, Cusick's speedwell, bracted lousewort, Sitka valerian, and many others.

In 1 mile from where you started, the trail ends with a sign saying "End of Maintained Trail." The dirt pathway continues much more faintly after the sign, but this makes a fine place to turn back unless you decide to continue rambling and enjoying the ambiance.

15 Skyscraper Pass and Skyscraper Mountain

RATING/ DIFFICULTY	ROUNDTRIP	ELEV GAIN/ HIGH POINT	SEASON
★★★★★/4	8 miles	1775 feet/ 7078 feet	mid-July– Oct

Maps: Green Trails Mount Rainier East No. 270, Mount Rainier Wonderland No. 269SX; **Contact:** Mount Rainier National Park or Sunrise or White River Ranger Station; **Permit:** Mount Rainier Park Pass or America the Beautiful Pass; **Notes:** Sunrise/White River Road is open seasonally most years from late June to mid-Oct. Concession area and visitors center are open for limited daily hours and close for the season soon after Labor Day. Check with the park before you go for road and trail conditions. Pets and stock prohibited; **GPS:** N 46 54.884 W 121 38.542

Scoot up to the tippy-top of the wide-open meadow country of Skyscraper Mountain, and you'll feel

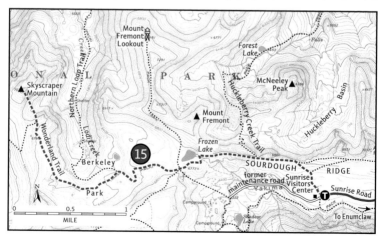

like you are sitting on top of the world with unobstructed views in almost every direction!

GETTING THERE

From Enumclaw, follow State Route 410 eastbound for just shy of 38 miles to a junction with the White River Entrance of Mount Rainier National Park. Turn right onto White River Road and continue for 15.5 miles, passing the entrance booths and ranger stations, to the Sunrise Visitors Center, which has ample parking. Restrooms available.

ON THE TRAIL

From the parking lot, locate the Sourdough Ridge Trail by heading to the north side of the parking lot and following the pavement between the snack bar and the restrooms for a couple of hundred feet until you reach the official gravel trail to the right (north). Wide, erosion-preventing stairs guide you northbound as you begin your ascent. Up, up, up you go toward the ridgeline, with views of Rainier to the southwest getting more and more beautiful. In 0.2 mile, arrive at a fork in the trail. Take the left fork (northwest) and continue the warm-up for another 0.2 mile until you reach the Sourdough Ridge Trail at the top. Ahead of you is a viewpoint for Huckleberry Basin, a great place for spotting bears nibbling on berries in the valley below.

Pass the Huckleberry Creek Trail junction and the viewpoint for Frozen Lake until you reach a five-way signed trail junction, located 1.1 miles from the ridgeline and 1.5 miles from the trailhead. Head right, following the Wonderland Trail westbound and gently descending.

In 0.8 mile from the five-way intersection, arrive at a trail junction with the Northern

Sweeping views make you feel like the "Monarch of the Mountain" as you bathe in the ambiance on top of Skyscraper Mountain.

Loop Trail, which drops into Berkeley Park. Stay on the Wonderland and continue rolling west. The huge, gorgeous meadows of the cirque you are crossing are popular with herds of mountain goats, so keep your eyes out for white dots grazing around the perimeter. Golden-mantled ground squirrels and hoary marmots also favor the tundra-like landscape, chowing on the low-growing flowering plants and popping up from their burrows to spy on you. If you think you are being watched, you probably are!

Trickling creeks through this open country make fine water sources if you brought your filter or just need to stop and splash your face. In 1.2 miles from the Northern Loop Trail, the trail makes a hairpin turn and then delivers you to a small plateau known as Skyscraper Pass. You'll know you are here because Mount Rainier is in your face and bigger than life. What a view and what a mountain! Seats for resting are scarce around these parts, so the ground will have to do if you want to take a load off.

If you are still feeling energetic, look to your right (north) for an unmaintained and unsigned but well-traveled boot-beaten path heading up toward the top of Skyscraper Mountain. Trust me when I say that it looks farther than it is. It's only 0.5 mile and a few grumbles to the top! Penstemon and phlox bloom with reckless abandon in the sandy soil of the barren slopes as you travel higher and higher, zigzagging this way and that until you reach the summit. Be very aware of your footing and where you park your tail feathers because there isn't much margin for error in places on the rocky top, especially if you have a lot of people in your party jockeying for position. Views in all directions are eye-popping. If you brought your binoculars, look for bears

way down in the Berkeley Park valley to the west; one time I counted three! Mountain goats love this place almost as much as hikers do and often hang out up here. If you don't see any, you are likely to at least see their droppings. Forgive them; it's hard to hold a trowel with a hoof!

When you've rested your quads, shoulders, and posterior, haul yourself back to Sunrise and enjoy the memories you've made.

16 Sourdough Ridge

RATING/ DIFFICULTY	ROUNDTRIP	ELEV GAIN/ HIGH POINT	SEASON
★★★★/2	4.7 miles	800 feet/ 7000 feet	July–Oct

Maps: Green Trails Mount Rainier East No. 270, Mount Rainier Wonderland No. 269SX; **Contact:** Mount Rainier National Park or Sunrise or White River Ranger Station; **Permit:** Mount Rainier Park Pass or America the Beautiful Pass; **Notes:** Sunrise/White River Road is open seasonally most years from late June to mid-Oct. Concession area and visitors center are open for limited daily hours and close for the season soon after Labor Day. Check with the park before you go for road and trail conditions. Pets and stock prohibited; **GPS:** N 46 54.884 W 121 38.542

 *If you want mindblowing views of Mount Rainier, look no further than this splendid romp through wildflower meadows to a ridgeline teeming with vistas. Not only that, but this hike starts off from the Sunrise Visitors Center, which offers exhibits, a gift shop, and a snack bar, so you'll have everything you need to keep your mind, your tummy, and your hiking feet happy.*

GETTING THERE

From Enumclaw, follow State Route 410 eastbound for just shy of 38 miles to a junction with the White River Entrance of Mount Rainier National Park. Turn right onto White River Road and continue for 15.5 miles, passing the entrance booths and ranger stations, to the Sunrise Visitors Center, which has ample parking. Restrooms available.

ON THE TRAIL

The Sourdough Ridge hike is very versatile and can be as long or short as you want it to be, depending on your group's abilities and your time frame. Don't discount how much time you'll spend clicking away with your shutter at all the glory of this majestic landscape; it's worth every snap!

From the visitors center, find the trailhead by following the wide paved pathway (and the throngs of hikers) to the west of the store/snack bar and east of the restrooms. In roughly 200 feet, the trail heads north, taking you off the pavement and onto gravel, staying wide at first. Erosion-preventing trail stairs help you gain elevation as you climb higher amid meadows of wildflowers, such as western anemone, purple lupine, and aster. The backdrop of Mount Rainier is ever present with magnificent Emmons Glacier to the southwest. From here in summer months you can often see a well-worn climbers' path, especially on a stretch lower on the mountain known as Steamboat Prow.

At 0.2 mile, reach a fork and a challenging decision on which way to go, east or west. Both ways are beautiful and take you to the same ridge. For now, go left (northwest) and continue your climb for another 0.2 mile until you reach Sourdough Ridge. Once here, stop, collect your thoughts, and catch your breath. Views below you to the north are of deep and lush Huckleberry Basin, with trickling waterways, clumps of evergreen trees, and divine meadows. Look closely and pull out the binoculars if you brought them. Bears

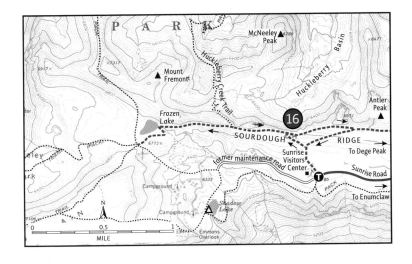

Sunrise at sunrise is a vision in summer months, provided you can get your sleepyhead out of bed in the wee hours.

love this area, particularly in late summer, when, true to its name, the basin produces tiny, sweet berries that provide delicious sustenance for the hungry bruins.

From here, wander the ridgeline to the left (west) as it cruises up and down, passing a junction with the Huckleberry Creek Trail and rolling onward with great views and whistling marmots scurrying about. Look for gray, white, and black Clark's nutcrackers flitting through the trees in this area, a popular feathered friend in this neck of the woods.

In 1.2 miles from where you joined the ridgeline, look for Frozen Lake to the right (north), true to its name much of the year. This small lake provides the water for use at the Sunrise Visitors Center as well as park staff housing, so its shoreline is off-limits to visitors. Just beyond the lake, reach a five-way trail intersection of the Wonderland, Mount Fremont, and Burroughs Mountain trails. Make notes to come back and hike those another day, but for now, this is your turnaround spot. If your tummy is rumbling, a few rocks here provide a spot to sit and enjoy your PB&J; just watch for golden-mantled ground squirrels that feel they are entitled to your bounty!

Head back the way you came, and once you reach the point where you first joined the ridge, continue walking east. The trail now offers lofty views of the Sunrise area—bountiful meadows, the bustling visitors center, a ribbon of road, and all!

In 2.1 miles from the five-way trail intersection, find yourself standing on the broad shoulder of Antler Peak. Several unofficial trails scoot around to various rocky vistas; just use extreme caution as loose rocks mean precarious footing. This angle offers a slightly different view of Huckleberry Basin and Sunrise and is well worth a picture or two. Those with leftover energy may want to make an extra full day of it and continue east, hiking up Dege Peak (Hike 5) and/or making a car shuttle and ending at Sunrise Point.

When your camera battery is spent, head back to the car the way you came, with a slight modification. Follow the signs back to Sunrise using the eastern branch of the forked portion of the trail instead of the west. Because this area is wide-open subalpine country, it's pretty hard to get lost.

17 Summerland and Panhandle Gap

RATING/ DIFFICULTY	ROUNDTRIP	ELEV GAIN/ HIGH POINT	SEASON
★★★★/5	11.8 miles to Panhandle	2950 feet/ 6800 feet	mid-July– early Oct

Maps: Green Trails Mount Rainier East No. 270, Mount Rainier Wonderland No. 269SX; **Contact:** Mount Rainier National Park or Sunrise or White River Ranger Station; **Permit:** Mount Rainier Park Pass or America the Beautiful Pass; **Notes:** In snowy conditions, the trails to Summerland and Panhandle Gap can be hazardous. Route-finding above Summerland in inclement weather can be deadly; use extreme caution. Park-service-placed snow wands are often present to lead hikers through permanent snowfields but good navigation skills are a must. Stock and pets prohibited; **GPS:** N 46 53.314 W 121 36.668

 *This hike is one of the most popular in the park and for good reason; high alpine environments to the south of Summerland, known as Panhandle Gap, give hikers views of hanging glaciers and herds of mountain goats. Wildflowers of all colors of the rainbow gently scent the breeze, and Mount Rainier as seen from Summerland is a vision! While this is one of the most beautiful hikes in the park, it is also one of the most crowded. For the best opportunity to enjoy this area without having to throw trail elbows, visit on a weekday, and if possible in September, after the summer rush is over.*

GETTING THERE

From Enumclaw, follow State Route 410 eastbound for just shy of 38 miles to a junction with the White River Entrance of Mount Rainier National Park. Turn right on Sunrise/ White River Road and follow the road past the entrance booths and official entrance. In roughly 2.9 miles beyond the entrance, cross over Fryingpan Creek and locate the parking area on a hairpin turn to the right (northeast). The signed trail is across the road (southwest). Restrooms and White River Wilderness Information Center are just after the entrance booths. No facilities at trailhead.

ON THE TRAIL

The adventure kicks off in a forest of thick, sunlit conifers on a trail so wide you can walk comfortably arm in arm with your hiking companion. Because it's often so busy, you might want to opt for single file. Regardless, the gentle grade welcomes you to the area and slowly warms up the quads and calves for what's ahead. Water is flowing in many places along the way, so carry only what you need, and filter when you dry up.

Famed most for the amazing wildflower display during the summer months, Summerland is also a sight to see in the fall when the meadows take on autumn hues.

The gentle grade turns slightly steeper as the trail turns to the west and follows the Fryingpan Creek gorge to the trail's left (south). The trail flirts with the gorge at least three times, each time giving hikers a vista of the swift water in the valley, the steep avalanche chutes from Tamanos Mountain high above, and an opportunity to catch their breath.

The trail ducks back into the woods for a short distance, then pops out at a brushy, riparian stretch of trail where salmonberries, thimbleberries, and fireweed try their best to grab your shirt and make you stop to check them out. Tell them who's boss with a whack of your trekking poles if necessary. Keep your eyes out for bears and make some noise in this dense section, particularly if you are here when the crowds are minimal. Goat Island Mountain just above seems to have a few bruin residents that enjoy nibbling the berries.

Little Tahoma and Rainier's summit come into view as you make your way to a crossing of the swift headwaters of Fryingpan Creek and a glad-it's-there log bridge at roughly 3.5 miles from the trailhead. Once across, the trail turns to the south and switchbacks steeply across a hillside before delivering you to the Summerland area and its fragile meadows; note the sign reminding you to stay on the trail. Wildflower meadows and eye-candy views of Mount Rainier are found to the trail's right (west), while to the left (east), the official wilderness camp of Summerland arrives. At the camp, a mostly odor-free, composting outhouse propped up high via a wooden structure (a true throne) is available. Also in the camp is a historic three-sided stone shelter built by the Civilian Conservation Corps in the 1930s that now serves as the camp's group site. Bears are frequent visitors to Summerland

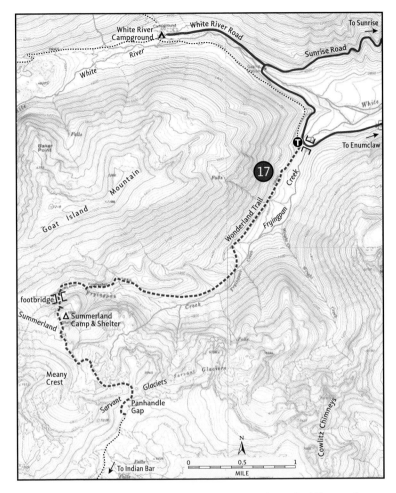

and with any luck you might get a photo op of one grazing on nearby hillsides, especially toward evening.

In 1888, Major Edward S. Ingraham, the first superintendent of the Seattle Public Schools and an accomplished mountaineer, named this area Summerland for the amazing meadows of wildflowers that are on display in the summer months.

Many hikers choose to stop at Summerland, fish out their lunch, enjoy the views, and then head back. Others aren't content until they reach Panhandle Gap, the very tippy-top of the alpine area to

Summerland's south and the highest point on the Wonderland Trail. If you are one of those folks, continue past Summerland and cross two lovely little unnamed creeks and large boulders where marmots, and often their pups, hang out. Follow the wooden, erosion-resistant trail stairs as they lead you up, up, and away from where you just were. The landscape quickly changes from subalpine meadows to rocky and often snowy alpine terrain where you may need to follow cairns or snow wands if the path isn't obvious. Several log bridges take you over glaciated creeks coming off the Sarvant Glaciers, which in early season can be raging. To the trail's right (southwest) pass a large unnamed tarn, which will be either brilliantly turquoise in color or muddy brown, depending on the time of year. Either way, it's a beautiful thing to behold in this somewhat desolate setting. Don't forget to look behind you at Summerland, which begins to look like a small dot as you climb higher and higher. At 1.4 miles beyond Summerland, reach the top of the crest, Panhandle Gap, at 6800 feet. Once here, views to the south on a clear day reveal Mount Adams and tundra-like meadows with pockets of

grasses where mountain goats often are seen enjoying greens. When time is up, turn around and call it a day.

18 Sunrise Lake

RATING/ DIFFICULTY	ROUNDTRIP	ELEV GAIN/ HIGH POINT	SEASON
★★★/2	1.2 miles	425 feet/ 6155 feet	mid-July– Oct

Maps: Green Trails Mount Rainier East No. 270, Mount Rainier Wonderland No. 269SX; **Contact:** Mount Rainier National Park or Sunrise or White River Ranger Station; **Permit:** Mount Rainier Park Pass or America the Beautiful Pass; **Notes:** Sunrise/White River Road is open seasonally most years from late June to mid-Oct. Concession area and visitors center are open for limited daily hours and close for the season soon after Labor Day. Check with the park before you go for road and trail conditions. Pets and stock prohibited; **GPS:** N 46 55.063 W 121 35.254

This short hike provides access to a shallow, tranquil lake that is visible from a viewpoint near Sunrise. Subalpine

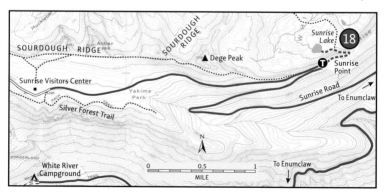

On a tight schedule? Make a short visit to the peaceful waters of Sunrise Lake.

meadows and spindly firs dot the lake's shoreline while fritillary butterflies flutter among the heather and paintbrush in the area. Kids and those unable to do longer hikes will enjoy an accessible goal, while folks with lengthier ambitions can use this as a starting point to continue on to Clover and Palisades lakes.

GETTING THERE

From Enumclaw, follow State Route 410 east for just shy of 38 miles to Sunrise/White River Road and the White River Entrance of Mount Rainier National Park. Turn right onto Sunrise/White River Road, and continue for roughly 12 miles, passing the entrance booths and White River Campground, until you reach a hairpin turn with a parking area and viewpoint known as Sunrise Point. Park here and cross the road to the northeast to locate the trailhead. The lake is visible from above.

ON THE TRAIL

The trail starts off near the often-crowded overlook. Quickly, you are whisked off into the forest, where the trail narrows and the crowds diminish. It's obvious that you'll need to save some energy to make it back up this hill as you steeply descend the dusty trail and let your quads do the braking.

The trail traverses to the east, following a sloping ridgeline, before it turns sharply back to the west and continues downhill. Rocky patches of scree play hopscotch with patches of pink heather and small firs. In warm summer months, the trail becomes dusty and every step creates a mini puff of dirt to decorate your boots. Watch your step as you wander since pointy rocks can hide underneath the trail fluff.

Keep your eyes on the high slopes above for herds of mountain goats grazing on the grassy meadows of the Sourdough Mountains to the west. Bears also frequent these hillsides, and a keen eye or a good monocular can often locate them dining on greens and berries. In the scree fields surrounding the trail, pikas, small members of the rabbit family, occasionally pop up from their burrows with a resounding "eeeeepppp," causing you and your hiking partners to pause. Because they are almost perfectly camouflaged, they are hard to spot! I like to play a little game of "pick a pika on the pumice" and see who spots one first.

In 0.5 mile, arrive at a sign noting the end of the maintained trail. The Palisades Lake Trail, otherwise known as the one you've been following, makes a hairpin turn to the right (north) here, while an unmaintained spur trail continues to Sunrise Lake. Continue forward (west) for another 0.1 mile to arrive at the shoreline of shallow, turquoise Sunrise Lake. Frogs hop near the lake's marshy edges waiting for hatching insects. A few rocky patches allow for spots to drop the pack for pictures or snacks before heading back or exploring more of the Palisades Lake Trail.

19 White River Valley to Sunrise

RATING/ DIFFICULTY	ROUNDTRIP	ELEV GAIN/ HIGH POINT	SEASON
★★★/4	6.7 miles	2000 feet/ 6225 feet	late July– Oct

Maps: Green Trails Mount Rainier East No. 270, Mount Rainier Wonderland No. 269SX; **Contact:** Mount Rainier National Park or

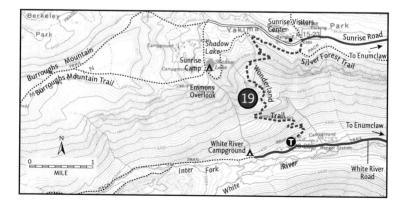

If you're looking to burn enough calories to warrant a treat from the Sunrise snack bar, climb your way through evergreens to the high country.

Sunrise or White River Ranger Station; **Permit:** Mount Rainier Park Pass or America the Beautiful Pass; **Notes:** Sunrise/White River Road is open seasonally most years from late June to mid-Oct. Concession area and visitors center are open for limited daily hours and close for the season soon after Labor Day. Check with the park before you go for road and trail conditions. Pets and stock prohibited; **GPS:** N 46 54.136 W 121 38.474

Hiking from White River Campground to the Sunrise Visitors Center is all about the workout and the destination. The trail climbs through thick forest and will have *you huffing and puffing until you reach the large subalpine meadows and amazing vistas high above. When you get to Sunrise, you have many options, including checking out the exhibits of the Sunrise Visitors Center, grabbing lunch at the Sunrise Day Lodge, or wandering to your heart's content through wildflower meadows with grand vistas of Mount Rainier.*

GETTING THERE

From Enumclaw, follow State Route 410 east for just shy of 38 miles to Sunrise/White River Road to the White River Entrance of Mount Rainier National Park. Continue on Sunrise/

White River Road for 5.3 miles, passing the entrance booths, restrooms, and ranger station. Turn left (west) into White River Campground and look for the day-use parking area to the left (south). Restrooms and picnic areas available.

ON THE TRAIL

Once you get the backpack strapped on, finding the trail can be tricky. Follow White River Road to the left (west) from the parking lot for 0.1 mile until you reach a historic ranger patrol cabin to the right (north). The cabin, built in 1927, is a reminder of when rangers used this structure as a base camp to track poachers, watch for wildfires, and provide aid to park visitors. Feel free to walk inside and let your mind wander back to a different era. Once you've enjoyed your trip back in time, follow the path around the back of the cabin and locate the Wonderland Trail, which will lead you to Sunrise.

Pass a sign for the Wonderland Trail walk-in campsites and begin your climb up, up, and away. Seasonal creeks lined with mossy rocks dribble in places as you ascend through sunlit Douglas fir and western hemlock. Wide, sweeping switchbacks climb moderately, so you never really feel like the trail is gnawing at your quads as you continue.

Several small trail bridges cross dripping creeklets and make you thankful for trail crews who work hard to keep these park trails in tip-top condition, allowing you to cross waterways with little effort.

The evergreens become sparser the closer you get to Sunrise, and before you know it, you arrive at the top, where meadows filled with aster, lupine, and Sitka valerian await.

Here a signed junction with the Wonderland Trail provides options. You could choose to head right (southeast) to visit the Sunrise Visitors Center and Day Lodge in just 0.5 mile. Going right also takes you to the Silver Forest Trail (Hike 14). Turning left (west) at the signed junction takes you along the Wonderland Trail toward shallow Shadow Lake as well as Sunrise Camp, where Wonderland Trail hikers can enjoy meals and relax after long days. Continuing past Sunrise Camp puts your boots on the Burroughs Mountain Trail (Hike 2), where a long loop (connecting with the Glacier Basin Trail, Hike 8) is possible.

Whichever direction you decide to go, you'll enjoy the sights and sounds of the very beating heart of Mount Rainier's east side.

When you've had your fun at Sunrise, wander back the way you came; thankfully, this direction it's all downhill.

Views from Summit Lake on a clear day are hard to beat (Hike 30).

carbon river/
mowich lake area

In the northwest corner of the park, the Carbon River and Mowich Lake areas provide wonderful opportunities to explore deep primeval forests, sublime subalpine scenery, and primitive river valleys. Your senses will come alive as you wander through temperate rainforests laden with moss and lichen, and your camera will get its own workout as you pause to photograph waterfalls, quiet lakes, knocking woodpeckers, or the occasional black bear. Rich history from a distant past has left behind a few relics, while nature has taken back what it rightfully owns. Whatever you fancy in a hike, you're likely to find it here.

20 Bearhead Mountain

RATING/ DIFFICULTY	ROUNDTRIP	ELEV GAIN/ HIGH POINT	SEASON
★★★/4	6.2 miles	1810 feet/ 6089 feet	mid-July– Oct

Map: Green Trails Enumclaw No. 237; **Contact:** Mount Baker–Snoqualmie National Forest, Snoqualmie Ranger District, Enumclaw Office; **Permit:** Northwest Forest Pass; **Notes:** Road to trailhead is extremely rough with large stones and potholes, so high-clearance vehicles strongly recommended. Wilderness regulations apply. Horses and dogs permitted; **GPS:** N 47 01.880 W 121 49.615

Most folks who come out this way are headed to Summit Lake, which uses a portion of the same trail and can be very crowded, especially on weekends. Going to Bearhead Mountain means fewer people, more solitude, and a great place to sit and ponder all good things. Great Rainier views are sublime from the lofty perch of this former fire-lookout tower site. Combine it with Summit Lake (Hike 30) for a full, vista-filled day.

GETTING THERE

From State Route 410 in Buckley, turn south onto SR 165. In roughly 200 yards, the road makes a hard right. Follow SR 165 south (heading southwest) for 1.6 miles before turning left (south) and continuing through the towns of Wilkeson and Carbonado until you reach the one-lane Carbon River Gorge/ Fairfax Bridge, 9.7 miles from Buckley. In 0.7 mile past the bridge, the road forks. Stay left and continue for 7.5 miles, past the Carbon River Ranger Station, to find Forest Road 78 and a big metal, one-lane bridge to the left (north) just before the Mount Rainier National Park Entrance.

Turn left (north) and wait your turn to cross the bridge over the Carbon River. In 0.4 mile, stay right (northeast) at the fork in the road. Stay straight at two other road spurs, located 3.2 miles and 3.9 miles beyond turning onto FR 78. At 5.4 miles after turning onto FR 78, turn left (west) at a Y in the road with a sign pointing toward the Summit Lake trailhead as well as a sign noting that you are now on FR 7810. Follow FR 7810 for 1.5 miles, where the road ends, and locate the parking lot for the Summit Lake trailhead, where there is room for roughly 15 vehicles. Picnic table available but no privy.

ON THE TRAIL

Summit Lake Trail No. 1177 kicks off with a dusty, rocky climb that passes a picnic table in the forest for those who want lunch before they head out. Pleasantly graded switchbacks cross a tributary creek on a wooden bridge 0.4 mile from the trailhead; water is plentiful in the creek should you need to top off.

The moderate ascent delivers you to the Clearwater Wilderness, marked by a tree sign, 0.8 mile from where you started. Created by Congress in 1984, the Clearwater

On a clear day, Mount Rainier is front and center from the summit of Bearhead Mountain, the highest point in the Clearwater Wilderness.

Wilderness is a small one, coming in at 14,192 acres, with eight small lakes, the Clearwater River, and many small, sparkling streams. The peak you are headed up is the highest one in the wilderness area and one of the best places to take it all in.

In 1 mile from the trailhead, the landscape hosts a more open feeling, with huckleberry bushes, beargrass, and marshy meadows, before it arrives at the quiet waters of Twin Lake, which seasonally can be more swamp than lake. Despite that, it's still tranquil and an important part of the ecosystem. Keep your eyes out for the deer, elk, and bears that call this area home.

At Twin Lake, a wooden sign points you to the right to Bearhead Mountain and Martin Gap, while the arrow to the left directs you to Summit Lake. Be sure to check out Summit Lake (Hike 30) when you have the time, but for now, head right (you are technically now on Carbon Trail No. 1179, although it's not signed at this point) and begin ascending through sparse conifers that eventually become thicker. Up you go, reaping rewards of Mount Rainier views as you huff and puff along. Pockets of wildflowers show up seasonally in between evergreen thickets and add to the overall ambiance of the stunning mountainside.

In 1.2 miles from Twin Lake, arrive at a trail junction with wooden signs on an aging tree pointing the way. To the left is your trail, Bearhead Mountain (Trail No. 1179a, or 1179.1 on some maps), while to the right is the continuation of Carbon Trail No. 1179. Head left and immediately pass a small viewpoint leading to a rocky perch. If you need a break, this is a good spot to stop and rest as well as look and listen for mountain goats that love to clickety-clack through surrounding talus fields and cliff bands.

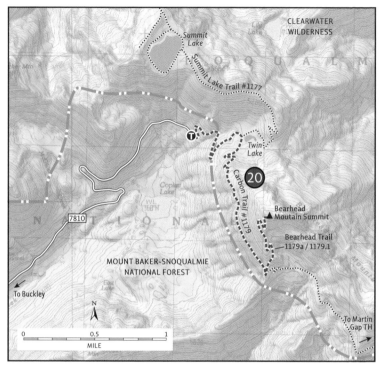

Keep your feet under you as the trail gets slightly rockier and delivers you to a ridgeline 0.8 mile from the last junction. You are standing on Bearhead Mountain at this spot, but the true summit, and the site of the former lookout tower, is 0.1 mile to the left—a rocky, open area with a metal benchmark placed in 1955.

In 1931, the Civilian Conservation Corps built a classic L4-style lookout tower on this peak, where fire watchers used it for 26 years. It's been gone since 1957 and very little evidence of it remains.

When you are done flirting with your camera and purring at the views, trace your steps back the way you arrived.

21 Carbon Glacier

RATING/ DIFFICULTY	ROUNDTRIP	ELEV GAIN/ HIGH POINT	SEASON
★★/5	18 miles	1640 feet/ 3200 feet	June–Oct

Maps: Green Trails Mount Rainier West No. 269, Mount Rainier Wonderland No. 269SX; **Contact:** Mount Rainier National Park, Carbon River Ranger Station; **Permit:** Mount Rainier Park Pass or America the Beautiful Pass. Park pass available at Carbon River Ranger Station or entrance booth at park's entrance; **Notes:** Carbon River Road open to bicycles. All park trails are hiker only. Pets and stock prohibited; **GPS:** N 46 59.709 W 121 54.939

Since the closure of Carbon River Road after the floods of 2006, this hike is no longer just a simple walk in the park. You have to hike 5.1 miles of defunct roadway to reach the trailhead. While the grade is gentle on both the road and trail, the distance might be too much for the average day hiker. Thankfully, bicycles are permitted on Carbon River Road, which may help you if you want to pedal your way to the trailhead and shave off some time. Whether you walk or crank your pedals, you'll enjoy visiting Carbon Glacier, the lowest-elevation glacier in the contiguous 48 states. Additionally, you can sway your way across one of the park's most famous features, the Indiana Jones–style Carbon River Suspension Bridge, which provides great views of the nearby glacier while testing your inner adventurer.

GETTING THERE

From State Route 410 in Buckley, turn south onto SR 165 and continue onward as it makes a hard right. Follow SR 165 through the towns of Wilkeson and Carbonado until you reach the one-lane Carbon River Gorge/Fairfax Bridge. Just past the bridge, the road forks. Stay left and continue for 7.7 miles, passing the Carbon River Ranger Station, until the road dead-ends at the Carbon River Entrance. Privy available.

ON THE TRAIL

Walk around the gate at Carbon River Road and begin your hike or spin east on the gravel-surfaced pathway. At first, you might wonder why the road is closed, but you find out after a couple of miles. Before 2006, Carbon River Road washed out every few years,

requiring costly repairs. In the historic flood of 2006, where 18 inches of rain fell in 36 hours, the road was so badly damaged the Park Service declared it nonrepairable and closed it forever. These days, large chunks of road are missing and the road has been rerouted at times into a single-track trail. Ancient, behemoth Douglas fir, western red cedar, and western hemlock provide a shady green canopy, while moss in almost every direction hints at the rainy climate this area is known for. Bike or hike your way for 5.1 miles until you reach Ipsut Creek Campground, now a true wilderness camp, meaning a backcountry permit is required for overnight stays and campfires are prohibited.

The historic patrol cabin standing here has made its return! In the floods of 2006, the cabin, in a slightly different location, was so badly undercut from the riverbank that it had to be taken down and moved off-site for restoration. It is back now in its familiar landscape and just as grand as ever. Be sure to check it out, as it's on the National Register of Historic Places because the Civilian Conservation Corps built it way back in 1933. Imagine all the changes this mass of weathered wood has seen! The cabin sits on what used to be the parking area for the trailhead back when cars zipped up and down this stretch, carrying campers with coolers of deliciousness. These days, with feet and pedals only, the white noise is not from motors but from the purr of the nearby Carbon River and Ipsut Creek.

Find the Ipsut trailhead at the road's dead end and turn right (southeast) for 0.2 mile to reach a signed spur trail for Ipsut Falls. The waterfall (Hike 24) is a great place to stop for a photo or just to gawk at the sheer power of water falling through a channel in a mossy forest glen. From there, reach a signed junction with the Wonderland Trail pointing right (southwest) toward Mowich Lake and Ipsut Pass, but continue straight ahead (southeast) toward your goal, Carbon Glacier. Pass several areas of washouts where the trail has been rerouted to accommodate moody, silted Carbon River. When in doubt, look for cairns (purposefully placed stacks of rocks) that lead the way through the sea of river-strewn stones. Be sure to note the dead standing trees with their roots buried in silt and sand from the wandering river.

In 1.7 miles from the Wonderland junction, arrive at a signed detour for the Wonderland Trail. In 2006, the Carbon River completely destroyed this particular stretch of pathway,

stripping it down to steep, impassable slopes of bedrock. The trail here used to continue up the western slopes of the Carbon River to the Carbon River Suspension Bridge. Today, you are guided across the Carbon River on log footbridges downstream of the old crossing. As with all "bridges over troubled water," be sure to focus on the opposing bank or the bridge itself instead of the rushing water under your feet. Once across, enjoy a peaceful hike among big conifers on the western side of the river, a trail that once served as part of the Northern Loop. In 1.5 miles from the detour, arrive at the Carbon River Suspension Bridge and a view of Carbon Glacier!

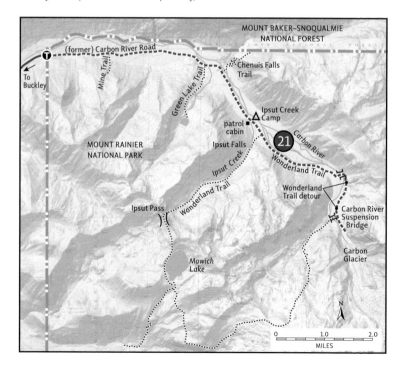

Getting a front-row seat to the Carbon Glacier, the lowest-elevation glacier in the Lower 48, is possible with a little time and effort.

Cross the bridge just for fun and grab a few pictures as you teeter across, or simply continue on the Wonderland, climbing along the shoulders of the Northern Crags. Most folks don't realize that glaciers, especially near their toes or snouts, aren't usually white. Carbon Glacier is exactly that, a dark carbon color from sediment and volcanic minerals ground down through the years. While it's tempting to hop off the trail and head down to the glacier for a closer look, it is not safe! Glaciers have a nasty habit of unexpectedly throwing rocks and dropping ice chunks. Play it safe and don't tempt fate since nothing ruins your day like a crack on the noggin from falling debris.

Instead, enjoy the sweet taste of Mount Rainier's gentle breezes as you make your way back to your waiting vehicle.

22 Chenuis Falls

RATING/ DIFFICULTY	ROUNDTRIP	ELEV GAIN/ HIGH POINT	SEASON
★★★/2	8.4 miles	400 feet/ 2200 feet	May–Oct

Maps: Green Trails Mount Rainier West No. 269, Mount Rainier Wonderland No. 269SX; **Contact:** Mount Rainier National Park, Carbon River Ranger Station; **Permit:** Mount Rainier Park Pass or America

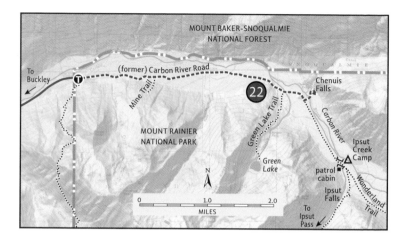

the Beautiful Pass. Park pass available at Carbon River Ranger Station or entrance booth at park's entrance; **Notes:** Carbon River Road open to bicycles. Bridges to Chenuis Falls wash out almost every season. Check with park staff for trail conditions before setting out. All park trails are hiker only. Pets and stock prohibited; **GPS:** N 46 59.709 W 121 54.939

Since the closure of Carbon River Road after the floods of 2006, this once short hike is much longer. But don't be discouraged! The road itself has turned, in places, into a single track of sorts with plenty of eye candy in the form of old-growth Douglas fir, western red cedar, western hemlock, and Sitka spruce so large you are mostly eyeball-to-eyeball with their roots. In fact, it's a worthy destination on its own! Add to it a cascading waterfall coming off Chenuis Creek, and it might just be the perfect hike for an easy, albeit somewhat lengthy, adventure.

GETTING THERE

From State Route 410 in Buckley, turn south onto SR 165 and continue onward as it makes a hard right. Follow SR 165 through the towns of Wilkeson and Carbonado until you reach the one-lane Carbon River Gorge/Fairfax Bridge. Just past the bridge, the road forks. Stay left and continue for 7.7 miles, passing the Carbon River Ranger Station, until the road dead-ends at the Carbon River Entrance. Privy available.

ON THE TRAIL

Mount Rainier can be a real pain when it comes to washouts. In 2006, 18 inches of rain fell in a 36-hour period, destroying Carbon River Road and washing out almost every single footbridge in the park's backcountry. So much damage was done that the park was closed for a historic six-month period. Prior to 2006, the moody Carbon River had been flooding for decades, requiring costly repairs. In 2006, the Park Service finally threw in the towel and closed the road for good. For us, it is now a trail.

When you want to get away from the rat race with a picnic in a picturesque spot, look no farther than Chenuis Falls.

Walk the Carbon River Road for 3.7 very green miles. Around you in all directions are huge, mossy trees and a landscape similar to a temperate rain forest due to the consistent high amounts of rainfall this area receives. Water trickles from mountains high above to reach the milky, glaciated Carbon River to the north. Above you, birds flit from branch to branch, choreographing your walk with a symphony of tweets and calls. Pass the Mine Trail (Hike 26) and the Green Lake Trail (Hike 23) to the south and arrive at the signed Chenuis Falls trailhead to the north. The former parking area is now covered in grass and riparian brush.

From here, the trail cruises through alders and riparian forest before reaching the rocky shoreline of the silty Carbon River. A log bridge, which is known for washing out, crosses over the rushing river. Hang on to the handrails tightly and focus on the shoreline instead of the white water under the bridge. A small rocky island in the center leads you to the next bridge, where you test your courage again and tiptoe gently across.

A short forest walk follows before you pop out at the roaring waterfall gushing from Chenuis Mountain high above. This is a perfect place to spread out a picnic and take a few pictures. An unmaintained trail continues up the edge of the waterfall, giving you a different perspective if you choose to follow it. Eventually, all good things must come to an end, so head back when you've enjoyed all there is to enjoy.

23 Green Lake and Ranger Falls

RATING/ DIFFICULTY	ROUNDTRIP	ELEV GAIN/ HIGH POINT	SEASON
★★★★/3	10.4 miles	1720 feet/ 3215 feet	May–Oct

Maps: Green Trails Mount Rainier West No. 269, Mount Rainier Wonderland No. 269SX;

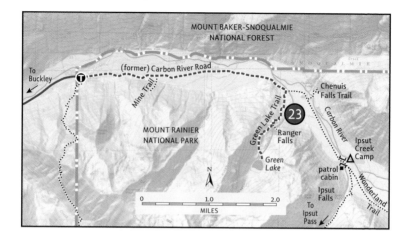

Contact: Mount Rainier National Park, Carbon River Ranger Station; **Permit:** Mount Rainier Park Pass or America the Beautiful Pass. Park pass available at Carbon River Ranger Station or entrance booth at park's entrance; **Notes:** Carbon River Road open to bicycles. All park trails are hiker-only. Pets and stock prohibited; **GPS:** N 46 59.709 W 121 54.939

For years, the Park Service struggled to maintain Carbon River Road since washouts were common and repairs costly. In 2006, the Carbon River threw a tantrum that finally caused the Park Service to officially close the road. The trail to Green Lake now requires walking or bicycling defunct Carbon River Road for 3.2 miles before you arrive at the trailhead and start up the trail that is only for feet. Despite the added mileage, the road walk/ride is enjoyable as it weaves through huge old-growth conifers and temperate rain forest before reaching the trail and climbing toward rushing Ranger Falls and the peaceful, true-to-its-name Green Lake. It takes a full day now, but is a great way to enjoy getting away from it all.

GETTING THERE

From State Route 410 in Buckley, turn south onto SR 165 and continue onward as it makes a hard right. Follow SR 165 through the towns of Wilkeson and Carbonado·until you reach the one-lane Carbon River Gorge/Fairfax Bridge. Just past the bridge, the road forks. Stay left and continue for 7.7 miles, passing the Carbon River Ranger Station, until the road dead-ends at the Carbon River Entrance Privy available.

ON THE TRAIL

Walk around the gate and begin your gravel-road walk through ancient western red cedar and Douglas fir. These large giants have been here a long time, and it's fun to imagine what kinds of changes they've seen over hundreds of years. In 3.2 miles, find the official trailhead noted by a sign on the right (south). A bike rack near the trail allows you to lock up your wheels if you decided to pedal.

Despite the closed road, or perhaps because of it, Green Lake and Ranger Falls are a wonderful place to disappear into the hinterlands.

Immediately, the trail begins climbing south. The grade is gentle at first and then takes on a consistent steepness that it maintains for most of the climb. The large conifers sway back and forth above your head while small songbirds, such as winter wrens, provide a symphony of melodic tunes to distract you from the huff and puff. Trail stairs here and there help with runoff issues when the persistent rains come to this area. At your feet, moss, licorice fern, and vanilla leaf provide a carpet of green trailscaping.

In 0.9 mile beyond the official trailhead, reach a cutoff to the trail's left (east) noted by a sign for Ranger Falls. Ranger Falls has a slight identity crisis and is known on some maps as Ranger Creek Falls since it comes off Ranger Creek. Whatever you decide to call it, follow the cutoff trail as it drops roughly 400 yards to a wooden railing near a viewpoint for the over 150-foot-high, multisection, multitier waterfall. While the creek babbles year-round, the best time to visit the falls is in the springtime when snowmelt has that mama roaring!

Follow your steps back to the main trail and continue climbing south toward Green Lake, switchbacking tightly a few times before leveling out and giving the quads a break. A log footbridge with a sturdy handrail crosses the now-much-quieter Ranger Creek just prior to arriving at the tranquil shores of Green Lake, 2 miles beyond the official trailhead. True to its name, the lake reflects the emerald color of the wooded peaks above, while logs perfect for sitting wait for you to take a seat. An unmaintained trail cruises around the lake's shoreline, allowing you to pop out at various vistas and gawk at the lake from different angles, provided you don't mind a bushwhack and the occasional spiderweb in your eyeball.

When you've had your lunch and taken enough pictures, head back the way you came.

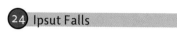

24 Ipsut Falls

RATING/ DIFFICULTY	ROUNDTRIP	ELEV GAIN/ HIGH POINT	SEASON
★★/4	10.8 miles	1675 feet/ 2650 feet	June–Oct

Maps: Green Trails Mount Rainier West No. 269, Mount Rainier Wonderland No. 269SX; **Contact:** Mount Rainier National Park, Carbon River Ranger Station; **Permit:** Mount Rainier Park Pass or America the Beautiful Pass. Park pass available at Carbon River Ranger Station or entrance booth at park's entrance; **Notes:** Carbon River Road open to bicycles. All park trails are hiker only. Pets and stock prohibited; **GPS:** N 46 59.709 W 121 54.939

Ipsut Falls used to be accessible by a simple walk in the woods after parking near Ipsut Campground at the end of Carbon River Road. But, sadly, after several road washouts, the trailhead is officially inaccessible to cars. Thankfully, the

Park Service allows bicycles on the decommissioned road to help you zip your way to the trailhead if you please. Once there, a short walk leads to a 60-foot tiered waterfall bursting from Ipsut Creek and creating a tranquil place for a picnic or a splash on a warm summer's day.

GETTING THERE

From State Route 410 in Buckley, turn south onto SR 165 and continue onward it as it makes a hard right. Follow SR 165 through the towns of Wilkeson and Carbonado until you reach the one-lane Carbon River Gorge/ Fairfax Bridge. Just past the bridge, the road forks. Stay left and continue for 7.7 miles, passing the Carbon River Ranger Station, until the road dead-ends at the Carbon River Entrance. Privy available.

ON THE TRAIL

The trail to Ipsut Falls follows defunct Carbon River Road, which officially closed to cars in 2006 after a historic flood. To get there, walk around the gate and begin your

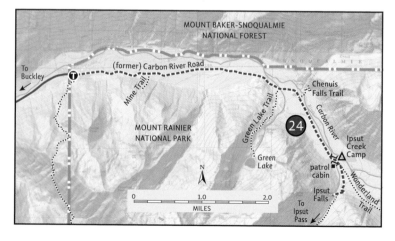

walk or your bicycle ride up the wide gravel road. Huge conifers, including Douglas fir, western red cedar, and western hemlock, sway high above and keep our place in the universe in perspective. Due to the high volume of rain in this area, the mossy bark and understory swim in a sea of lime green.

The road ebbs and flows between a wide cruising lane and a narrow, washed-out single track. At 3.2 miles, pass the trailhead for the Green Lake Trail (Hike 23) to the right (south) and make a mental note to come back and hike it another time. In 0.5 mile beyond that, to the left (northeast) pass the Chenuis Falls Trail (Hike 22) and continue on your way.

At 5.1 miles beyond where you started, reach Ipsut Creek Campground. This campground was once a bustling car-camping area with tents, coolers, and campfires at almost every site. These days, due to the road closure, Ipsut Campground is a true backcountry camp, so fires are not allowed and a prearranged permit is required for overnight stays. A privy and a picnic table are still available for those enjoying the area for the day.

Be sure you also take the time to check out the historic patrol cabin that you'll see here. Damaged in the 2006 floods, when it stood in a slightly different location, the cabin had to be moved off-site for repair. Happily, the restoration was completed successfully and the structure, which is on the National Register of Historic Places, has been reinstated close to its original setting. Just as striking as ever, the cabin was originally built back in 1933 by the Civilian Conservation Corps and has stood witness to who knows what frolicking and changes over the years. May it continue to do so for many more!

The road dead-ends at a large sign noting the various trails in the area that all commence to the sign's right (southwest). Follow the well-used trail as it heads off, crossing a couple of creeks on footbridges before arriving at a signed spur trail toward Ipsut Falls to the right (west), 0.2 mile from

The purring cascades of Ipsut Falls provide a good destination for those looking to ride a bike or walk up the former Carbon River Road and hike to the playful water.

the sign. Roughly 100 feet later, arrive at the flowing, tiered falls and the playful waters of Ipsut Creek. The word *ipsut* means "hidden" in Chinook, a Native American trading language. Standing at the base of the falls surrounded by large conifers, you feel as if you are worlds away from the hustle and bustle of the rat race.

Head back the way you came when you are done enjoying the falls, or wander along the Wonderland Trail near the Ipsut Falls spur trail junction for more adventure. (See Hike 21.)

25 Ipsut Pass

Easy Way

RATING/ DIFFICULTY	ROUNDTRIP	ELEV GAIN/ HIGH POINT	SEASON
★★/2	3 miles	960 feet/ 5100 feet	late July– Oct

Hard Way

RATING/ DIFFICULTY	ROUNDTRIP	ELEV GAIN/ HIGH POINT	SEASON
★★★/3	18.4 miles	4100 feet/ 5100 feet	June–Oct

Maps: Green Trails Mount Rainier West No. 269, Mount Rainier Wonderland No. 269SX; **Contact:** Mount Rainier National Park, Carbon River Ranger Station; **Permit:** Mount Rainier Park Pass or America the Beautiful Pass. Park pass available at Carbon River Ranger Station or self-service payment booth at the park entrance or near the Paul Peak trailhead off Mowich Lake Road; **Notes:** Carbon River Road open to bicycles. Road to Mowich Lake is very rough but passenger cars will make it by going slowly. All park trails are hiker-only. Pets and stock prohibited; **GPS:** (easy way) N 46 56.251 W 121 52.076, (hard way) N 46 59.709 W 121 54.939

 Here are two ways to get to Ipsut Pass, the short way and the long way. Or I should say, the easy way and the hard way. Each has interesting viewing opportunities and very different scenery. (To reach the waterfalls and historic site noted above for this hike, you have to go the long way.) You can combine the two and make it a thru-hike if you leave one car at Carbon River Road and one at Mowich Lake. I'll describe both options here so you can talk it over with your hiking partners and decide which option is best.

The easy way begins at Mowich Lake trailhead and follows the Wonderland Trail around the west side of Mowich Lake until it heads north and reaches the very top of Ipsut Pass, where a viewpoint showcases the valley below. The hard way begins by biking or hiking up closed Carbon River Road to the end, then hiking to the trail. Because 18.4 miles is a little long for a day hike, most folks choose to bicycle up the road, then lock their bikes and begin the day hike up to Ipsut Pass. Whichever route you choose, Ipsut Pass and the Wonderland Trail near Ipsut Creek are visions of old-growth conifers, large, jagged peaks, and avalanche-valley seasonal wildflowers.

GETTING THERE

To reach Ipsut Pass via Mowich Lake (easy way), from State Route 410 in Buckley, turn south onto SR 165 and continue onward as it makes a hard right. Follow SR 165 through the towns of Wilkeson and Carbonado until you reach the one-lane Carbon River Gorge/Fairfax Bridge. Just past the bridge, the road forks. Stay right and follow the signs for Mowich Lake. Continue on this road, which turns to gravel, for roughly 17 miles until you see Mowich Lake to the left (north). Park along the road near the lake's southwestern

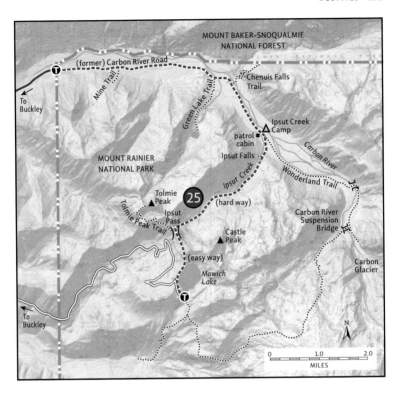

end and locate the trailhead, marked by a sign for the Wonderland Trail on the outskirts of the forest.

To reach Ipsut Pass via Carbon River (hard way), from SR 410 in Buckley, turn south onto SR 165 and continue onward as it makes a hard right. Follow SR 165 through the towns of Wilkeson and Carbonado until you reach the Carbon River Gorge/Fairfax Bridge. Just past the bridge, the road forks. Stay left and continue for 7.7 miles, passing the Carbon River Ranger Station, until the road dead-ends at the Carbon River Entrance. Privy available.

ON THE TRAIL

Ipsut Pass via Mowich Lake (Easy Way)

Duck into the forest near the parking area and locate the Wonderland Trail along the east edge of Mowich Lake. Go left (north) and meander along the lake's forested shoreline for roughly 0.9 mile (or 0.4 mile if you park along the road near the lake's far western shore) until the trail peels away from the lake and crests a small rise. On the rise's north side, continue along for another 0.6 mile until you reach a signed junction for Eunice Lake/Tolmie Peak that veers left (northwest). Make a note to pop over there

Whether you take the easy way or the hard way, Ipsut Pass offers views of rugged Castle Peak with seasonal wildflowers lightly scenting the air.

and check that trail out if there is time (Hike 31). Your trail stays straight and continues onward until it reaches Ipsut Pass in roughly 200 feet. Enjoy the views of the Carbon River valley and the jagged stone cliffs of Castle Peak to the right (east) before heading back the way you came.

Ipsut Pass via Carbon River (Hard Way):

The trail to Ipsut Pass follows defunct Carbon River Road, which in places is only big enough for a bicycle tire or a bootprint. Walk around the barriers and begin your traipse eastbound along the old road. Riding your bicycle up this road is a much faster way to get to the trailhead and is strongly

advised if you intend to hike all the way to Ipsut Pass.

Pass the gorgeous, huge old-growth evergreens that sway in the wind high above the valley. There is so much green in the forest that it almost hurts your eyes! The rushing white noise of the Carbon River provides a musical background as you pedal or stroll along.

At 5.1 miles beyond where you started, reach Ipsut Creek Campground, which is no longer full of coolers, cars, and campers, thanks to the impassable road. Now it is a backcountry camp and requires a prearranged permit for camping and prohibits campfires. A privy and a picnic table are still available for those enjoying the area for the day.

You should also take the opportunity to inspect and appreciate the historic patrol cabin that now stands nearby. It suffered in the floods of 2006 when the Carbon River ran wild and the damaged structure had to be taken down and shifted off-site for extensive restoration. Now it's back, near its original location, and just as grand as ever. Built by the Civilian Conservation Corps back in 1933, the cabin is listed on the National Registry of Historic Places. Pause to consider the marvels and changes that this noble old structure has witnessed.

The road ends at a trailhead sign noting the wide variety of trails in the Carbon River area that all commence to the sign's right (southwest). Follow the well-used trail as it heads off, crossing a couple of creeks on footbridges before arriving at a signed spur trail toward Ipsut Falls to the right (west), 0.2 mile from the sign. If time permits, check out the plummeting falls, located roughly 100 feet off the trail. If not, continue onward for another 200 feet to reach two stacked signs for the Wonderland Trail, one pointing toward Carbon Glacier and the other pointing toward Mowich Lake and Ipsut Pass. You want the latter trail, so go right (southwest) and, sadly, uphill. Thankfully, the climbing isn't too grueling until the very top.

Several beautiful small bridges over playful creeks arrive to break up the monotony of trees, trees, and more trees. At 1.1 miles from the signs, look to the left to spot a dead tree so large that its roots have rotted completely, creating a perfect hollow spot to hide. Go ahead: check it out and grab a picture! Some folks choose to stop here while others keep going to the water, and the hardiest of hikers make it all the way to Ipsut Pass.

Just 0.3 mile beyond the hollow tree, arrive at a wooden bridge that escorts hikers over a tributary waterfall that careens down the hill and pours into Ipsut Creek in the valley to the trail's right (west). More moderate climbing continues until, in roughly 3 miles from the signs, the trail pops out of the forest and begins switchbacking up a steep, flowered slope. The vegetation on this slope, while beautiful and fragrant when blooming, can be aggravating since it grows with reckless abandon and, despite its best efforts, the Park Service can't seem to keep up with trail maintenance. When the greenery is wet with dew, you'll likely get soaked even when it's not raining. Thankfully, the views of nearby jagged Castle Peak and countless other large stone faces take your mind off the bushwhack.

Reach the top of the pass in 3.7 miles from the sign and stop to take it all in. If you left a car for a thru-hike at Mowich Lake, proceed on the Wonderland Trail as it winds around the lake and delivers you to the Mowich Lake parking area, 1.5 miles beyond here. If not, make your way back down into the giant conifers and prepare for the forested walk (or bike ride) back to your car along Carbon River Road.

26 Mine Trail

RATING/ DIFFICULTY	ROUNDTRIP	ELEV GAIN/ HIGH POINT	SEASON
★★★★/3	3 miles	270 feet/ 2140 feet	May–Oct

Maps: Green Trails Mount Rainier West No. 269, Mount Rainier Wonderland No. 269SX; **Contact:** Mount Rainier National Park, Carbon River Ranger Station; **Permit:** Mount Rainier Park Pass or America the Beautiful Pass. Park pass available at Carbon River Ranger Station or entrance booth at park

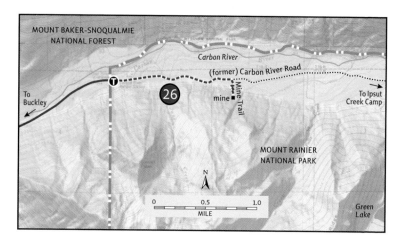

entrance; **Notes:** Carbon River Road open to bicycles. All park trails are hiker only. Pets and stock prohibited; **GPS:** N 46 59.709 W 121 54.939

  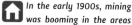 *In the early 1900s, mining was booming in the areas around Mount Rainier National Park. The Washington Milling and Mining Company managed mining operations just inside park boundaries near the Carbon River and workers arrived daily to pick away at the minerals. Due to conflicts with the park, mining efforts were short lived, only lasting three years before the whole kit and caboodle was shut down in 1910. Today, a hike to the mine's entrance puts your imagination to work thinking of what life must have been like over 100 years ago.*

GETTING THERE

From State Route 410 in Buckley, turn south onto SR 165 and continue onward as it makes a hard right. Follow SR 165 through the towns of Wilkeson and Carbonado until you reach the one-lane Carbon River Gorge/ Fairfax Bridge. Just past the bridge, the road forks. Stay left and continue for 7.7 miles, passing the Carbon River Ranger Station, until the road dead-ends at the Carbon River Entrance.

ON THE TRAIL

The trail begins by going around the gate and barriers at defunct Carbon River Road and following it for 1.2 miles. Over the years, Carbon River Road washed out many times, and after the 2006 flood, the Park Service threw in the towel and closed the road. These days, the road is a pleasant walk with large old-growth western red cedar and Douglas fir gracing the forest edges and providing plenty of shade on hot days. The roadway itself is open to bicycles, providing a good cross-training option and allowing you to get to the trails faster.

After 1.2 miles, look to the right (south) to locate a large former parking area and a small sign pointing the way to the mine. This is the beginning of the uphill "shlog" to the

Step back in time and visit historic relics of yesteryear on the Mine Trail.

mine's entrance. "Shlog" is the informal term I've coined for the grunt-worthy, huffy-puffy switchbacks that seem to go straight up in places. Thankfully, they are short lived and you arrive at the mine entrance before your quads start cramping. The mine, gated with steel bars since the 1980s, still has rusty, abandoned ore-cart tracks that once delivered precious metals to the surface from deep within the earth. Use extreme caution when approaching the accessible undercut areas of the mine and, as always, never enter an abandoned mine shaft.

According to retired Park Trails Foreman Carl Fabiani, this particular mine was called the Rudolph Discovery Mine. Its main mineral goal was likely copper, but in those days, it wasn't uncommon to also dig for precious metals and hope for a jackpot. A primitive road used to lead to the nearby mining town of Fairfax, and several buildings used to stand at the base of the

hill leading to the mine; however, Mother Nature has erased any evidence of their existence.

When you've taken pictures and explored the area, wander back to your waiting car with visions of yesteryear buzzing about. Or continue exploring along Carbon River Road and combine your adventure with another trail, such as Chenuis Falls (Hike 22).

27 Mowich River

RATING/ DIFFICULTY	ROUNDTRIP	ELEV GAIN/ HIGH POINT	SEASON
★★/2	8.4 miles	2330 feet/ 4930 feet	July–Oct

Maps: Green Trails Mount Rainier West No. 269, Mount Rainier Wonderland No. 269SX; **Contact:** Mount Rainier National Park, Carbon River Ranger Station; **Permit:** Mount Rainier Park Pass or America the Beautiful

Log bridges like this one abound along the north and south branches of the Mowich River.

Pass. Park pass available at Carbon River Ranger Station or self-service payment booth near Paul Peak trailhead off Mowich Lake Road; **Notes:** Road to Mowich Lake is very rough but passenger cars will make it by going slowly. All park trails are hiker only. Pets and stock prohibited; **GPS:** N 46 55.984 W 121 51.789

The Mowich River valley is alive with powerful, glaciated water and is a good place to experience the devastation volcanic outbursts can create. Pack a lunch and hike down to the river valley for some rocky beach time or to visit one of the Wonderland Trail's backcountry camps and an aging lean-to built years ago by the Civilian Conservation Corps. Just be sure to save enough gumption to hike back out of the valley, since this puppy descends before the "return burn."

GETTING THERE

From State Route 410 in Buckley, turn south onto SR 165 and continue onward as it makes a hard right. Follow SR 165 through the towns of Wilkeson and Carbonado until you reach the one-lane Carbon River Gorge/Fairfax Bridge. Just past the bridge, the road forks. Stay right and follow the signs for Mowich Lake. Continue on this road, which turns to gravel, for roughly 17 miles until the road ends at Mowich Lake. Privies and picnic areas available.

ON THE TRAIL

From the parking area, head toward the privies and locate the Wonderland Trailhead in the evergreens on the south end of the campground. The pathway wastes no time descending into a sea of green along several steep switchbacks before arriving at a

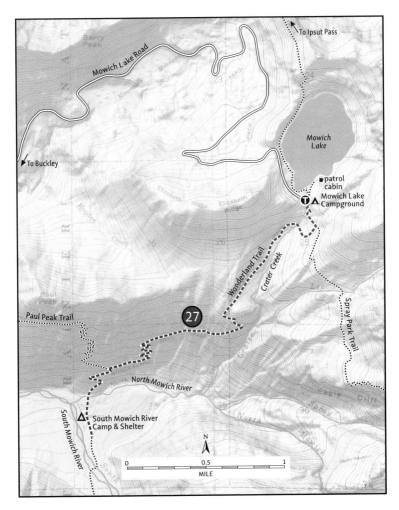

junction with the Spray Park Trail coming in from the left (south). Bear right (southwest) and remain on the Wonderland Trail.

After the junction, the trail takes a turn to the west and crosses seasonal Crater Creek before returning southwest and working its way down toward the valley. Tall conifers, such as Douglas fir, western hemlock, and western red cedar, guide you along, their boughs whispering of years past as they sway in the wind. At your feet, Oregon grape, vanilla leaf, small saplings, and plenty of moss on surrounding rocks remind you of how much rain this area gets.

Down, down, down you go, switchbacking under thick forest cover until you reach a junction with the Paul Peak Trail coming in from the right (northwest), 2.9 miles beyond the junction with the Spray Park Trail. The Mowich River is louder now, creating excitement for things to come. With most of your descent behind you, the trail crosses through a riparian area of lowland forest and sandy river shorelines before it arrives at a crossing of the North Mowich River. Each year, Mount Rainier's runoff rearranges how things look in this valley. In the past, creeklets tripped and played along this stretch of trail, but these days most are gone, save for the North Mowich. Because of the immense amount of water this area receives, log footbridges are often washed out. Only attempt to cross if the bridges are in place, or you may end up having more of an adventure than you bargained for!

Just ahead, in between the North Mowich and South Mowich river branches, locate South Mowich River Camp to the trail's right (west). Stop here to check out the weathered mass of wood of the South Mowich Shelter, which was constructed long ago and now is a mossy, wet mess with some comical graffiti inside, clearly written by those who don't know or care that such vandalism is frowned upon in national parks. My personal favorite is one by someone who, in all caps, questioned "Will it ever stop raining?" There is a primitive privy here as well as several forested campsites. The camp is a good goal for a turnaround spot, or wander out to the South Mowich River, just a little beyond the camp, to stake out a picnic spot on the sandy and rocky shoreline before heading back.

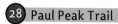

28 Paul Peak Trail

RATING/ DIFFICULTY	ROUNDTRIP	ELEV GAIN/ HIGH POINT	SEASON
★★/4	7.8 miles	1150 feet/ 3650 feet	June–early Oct

Maps: Green Trails Mount Rainier West No. 269, Mount Rainier Wonderland No. 269SX; **Contact:** Mount Rainier National Park, Carbon River Ranger Station; **Permit:** Mount Rainier Park Pass or America the Beautiful Pass. Park pass available at Carbon River Ranger Station or self-service payment booth near Paul Peak trailhead off Mowich Lake Road; **Notes:** Road to Mowich Lake is very rough but passenger cars will make it by going slowly. All park trails are hiker only. Pets and stock prohibited; **GPS:** N 46 54.882 W 121 53.610

🏠 *This trail doesn't go to a true peak but leads to a lovely river valley. If you are a big fan of deep forest, songbirds, white trillium, and gentle breezes, this trail is perfect for you. The Paul Peak Trail presents "dessert first" as you start by steeply descending into the Mowich River basin on the shoulders of Paul Peak before climbing back out on your return. Along the way, the ancient trees almost talk as they sway gently far above your head, beckoning you to continue exploring their sea of green.*

GETTING THERE

From State Route 410 in Buckley, turn south onto SR 165 and continue onward as it makes a hard right. Follow SR 165 through the towns of Wilkeson and Carbonado until you reach the one-lane Carbon River Gorge/ Fairfax Bridge. Just past the bridge, the road forks. Stay right and follow the signs for

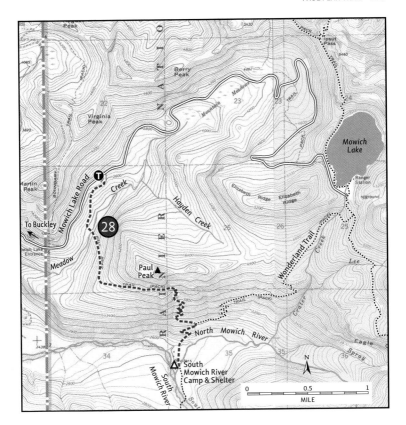

Mowich Lake. Continue on this road, which turns to gravel, for 11 miles until you reach the park boundary and the Paul Peak Trail to the road's right.

ON THE TRAIL

The Paul Peak Trail will charm you from the moment you leave the trailhead. Large conifers overhead gracefully offer the soul a respite from a busy world, while winter wrens sing their sweet melodies from high within the canopy. The forest floor is bursting with plants growing happily in the acidic soil, including Oregon grape, vanilla leaf, sword fern, mosses, and young saplings. A cushioned trail tread of decaying pine needles keeps the feet happy as you continue dropping toward the river valley. Because you are descending, you might get lost in the ease of the walk and forget just how much you have come down. Remember, what goes down, must come up!

Thanks to a damaging windstorm in 2004 that knocked down many large trees, a view

An enchanted forest with a lush understory awaits you on the Paul Peak Trail.

of Mount Rainier now exists to break up your switchbacking descent. The poor Park Service had the grueling task of cutting up massive logs in the debris field to keep the trail open for all of us to enjoy. Tip your hat to those hardworking men and women as you continue going down, down, down through the emerald tunnel.

The South Mowich River begins to loudly and proudly sing its white-noise song as you get closer to the valley bottom. The mossy forest thickens and the trail vegetation gets lusher, looking like a true temperate rain forest, building anticipation for your arrival.

In 3.1 miles from the trailhead, reach a junction with the Wonderland Trail. Turn right and follow the Wonderland until you arrive at the South Mowich River, whose tributaries and forks change every year. Find a nice rocky beach to park yourself for a picnic or continue onward roughly 1 mile from the Wonderland's junction to find South Mowich River Camp and an old lean-to built by the Civilian Conservation Corps in the 1930s. Sadly, graffiti has been splashed all over the old, leaky structure by those who (ahem) likely didn't know better. If nature calls, a primitive backcountry privy is found at this camp.

When you've enjoyed all this scenic area has to offer, huff and puff back the way you came, but uphill this time, to your waiting vehicle.

29 Spray Falls, Spray Park, and Seattle Park

RATING/ DIFFICULTY	ROUNDTRIP	ELEV GAIN/ HIGH POINT	SEASON
★★★★/3	7 miles	2200 feet/ 6400 feet	late July– mid-Oct

Maps: Green Trails Mount Rainier West No. 269, Mount Rainier Wonderland No. 269SX; **Contact:** Mount Rainier National Park, Carbon River Ranger Station; **Permit:** Mount Rainier Park Pass or America the Beautiful Pass. Park pass available at Carbon River Ranger Station or self-service payment booth near Paul Peak trailhead off Mowich Lake Road; **Notes:** Road to Mowich Lake is very rough but passenger cars will make it by going slowly. All park trails are hiker-only. Pets and stock prohibited; **GPS:** N 46 55.984 W 121 51.789

They say it's not the breaths you take but the moments that take your breath away that make up a great life. Spray Park will take your breath away; it's simply that majestic! Imagine a place with a 345-foot waterfall, brilliant subalpine meadows, wildflowers that lightly scent the air, bears grazing on hillsides, spectacular up-close Mount Rainier views, marmots snoozing on sun-warmed boulders, and mountain goats frolicking on rocky peaks. That is Spray Park. Get there, but if possible, do it on a weekday to avoid the crowds who love it as much as you will.

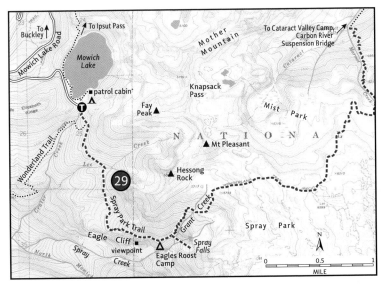

GETTING THERE

From State Route 410 in Buckley, turn south onto SR 165 and continue onward as it makes a hard right. Follow SR 165 through the towns of Wilkeson and Carbonado until you reach the one-lane Carbon River Gorge/Fairfax Bridge. Just past the bridge, the road forks. Stay right and follow the signs for Mowich Lake. Continue on this road, which turns to gravel, for roughly 17 miles until the road ends at Mowich Lake. Walk toward the camping area and the toilets and locate the trailhead for the Wonderland Trail to the south. Privy and picnic areas available.

ON THE TRAIL

Starting off, it might not look like much. Mowich Lake twinkles and the parking-lot-turned-camping-area is a decent place for folks to spend a night or two, but large conifers surround the landscape, so you might ask, where are these subalpine meadows you speak of? Oh, you just wait!

Found to the south of the camping area, the Spray Park Trail follows the Wonderland Trail southbound and quickly begins descending in a series of small switchbacks. In a short 0.3 mile, a junction with the Spray Park Trail arrives to the left (south). Turn left and begin your official trek to the Spray Park area. In roughly 1.5 wooded miles from the junction, arrive at a spur trail for Eagle Cliff, a sneak peek of coming attractions. The spur trail leads hikers down a slightly overgrown landscape to a rocky outcropping with views of Mount Rainier. Use caution with your footing since it is a cliff and you don't have wings. Below you is the site of the former North Mowich Glacier Mine, once a bustling operation with ore cars, a railroad

Wildlife, including mountain goats and bears, are frequent visitors to Spray Park. Keep your camera handy!

track, two tunnels, flumes, water pipes, and heavy machinery. The mine was abandoned in 1908 and the mountain has reclaimed all evidence that humans once were there.

Back on the Spray Park Trail, find the backcountry camp of Eagles Roost to the right (south) by descending a pathway in the large conifers. If nature calls, a primitive privy is located here. If not, keep rolling.

In roughly 2.2 miles from where you started, arrive at a junction for a side trip to Spray Falls, a gorgeous misty waterfall that tumbles 345 feet over andesite rock and is well worth a visit. The roundtrip distance to the falls adds only 0.5 mile to your day and is a great place to cool off and splash around if it's a warm day.

From the Spray Falls spur trail, a steeper climb awaits. Put it in four-wheel drive and huff and puff your way up the tight switchbacks until the trail eventually traverses right and begins to open up. If hiking during berry season in the later months of summer, keep your eyes open for bears from this point forward. They come here to graze and will sometimes cross the trail right in front of you in their quest to get from one berry patch to the next.

The trail climbs a bit more on a series of park-made trail steps before it arrives at a more gentle grade and wanders northeast with great views of Mount Rainier, fragile flowered meadows, rocky buttresses in all directions, and dribbling water pockets. Small tarns dotted around provide water for the creatures, such as hoary marmots and mountain goats, that call this area home. Due to the large volume of visitors this delicate area receives, please do your part and avoid walking off-trail. Eventually, if you keep walking northeast, Spray Park turns into Seattle Park, with little delineation of borders except that Seattle Park is much more alpine than

subalpine and contains permanent snowfields and large talus patches. Follow the cairns through the snow and stones to your heart's content or simply walk until you have worn out your camera. When you are done, turn back the way you came.

EXTENDING YOUR HIKE

Hardy hikers may want to make a full day's adventure out of it and hike the Spray Park Trail in a loop. To do so, follow the directions above, but instead of turning around and heading back to Mowich Lake, continue heading northeast toward the Carbon River basin. The trail descends steeply to Cataract Valley Camp before reaching the Carbon River Suspension Bridge. Once across, follow the detour of the Wonderland Trail southbound and cross the Carbon River again, westbound, at the lower crossing. From here, follow the Wonderland Trail toward Ipsut Creek and turn left (southwest), staying on the Wonderland Trail until you reach Ipsut Pass. From Ipsut Pass, it's roughly 1.5 miles back to Mowich Lake Campground, making for a challenging hike of approximately 17 miles roundtrip.

30 Summit Lake

RATING/ DIFFICULTY	ROUNDTRIP	ELEV GAIN/ HIGH POINT	SEASON
★★★★/3	5.2 miles	1145 feet/ 5425 feet	July–Oct

Map: Green Trails Enumclaw No. 237; **Contact:** Mount Baker–Snoqualmie National Forest, Snoqualmie Ranger District, Enumclaw Office; **Permit:** Northwest Forest Pass required at trailhead; **Notes:** Road to trailhead is extremely rough with large stones and potholes, so high-clearance vehicles strongly recommended. Campfires prohibited at the lake. Horses and dogs permitted; **GPS:** N 47 01.880 W 121 49.615

 Despite having an extremely challenging, bumpy, and rough road, the Summit Lake area is very busy. Word has spread of the cerulean water, the rainbow wildflower explosions near its shoreline, and the knoll to its west where a clear day offers a stunning view of Mount Rainier. Folks flock to this relatively gentle trail, even on weekdays, to marinate in backcountry bliss. But who can blame them? Once you visit, you too will have "Summit fever."

GETTING THERE

From State Route 410 in Buckley, turn south onto SR 165 and continue onward as it makes a hard right in roughly 200 yards. Continue on SR 165 south (heading southwest) for 1.6 miles before turning left (south) and continuing through the towns of Wilkeson and Carbonado until you reach the one-lane Carbon River Gorge/Fairfax Bridge, 9.7 miles from Buckley. In 0.7 mile past the bridge, the road forks. Stay left and continue for 7.6 miles, past the Carbon River Ranger Station, to find Forest Road 7810 and a big metal, one-lane bridge to the left (north) just before the entrance to Mount Rainier National Park. Turn left (north) and wait your turn to cross the bridge over the Carbon River. Set your odometer to zero just before the bridge. Stay straight on FR 7810, ignoring all spur roads, for 5.3 miles until you reach a Y and a signed junction for Summit Lake with an arrow to the left. Turn left (west) and stay on FR 7810 for 1.5 miles to the road's end, and locate the parking lot for the Summit Lake trailhead, where there is room for roughly 15 vehicles. No privy available.

ON THE TRAIL

The trail starts off with a view of a picnic table for folks who survived the bumpy road and want to grab a morsel before they break a sweat. Climbing steadily on a rocky tread, the trail guides you around a switchback and crosses a tributary creek on a wooden bridge 0.4 mile from the trailhead.

The moderate ascent continues and at 0.8 mile from the trailhead, the trail pops into the Clearwater Wilderness, denoted by a sign mounted on a tree. Compared to many in the state, the Clearwater Wilderness is fairly small, at 14,192 acres, but is popular due to the many prominent vistas of Mount Rainier.

The landscape becomes more open just beyond the wilderness boundary and arrives at Twin Lake 1 mile from the trailhead. The quiet, shallow waters of Twin Lake are peaceful but weedy and not inviting for a swim unless you are a pollywog. At Twin Lake, the trail splits and is well signed to help you avoid any confusion. The right branch, Carbon Trail No. 1179, heads south toward Bearhead Mountain (Hike 20), the highest point in the Clearwater Wilderness, and also toward the washed-out Martin Gap trailhead, while the left branch takes you where you are headed, Summit Lake.

Almost immediately after heading left, a sign appears on a tree reminding you that campfires are not permitted in the Summit Lake basin. You are still 1.5 miles from the lake, so don't let this sign fool you into thinking it's a hop, skip, and a jump up the hill. Thankfully, the climb to get there is a moderate to gentle grade. A small tarn shows up to the trail's right just after the sign and kicks off your ascent through the forest, winding north in your quest for the goal.

Scout the collie grins from ear to floppy ear on top of an unnamed knoll to the south of Summit Lake.

In 2.1 miles from the trailhead, 1.1 miles from Twin Lake, a small meadow breaks up the forest and gets you excited for coming attractions. From here, the trail crests a ridgeline, then drops toward the lake basin. Another "NO CAMPFIRES IN LAKE BASIN" sign is mounted on a tree here, in case you missed the first one. Just beyond this sign is an unsigned Y in the trail, causing hikers to scratch their heads and wonder which trail to take. The left fork leads to a small tarn and a trail toward Summit Lake and a few scattered campsites. Go right to keep on the main trail which drops you onto the tranquil, wildflower-filled shores of Summit Lake.

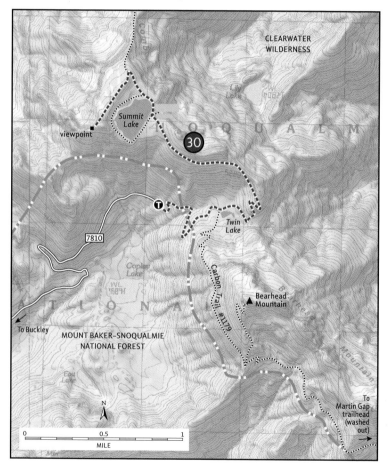

This popular area is starting to show signs of wear and tear so the Forest Service has roped off various areas to restore them. Please respect the signs and spread out your picnic only where permitted. If nature is calling, continue following the main trail around to the right, where a spur trail shoots off to the right and leads to a primitive toilet.

If time permits, you can view Mount Rainier in all its glory keeping watch high above the lake by hiking up the knoll to the south. To get there, proceed right along the main pathway, passing the toilet spur trail. In 0.2 mile beyond the toilet spur, stay right at a Y in a small meadow. After that, a gradual climb gains the ridgeline, where you make a hard left (southwest) turn toward the viewpoint almost without realizing it. Enjoy plenty of great views until you reach the tippy-top, 3.3 miles from the trailhead and 0.8 mile beyond the lake. Swoon at the spectacular sights from your perch and head back when your soul's cookie jar is full to the brim.

31 Tolmie Peak and Eunice Lake

RATING/ DIFFICULTY	ROUNDTRIP	ELEV GAIN/ HIGH POINT	SEASON
★★★★★/3	6.4 miles	1250 feet/ 5940 feet	late July– early Oct

Maps: Green Trails Mount Rainier West No. 269, Mount Rainier Wonderland No. 269SX; **Contact:** Mount Rainier National Park, Carbon River Ranger Station; **Permit:** Mount Rainier Park Pass or America the Beautiful Pass. Park pass available at Carbon River Ranger Station or self-service payment booth near Paul Peak trailhead off Mowich Lake Road; **Notes:** Road to Mowich Lake is very rough but passenger cars will make it by going slowly. All park trails are hiker only. Pets and stock prohibited; **GPS:** N 46 56.251 W 121 52.076

 *If your time is limited and you want to be blown away, this hike might just be*

On a clear day, the panoramas from Tolmie Peak's historic lookout might just make you misty.

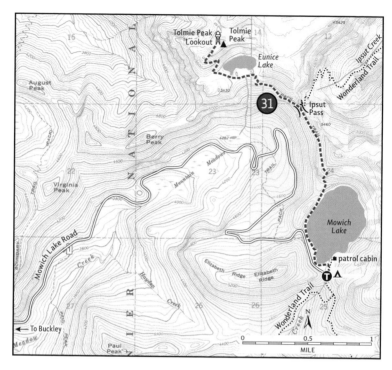

the best possible option. Not only will you be treated to spectacular large boulders en route, but the destination boasts a sparkling mountain lake and one of the last remaining historic fire-lookout towers in the park. What's more, you'll have unobstructed, swoon-worthy views of Mount Rainier from high on the peak. Just remember to bring your camera!

GETTING THERE

From State Route 410 in Buckley, turn south onto SR 165 and continue onward as it makes a hard right. Follow SR 165 through the towns of Wilkeson and Carbonado until you reach the one-lane Carbon River Gorge/ Fairfax Bridge. Just past the bridge, the road forks. Stay right and follow the signs for Mowich Lake. Continue on this road, which turns to gravel, for roughly 17 miles until you see Mowich Lake to the left (north). Park along the road near the lake's southwestern end and locate the trailhead, marked by a sign for the Wonderland Trail on the outskirts of the forest.

ON THE TRAIL

Duck into the conifers on a spur trail heading northeast toward Mowich Lake and connect with the Wonderland Trail in roughly 300 feet. From here, turn left (northeast) and follow the Wonderland along the lake's western shoreline until the trail crests a small ridge and meets up with a junction to the Tolmie Peak Trail in 1 mile. Bear left and begin your official trek to Tolmie Peak.

Large boulders dot the landscape as you traverse the south shoulders of an unnamed ridge above. At 1.5 miles from where you started, a small spur trail breaks off to the left (southwest) and explores a playful creek with dancing waters. Continue onward, switch-backing now six times before reaching the huckleberry-laden shoreline of sapphire Eunice Lake, 2 miles from the trailhead. Several spur trails head north to the lake and beg you to check them out. If you have small kiddos or folks who aren't used to hiking, the lake may be a wonderful turnaround or lunch spot. Several rocky perches around the area provide Leave-No-Trace places to sit and enjoy the tranquillity of the quiet shoreline. If you stop here, be sure to do a quick skyline scan to the lake's left (northwest) and spot the lookout tower, which looks itty-bitty from your vista. Extra points to those who can spot the hikers on their way to the tower, or better yet, standing on its walkways.

Hardy hikers will want to give their quads a pep talk and continue heading west along the lake's southern shoreline until the trail begins a series of three long switchbacks along open, subalpine slopes. Reach the historic tower in 3.2 miles beyond the trailhead. This weathered yet well-cared-for tower was constructed by the Civilian Conservation Corps in 1933, and is one of only four remaining lookout towers in Mount Rainier National Park and one fewer than a hundred left in the state. While small aircraft and satellites now do most fire spotting, Park Service personnel still occasionally use the tower for patrols. The tower offers one of the best views of Mount Rainier in the entire park, and on a clear day you can also see grand vistas of Mount St. Helens, the Olympic Mountains, and Mount Baker. Get out the camera if you haven't already; you are going to need it!

The peak and the lookout tower are named after Dr. William Frasier Tolmie, a Scottish-born botanist who went on a 10-day excursion on Mount Rainier in 1833 to collect and catalog medicinal plants and to observe the glaciers near the northwest corner of the park. This inspired several subsequent trips, during one of which he discovered a new species of saxifrage that also bears his name.

32 West Boundary Trail

RATING/ DIFFICULTY	ROUNDTRIP	ELEV GAIN/ HIGH POINT	SEASON
★★/5	7.3 miles	3810 feet/ 5430 feet	July–early Oct

Maps: Green Trails Mount Rainier West No. 269, Mount Rainier Wonderland No. 269SX; **Contact:** Mount Rainier National Park, Carbon River Ranger Station; **Permit:** Mount Rainier Park Pass or America the Beautiful Pass. Park pass available at Carbon River Ranger Station or entrance booth at park's entrance; **Notes:** Due to its steepness, this unmaintained trail does not get a great deal of traffic and may be challenging to follow at times. A scramble requiring hands and feet is necessary to reach high points and should only be attempted by those with rock climbing skills and previous experience in scrambling. Carbon River Road open to bicycles. All park trails are hiker only. Pets prohibited; **GPS:** N 46 59.709 W 121 54.939

This hike is not for everyone. The majority of the pathway is set in thick woods with a steep incline that rarely lets hikers rest. The monotony of the emer-ald tunnel and steep grade might make you start to mentally tap out unless you are aware of the goal and are in shape enough to reach it. Not only does this trail lead to a couple of

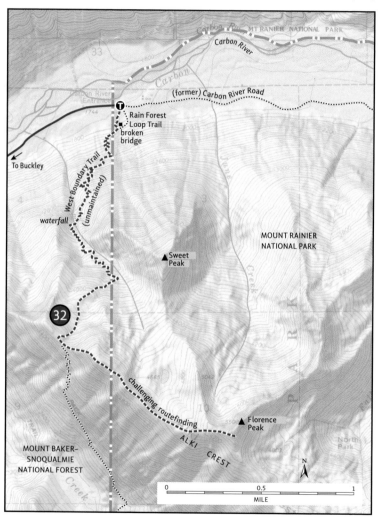

serene cascading waterfalls, but it also continues onward to a scramble where hands and feet obtain the pseudo summit of Florence Peak. From there, views, including those of Mount Rainier, abound!

GETTING THERE

From State Route 410 in Buckley, turn south onto SR 165 and continue onward as it makes a hard right. Follow SR 165 through the towns of Wilkeson and Carbonado until you reach the one-lane Carbon River Gorge/ Fairfax Bridge. Just past the bridge, the road forks. Stay left and continue for 7.7 miles, passing the Carbon River Ranger Station, until the road dead-ends at the Carbon River Entrance.

ON THE TRAIL

Unlike many trails in this area, the West Boundary Trail doesn't begin by following defunct Carbon River Road. Instead, it starts right in the parking area along the Rain Forest Loop Trail. Unfortunately, due to some fallen trees, the Rain Forest Loop is no longer a loop but an out-and-back, unless you continue on the West Boundary Trail.

The West Boundary Trail was built in the early 1930s as a way for park rangers to patrol for vandals, poachers, and fires. When the need for patrols lessened some 40 years later, the trail was nearly abandoned. Thanks to the efforts of volunteers, such as the fine folks from the Washington Trails Association and the hardworking Park

While lush and beautiful, the unmaintained West Boundary Trail is a tough climb and should be reserved for those with polished navigational skills.

Service trail maintenance crews, the trail is now back in good shape and provides recreational opportunities for many, although the Park Service doesn't officially consider it "maintained."

The trail begins at a signpost noting the Rain Forest Loop and reminding folks that pets and bicycles are prohibited. Go right at the sign and begin your forest walk along the flat interpretive trail. This stretch of trail badly needs repair, so watch your footing on rotting, loose boardwalk planks and use caution where they are missing. Well-worn signs in this stretch educate hikers on the importance of temperate rain forests and provide opportunities along the way to stop and learn.

In 0.1 mile, arrive at a trail junction for the West Boundary Trail noted by a sign. Continuing around the Rain Forest Loop is no longer an option, thanks to a broken bridge. Luckily, your trail goes right (south) and begins climbing the switchbacks under a thick forest canopy. Note the large Douglas fir and western red cedar that cushion the trail with their thick needles in places. In 1 mile, the climb finally rewards you with peekaboo views into the Carbon River valley far below. In 1.3 miles, the trail meets up with a primitive spur trail heading off to the right (west). Follow this detour to check out a waterfall as it cascades down a stone face. In low-water seasons, it can be a trickle but is impressive if it's flowing. Watch how you step as the trail can be rocky and rooty in places and rather ankle-twisty. Folks who have had enough huffing and puffing can call this their trail destination, which is still high-five worthy!

Those who haven't experienced enough punishment can continue climbing, and shortly after the spur trail, cross the creek where the upper part of the waterfall can be seen. Roughly 0.7 mile beyond the creek crossing, the trail really kicks into high gear and gets your quads screaming as it climbs very sharply up to Alki Crest. Here you have options. The first is to continue following the West Boundary Trail until you feel like turning back or until it turns into a navigational challenge. The second option is to head up and check out Florence Peak. To cruise up Florence Peak, look for a faint, unsigned trail heading off to the left (southeast) and follow it as it bobs and weaves through a sea of green until it pops out at a rocky but relatively straightforward scramble requiring hands and feet in places. Stand on a perch and take in all the awesome peaks surrounding you, including a certain big snowy volcano! Technically, you aren't yet at the actual summit, but unless you are a skilled mountaineer and familiar with challenging alpine scrambling, it's best to let this be the "top."

When you need to refresh your soul,
work your way up to the top of Noble Knob (Hike 38).

greenwater/
crystal mountain

Just outside the park and often overlooked is the splendid Norse Peak Wilderness and the scenic—and usually uncrowded—Crystal Mountain and Greenwater areas. These places offer great vistas with sweeping panoramas as well as so-green-it-hurts forests with smooth trails under thick canopies where songbirds flit and trill as you wander along. Those with cameras will want to have them ready for the elk and mountain goats that frequent the area and seem to be happy to have the paparazzi snapping away as they graze on greens. If it's tranquillity you seek, you are sure to find it in these impressive landscapes.

33 Crystal Mountain Loop and Henskin, Miners, and Elizabeth Lakes

RATING/ DIFFICULTY	LOOP	ELEV GAIN/ HIGH POINT	SEASON
★★★★/3	8.3 miles	2910 feet/ 6872 feet	July–Oct

Maps: Green Trails Mount Rainier Wonderland No. 269SX, Crystal Mountain Smartphone Trail App (Google Play and iTunes); **Contact:** Mount Baker–Snoqualmie National Forest, Snoqualmie Ranger District, Enumclaw Office; **Permit:** None; **Notes:** Summit House Restaurant, gift shop, and gondola hours vary during summer months. Check Crystal Mountain Resort website for details. Stock and pets permitted; **GPS:** N 46 56.151 W 121 28.425

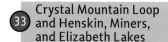 *Although this hike is near Crystal Mountain Resort, it offers plenty of solitude, few people, and several beautiful mountain lakes where you can relax on the shorelines without a single man-made creation in sight. What's more, elk and mountain goats hang out in this area in large herds, increasing your chances of seeing wildlife. The hike even delivers you to the Summit House Restaurant and gift shop, so with some good timing you can grab a burger before your descent!*

GETTING THERE
From Enumclaw, drive State Route 410 southeast for 31.5 miles and turn left onto Crystal Mountain Boulevard. Proceed for just over 6 miles until the road dead-ends and park in the large parking area for Crystal Mountain Resort. Privies and services available.

ON THE TRAIL
Locate the wide trail, which is an old road, that heads steeply up the northern slopes not far from the parking area and main lodge. This is the start of the Bullion Basin Trail. In 0.2 mile, come to an unsigned trail spur and go right. Follow the spur for 0.1 mile and then go right again near a sign directing folks coming from the other direction back to the resort. You are now on Silver Creek Trail No. 1163, although these trails are poorly signed and often slightly confusing.

In 0.5 mile, pass a few old mine buildings now used by the ski resort, and continue traversing the valley slopes near the ski hills. Back in the late 1800s, gold mining boomed in this area, and many landmarks still reference the industry, with such names as Pickhandle Ridge, Pickhandle Point, Pickhandle Basin, and Bullion Basin. Even the chairlift you are about to walk under is called Gold Hills.

With your mind drifting back to a much different time, you arrive at a puncheon bridge over a rocky, wet swath of trail, 0.7 mile from where you started. Here, clear as day, is a hole in the rock and an entrance to an old mine shaft, trailside left. If you aren't expecting it, the mine seems rather out of place on this quiet mountainside and looks more like a primitive cave. Don't stick around too long or a Neanderthal might just wander out! Remember, for your safety never enter a closed mine, as getting injured puts a real damper on a good day.

From here you climb through a variety of trees, including slide alder, hemlock, cedar, and fir, cross Silver Creek by rock hopping,

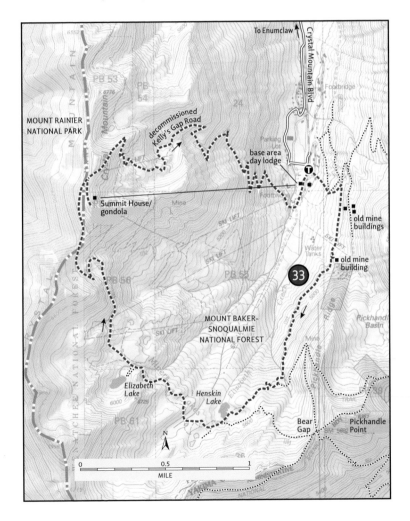

and make your way to a signed trail junction heading off to the left toward the Pacific Crest Trail (PCT) and a junction known as Bear Gap. Not far from here was a miner's camp called Jim Town in what was then the Summit Mining District. Several men named Jim prospected the area and so the town's name was born. Jim Town, sometimes spelled Jimtown, still appears on some maps even though the miners have been gone for many years.

A boot-beaten trail intersects the Silver Creek Trail but small signs save the day and keep you on the right track. In just 0.6 mile from the Jim Town intersection and 2.1 miles from where you started, find yourself in the Henskin Lake basin surrounded by evergreens that are reflected in the shallow water. In early season, the marshy grasses near the water's edge make for a feet soaker if you get too close, and the mosquitoes can be vicious. Still, it's worth fighting off the bitty biters as this place has a serene quality to it that makes you want to stay a while. Thankfully, a small camp on the lake's eastern shoreline invites you to take a load off and spread out a picnic if the bugs are driving you, well, buggy. It's hard to believe you are close to one of the most popular ski resorts in the state!

The lake got its name after a couple of visitors, Mr. and Mrs. Steffen, spent the night here and the wife complained of being cold. She'd brought along a thin cotton blanket known as a henskin that was not warm enough for the conditions. The thin blanket snafu became a running joke between the two, and Mr. Steffen, ever the prankster, clowned around

Sitting on the pristine edges of Henskin Lake, you have no idea you are so close to a commercial ski resort operation.

and marked the site of the chilly night with a one-word sign reading "Henskin." Folks visiting after that just assumed the sign represented the lake's name.

Several trails intersect as you continue along the Silver Creek Trail. A signed one at the far southern end of the lake takes off for the PCT and Bear Gap, and just 0.1 mile after leaving Henskin an unsigned trail junction to the left tempts you to visit Upper Henskin Lake. The upper lake is a smaller version of the one you just saw, so save it for another visit unless gumption and time are on your side.

Without your even realizing it, the trail you are following is now Crystal Mountain Trail No. 1163. Continue onward, passing Miners Lakes and a series of shallow ponds. At 0.9 mile from Henskin Lake, arrive at a sign for Elizabeth Lake to the left. A 0.1-mile spur delivers you to the emerald-colored lake set in a sublime high-country basin while rocky Silver King, The Throne, and Three Way Peak look on from above. Enjoy some time with your camera before heading back to the trail.

The Crystal Mountain Trail now morphs into a service road for a bit and then takes a hard turn to the right, 1.2 miles from the Elizabeth Lake junction. Back on a single-track trail, go under the Forest Queen Express chairlift and traverse a subalpine cirque complete with a couple of narrow stretches of rocky trail where you'll want to pay attention to your footing.

The trail then reaches the west side of a high ridgeline and reveals remarkable Mount Rainier views. It then hops onto a service road and heads north, delivering you to the top of the resort, 1.6 miles from Elizabeth Lake and 4.9 miles from where you started. Keep your eyes open for herds of elk; if you don't see them, I'll be shocked as they have been there on almost every one of my visits!

The gondola, the Summit House Restaurant, a gift shop, and a couple of chairlift towers all come together as if to rejoice in the lofty height. During peak summer months, this area is teeming with people from all over the world who ride the gondola up to this spot to see the views, enjoy a meal from the restaurant, and take in the scenery. To the west, Mount Rainier and the White River drainage are front and center and the view is awe inspiring. The gondola makes it possible for those with disabilities and physical challenges to see this view without hiking here. What a treat for all!

If you decide you've had enough hiking, you can enjoy a big meal, feast your eyes, and then bail out and buy a gondola ticket down from the gift shop. Or just keep hoofing it.

Make your way north to the Green Valley chairlift and locate the Green Valley Trail switchbacking underneath its towers. If you haven't seen elk yet, this might be your chance as they love these rich meadows and might be frolicking around their edges. Follow the Green Valley Trail as it switches through seasonal wildflower fields and evergreen thickets until you reach the bottom of the chairlift, roughly 2 miles from the top. From here, follow decommissioned Kelly's Gap Road for 2 miles down to the resort area. The road is extremely steep, hard on the knees, and in places it's downright easy to lose your footing on the sandy gravel and dirt. Just take your time and pack your patience as it's an important part of completing the loop. Kelly's Gap Road spits you out at another service road, where turning right puts you back at Crystal Mountain Resort in just 0.1 mile. Point your tired legs toward your waiting car and enjoy the memories of a big, wonderful day.

34 Federation Forest State Park

RATING/ DIFFICULTY	ROUNDTRIP	ELEV GAIN/ HIGH POINT	SEASON
★★/1	2.5 miles	160 feet/ 1670 feet	May–Oct

Map: Green Trails Greenwater No. 238; **Contact:** Washington State Parks and Recreation Commission; **Permit:** Discovery Pass; **Notes:** Trails may be muddy and slick during rainy periods. Interpretive Center hours vary, so see website for details. Years ago this area was known for the "Hobbit Trail," a series of small props that are now gone due to vandals. Camping prohibited. Bicycles permitted on paved roads only. Leashed dogs permitted; **GPS:** N 47 09.127 W 121 41.294

If you are looking for a mellow stroll among large conifers and a typical Northwest forest understory, this is the place. Gentle trails lead in all directions; some are in great shape, while others need attention, but overall, this is a serene place to take the kiddos or Fido for a short outing.

GETTING THERE:

From the last stoplight in Enumclaw on State Route 410 eastbound (284th Avenue SE/Farman and Roosevelt), proceed on SR 410 for 15.6 miles to the signed turnoff for Federation Forest State Park. Turn right (south) and follow the paved road past a couple of outbuildings to the Interpretive Center and large parking area. Privies and picnic tables available.

ON THE TRAIL:

Before you set out on the park's trails, you may want to cruise through the Catherine T. Montgomery Interpretive Center, named after the woman who first dreamed up the idea of the Pacific Crest Trail; a visitors center near a deep forest is a fitting tribute for such a woman. The Center houses exhibits explaining the cultural importance of the native tribes and also highlights the local conservation groups that work to preserve

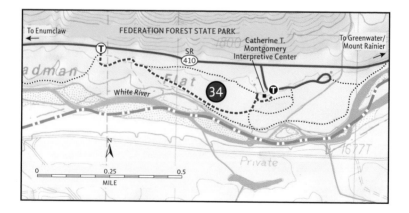

natural spaces. Around the center are native gardens with signage identifying the diverse plant life, although some areas could use a good gardener to reseed the plant beds and perk up the place. Be sure to use the restrooms here if nature is calling as there aren't any in the forest—except for bushes.

Start your wanderings among the 619 acres of evergreens to the Interpretive Center's southeast. A large, well-traveled trail guides you to your first junction where signs point the way to the Whispering Hemlocks Loop Trail to the left, as well as the Naches Trail, the Wind in the Woods Loop Trail, and the Esther Maltby Trail on the river to the right. Head right here and save the Whispering Hemlocks Loop Trail for later. In about 300 feet, arrive at another junction, this one unsigned. Trails lead in all directions, so take your pick! Sadly, some trails, like the one to the far right, end with a "trail closed" sign as a recent windstorm tossed big trees about, scattering them like toothpicks. Despite the closure, a large sign near the dead end explains the Naches Wagon Trail and gets your mind wandering back in time to when wagon trains made their way along this route. Check out the sign if you like, or simply go left and pass a directional sign pointing out trails and a commemorative rock bench honoring Esther Maltby, who helped map out the pathways around the park.

Next up are a couple of trail options, one leading you straight toward the White River, one leading you right toward the Naches Pass Trail and the Land of the Giants Interpretive Loop. Both are in need of some TLC in places but eventually take you to the same place—the world is your oyster! Whatever you decide, mosey your way along the trails heading northwest and eventually end up at a turnaround spot where the trails pop out

Tall evergreens guide the way through Federation Forest State Park as the sun tries hard to penetrate to the forest floor.

at SR 410 and a roadside parking area/trailhead. The trails run east and west near SR 410, so it's hard to get lost; you'll either end up at the road or at the White River if you get turned around.

When you've seen the large evergreens and noted the pecking woodpeckers and singing sparrows, retrace your steps or scoot off on a different trail for a change of scenery, eventually making your way back to the Interpretive Center.

Greenwater River, Greenwater Lakes, and Echo Lake

(35)

RATING/ DIFFICULTY	ROUNDTRIP	ELEV GAIN/ HIGH POINT	SEASON
★★★★/3	13.2 miles	2300 feet/ 4030 feet	late May– Oct

Map: Green Trails Lester No. 239; **Contact:** Mount Baker–Snoqualmie National Forest, Snoqualmie Ranger District, Enumclaw Office; **Permit:** Northwest Forest Pass; **Notes:** In early season or rainy weather, horses create mud bogs along the route. It may also be impossible to ford the river to reach Echo Lake early in the season. Bridges occasionally wash out, so check with rangers before heading out. In the summer of 2017, the Norse Peak Fire burned nearly 56,000 acres, and parts of this hike were affected. Again, contact the Forest Service before setting out to ensure the trail is open for use. Stock and pets permitted; **GPS:** N 47 06.311 W 121 28.512

Take someone you love or maybe even a first date on this hike, as the trail whispers of romance. A gentle pathway caresses the Greenwater River for a couple of easy-going miles before it breaks out near two quiet lakes where graceful waterfowl dine on aquatic insects. Those with gumption and stamina can keep walking, gaining more elevation and crossing into the Norse Peak Wilderness before arriving at large, fish-filled Echo Lake, where picnic opportunities abound.

GETTING THERE
From Enumclaw, drive east on State Route 410 roughly 18.8 miles to paved Forest Road

70, just 2 miles past the town of Greenwater. Turn left (northeast) and proceed 9.2 miles, then turn right (south) at a sign marked "Greenwater Lakes Trailhead, Trail #1176." Cross a bridge and find the trailhead and ample parking in 0.2 mile beyond the sign.

ON THE TRAIL
The trail starts out with lush vine maples lining the pathway, a vision of color in the fall, before it starts a small descent toward the Greenwater River valley. Near the river, white noise acts as a soundtrack as you continue your journey. Small spur trails heading right (southwest) toward the river beg you to follow to check out the rushing water, but the main trail is obvious. Large hemlocks, cedar, and Douglas fir stand proud over the pathway as you make your way to the first of many back-and-forth bridge crossings over the Greenwater River, 0.8 mile from the

Where there is water, there is life. Water fowl, songbirds, and small brook trout call this beautiful riparian zone near Greenwater River home.

trailhead. A large log with sturdy handrails takes hikers across, while horses have their own ford. Puncheon bridges over wetlands help keep the landscape healthy as you make your way through the lush forest.

Cross two more footbridges, which play hopscotch across the river, until you end up on the northeastern side and arrive at the first Greenwater Lake, 1.6 miles from the trailhead. The quiet water, really just a large

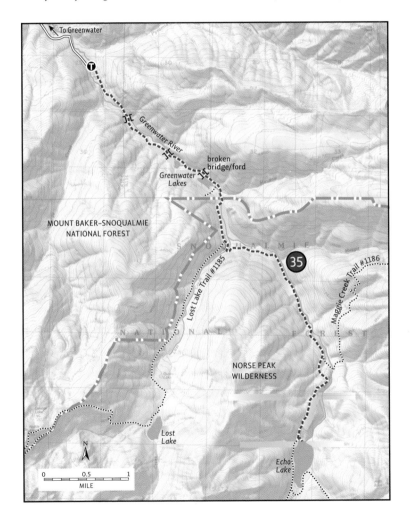

body of backed-up river, is true to its name and reflects a turquoise color. Canada geese preen on the shoreline while ducks gently glide across the calm lake surface.

Another bridge follows, and then you arrive at the second Greenwater Lake. Both have shoreline pathways leading to camps that make fine places to break out the sit pad and daydream. If the kiddos are in tow or you've seen enough, this makes a good turnaround spot. Otherwise, onward to Echo Lake!

In 0.2 mile beyond the second Greenwater Lake, a broken bridge makes crossing the Greenwater River an adventure. Because the water rages in the springtime, the Forest Service seems to have been defeated in efforts to repair it and year after year the bridge gets harder to cross. Early-season crossings will prove difficult if not treacherous, so contact the Forest Service before you go for up-to-date details. Some will be able to shimmy their way down the old bridge and teeter on downed logs to cross, while others might be happier to take off their shoes and enjoy a splish-splash. A small island with blowdowns guides you to yet another bridge, this one intact, which takes you to the other bank. This area is full of campsites and side trails, and even has a backcountry privy for all the creature comforts. Oh, happy day!

Cross into the Norse Peak Wilderness and climb away from the river before arriving at a junction with Lost Lake Trail No. 1185 to the right (southwest), 3 miles from the trailhead. Stay left (south) and follow the signs to Echo Lake.

The trail descends to a crossing with Lost Creek on a sturdy bridge, 0.1 mile from the junction, before traversing the lower shoulders of an unnamed ridge. The Greenwater River is never far away, purring and tumbling just below the path. Gentle ups and downs

follow, until the ups win and you find yourself huffing and puffing like mad. In 2.2 miles from the junction with the Lost Lake Trail, arrive at another junction, this time with Maggie Creek Trail No. 1186 coming in from the left (east). The ascent continues until you reach a small plateau with a swamp visible to the trail's right (west), 0.7 mile beyond the Maggie Creek Trail. From here, a rather steep descent allows you to see the lake through the trees and builds excitement for the coming attractions.

In 6.5 miles from the trailhead, a signed spur trail splits off and drops to campsites, a toilet, and the Echo Lake shoreline. Dip your feet in the water, take a swim, or simply sit by the lake's lapping edges and take it all in. Nature's creatures are everywhere, in the form of woodpeckers, fritillary butterflies, small rainbow trout, and small ants marching up and down logs. Does it get any more peaceful? Turn back when the clock says it's time.

36 Kelly Butte

RATING/ DIFFICULTY	ROUNDTRIP	ELEV GAIN/ HIGH POINT	SEASON
★★★/2	3.6 miles	1085 feet/ 5400 feet	June–early Oct

Map: Green Trails Lester No. 239; **Contact:** Mount Baker–Snoqualmie National Forest, Snoqualmie Ranger District, Enumclaw Office; **Permit:** None; **Notes:** Rough road to trailhead in places, but passenger cars will make it by going slowly. Ticks can be problematic in springtime. Stock and dogs permitted; **GPS:** N 47 09.789 W 121 28.454

 *Years ago, over 600 fire-lookout towers stood tall on high peaks in Washington State. Now fewer than 100 remain, including*

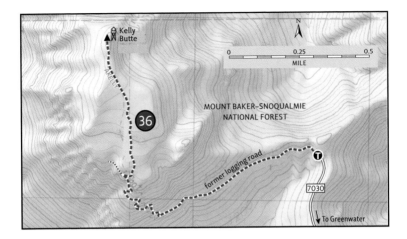

the recently restored tower on Kelly Butte. While the clear-cuts on surrounding hillsides are a bit of an eyesore, Mount Rainier in the distance looms large as a reminder that preservation of land for recreational enjoyment is a treasure. Thanks to the Washington Trails Association and the Forest Service, a proper trail to Kelly Butte now exists, winding its way up interesting geological formations and ending with a fantastic view from the historic tower.

GETTING THERE

From Enumclaw, drive east on State Route 410 roughly 18.8 miles to paved Forest Road 70, just 2 miles past the town of Greenwater. Turn left (northeast) and proceed 7.9 miles to signed FR 7030. Turn left onto FR 7030, which turns to gravel and reaches a T in 4 miles. Turn left at the T to stay on FR 7030. In 0.6 mile from the T, stay straight on FR 7030, indicated only by a scarcely legible sign riddled with bullet holes. In another 0.6 mile, reach a Y and go right, remaining on FR 7030. Proceed 1.3 miles to the signed trailhead and a parking area large enough

for three or four cars to the left. Kelly Butte is visible from the parking area.

ON THE TRAIL

The trail starts off gently down a former logging road, giving you and your quads plenty of time to warm up. At 0.7 mile, a trail to the right of the logging road shows up with a trail sign and a well-constructed rock support wall. Tip your hat to the folks who came here in 2007 and worked on this little beauty, providing a relatively safe way to reach the lookout. Begin your official climb at this point, saying good-bye to the logging road.

Switchback steeply through boulders on a rocky trail, bobbing and weaving through a sprinkling of wildflowers, such as Indian paintbrush, penstemon, spreading phlox, lupine, and beargrass. In just 0.2 mile from leaving the logging road, a viewpoint from a large boulder distracts you from the huff and puff as you look across the valley to the giant vanilla-ice-cream cone of Mount Rainier. What a majestic vision! Continuing onward, the switchbacks ease their tightness and begin longer sweeps, taking you higher and higher into the hinterlands. At 0.4 mile from the logging road, a faint trail comes in from the left. Stay right and continue climbing, unless you want to park yourself on a large boulder for a breather. If you do, look and listen for the marmots that live here and take siestas on the warm, inviting stones.

The grade eases as it continues climbing up, up, and up through beargrass meadows and subalpine fir trees, teasing you since the lookout has yet to show itself. In 0.9 mile from the logging road, the trail reaches a rocky ridgeline and drops over the west side before gently traversing to the lookout, just 0.2 mile beyond.

In 1926, a cupola cabin was built at this lookout site, but it was replaced with a tower in 1950. Over the years, vandalism and age took a toll, but today, thanks to the Forest Service, the tower has been restored and is in fantastic shape. From its perch, feast on the panoramic views of the Cascades, including Mount Rainier, Paranoia Peak, Goat Mountain, Kaleetan Peak, Chair Peak, Granite Mountain, and even Mount Baker. Enjoy the peace of this quiet place, and then head back the way you came when you've worn out your camera shutter.

The setting sun casts a brilliant golden hue over the lookout on Kelly Butte, while in the distance, Mount Rainier puts herself to bed.

37 Little Ranger Peak and Ranger Creek Shelter

RATING/ DIFFICULTY	ROUNDTRIP	ELEV GAIN/ HIGH POINT	SEASON
★★/4	10 miles	2405 feet/ 5120 feet	June–Oct

Map: Green Trails Greenwater No. 238; **Contact:** Mount Baker–Snoqualmie National Forest, Snoqualmie Ranger District, Enumclaw Office; **Permit:** Northwest Forest Pass; **Notes:** Use care at Little Ranger Peak's summit as the rocks can be slippery and there is little margin for error. Park at Skookum Flat Trailhead. Stock, dogs, and mountain bikes permitted; **GPS:** N 47 02.769 W 121 31.418

If a peaceful ascent through towering conifers appeals to you, this is your ideal hike. The playful white noise of Little Ranger Creek provides ambiance while the mossy understory of large evergreens keeps your eyes on the oh-so-green landscape. There is a peekaboo view of the White River basin from Little Ranger Peak roughly halfway up. Those who wish to continue have the chance to check out a well-maintained three-sided

Requiring tricky footwork to reach, the rocky viewpoint of Little Ranger Peak should be visited only by those who have excellent balance.

shelter built by the Boy Scouts years ago. Make a challenging loop by combining this trail with the Palisades Trail (Hike 40) and using a car shuttle or by adding the White River Trail.

GETTING THERE

From Enumclaw, follow State Route 410 east past the town of Greenwater to milepost 54. Turn right (southwest) just beyond the milepost at a sign marked "Buck Creek Recreation Area." Cross the sturdy bridge over the White River and turn left into the Skookum Flat's

parking area. Since there isn't much roadside parking at the trailhead of Little Ranger Peak, this is the best place to leave a car. To find the trailhead, walk back out to SR 410 and cross to the northeast side. Locate an obvious angled side trail heading north across an embankment and follow it to the trailhead.

ON THE TRAIL

Since Ranger Creek Trail No. 1197 doesn't have an official trailhead, the best approach is to follow the highway embankment trail

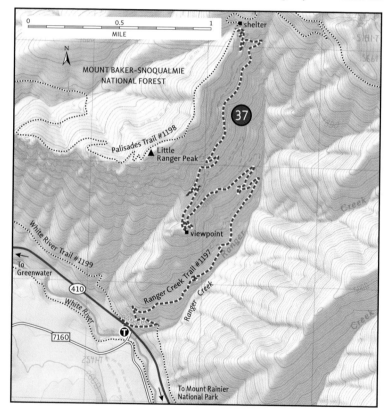

(see Getting There section) to a junction with White River Trail No. 1199. From there, a sign notes the direction of the Ranger Creek Trail to the right (southeast). In 0.3 mile from the sign, arrive at a junction with the path you want, Ranger Creek Trail No. 1197, which is also noted by a sign and turns left (north). Now you are officially on your way. Trust me when I say it sounds more complicated than it is.

Gently climb back and forth under swaying Douglas fir and western hemlock on a soft fir-needle-lined pathway. Since mountain bikers use this trail, keep your wits about you as you ascend moderate switchbacks lined with lush moss and vanilla leaf. At 2.7 miles, the trail reaches a ridgeline and a deteriorating sign noting the viewpoint for the summit of Little Ranger Peak. Head left for 0.1 mile through the sparse conifers and break out onto a cliff band. Those with a fear of heights and the coordination of a bloated buffalo should stay far away from the edges. The mossy rocks are slick when wet. Even when the rocks are dry, coordinated hikers still could go for a painful slide if they aren't careful and don't use good hand placement. Thankfully, the view from a safe distance is nearly the same as from the edges. It won't knock your socks completely off, but it's worth checking out.

Some folks will call Little Ranger Peak the destination for the day, spreading out a picnic and enjoying the ambiance. Others won't be satisfied until they keep climbing to the unique three-sided structure ahead, scratching their heads in wonder about those who chose to construct it in a dense forest accessible only by hiking up a fairly steep hill. If that's you, then onward!

Continue your ascent to a series of tight switchbacks that take you under some cliff bands and through a couple of creeks. Back and forth you go until you reach the shelter and a junction with Palisades Trail No. 1198, 4.9 miles from the trailhead. The shelter sits on flat land high on a ridgeline and deep in the forest. Perhaps the peace of this place inspired the building of this structure. It has received little vandalism over the years and is holding up beautifully, despite the harsh Northwest climate. It's the perfect place to stop, grab a snack, rest, and recover before heading back the way you came or connecting with the Palisades Trail to make a loop.

38 Noble Knob and George Lake

RATING/ DIFFICULTY	ROUNDTRIP	ELEV GAIN/ HIGH POINT	SEASON
★★★★★/3	5.1 miles	1560 feet/ 6011 feet	July–Oct

Maps: Green Trails Greenwater No. 238, Lester No. 239; **Contact:** Mount Baker–Snoqualmie National Forest, Snoqualmie Ranger District, Enumclaw Office; **Permit:** None; **Notes:** The Norse Peak Wilderness Fire of 2017 affected this hike: Use caution in burn zones and contact Forest Service for the most up-to-date trail conditions. Wilderness regulations apply. Stock and dogs permitted; **GPS:** N 47 03.892 W 121 30.094

Pack up the kids, grab the pup, and hit this trail that leads to breathtaking views. Fortunately, the hike is gentle enough that working for the reward is not a super-challenging adventure and most will make the top without issues. Once there, wide-open subalpine meadows and viewpoints greet you with vistas in nearly all directions.

GETTING THERE

Corral Pass has been closed for several years due to its rough, challenging condition. Until it opens, the best way to get to Noble Knob is the back way, with a high-clearance vehicle. Follow State Route 410 from Enumclaw roughly 20 miles to the town of Greenwater. At roughly 2 miles beyond Greenwater, turn left on Forest Road 70. Follow FR 70 east for roughly 5.8 miles, then turn right on FR 72. Drive 0.7 mile and then turn left on FR 7220. Drive 1 mile, then turn right onto FR

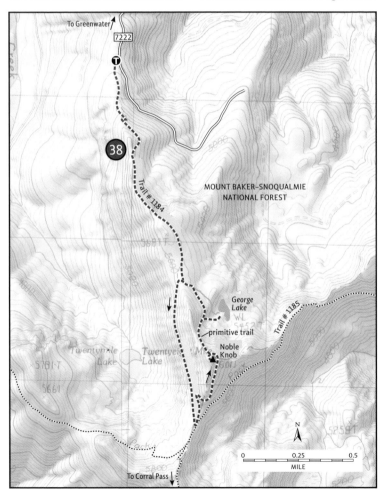

Penstemon grows along the rocky crevasses at the summit of Noble Knob while Mount Rainier looms large in the distance.

7222, which has no sign. Bear left at the forks, staying on FR 7222 until you arrive at a parking area to the right in 5.6 miles. Park here or drive just beyond it and tuck your vehicle in tightly along the side of the road.

ON THE TRAIL

From this entrance, there is no official trailhead with a sign, but you can find the well-worn trail, No. 1184, in two different ways. The first way is to walk the road south of the parking area and look to the right for a well-used trail. The second is to look for a faint trail heading south out of the parking area and follow it until it meets up with the main trail in 0.2 mile. Either way, follow the main trail as it climbs moderately through evergreens and then into huckleberry patches with expanding views.

In 1.2 miles, the trail splits. If you go left you follow the steep bootpath 0.4 mile to the top of Noble Knob. The trail to the left also heads down to George Lake, whose blue color beckons you to visit. Why not visit both?

For a fun loop to Noble Knob, instead go right, staying on Trail No. 1184, and go around the back side of the Knob to arrive at an unsigned trail intersection in 0.7 mile that connects with Trail No. 1185 near Dalles Ridge as well as another worn trail to the top of Noble Knob. Trail No. 1184 keeps going straight at the intersection and meets up with other trails ahead, but for this trip, make a hairpin turn and begin climbing up the unsigned dusty trail toward Noble Knob above.

This subalpine open country is dreamy, complete with tiny noble firs, mountain goats, rainbows of seasonal wildflowers, and the occasional whistling marmot. Does Washington State get more beautiful? What a show-off! Even Mount Rainier comes out to play to the southwest. Reach the tippy-top of Noble Knob in a huffy-puffy 0.5 mile from the intersection and stop to swoon. The peak you are standing on once held a classic L4-style fire-lookout tower. It was built in 1934, and sadly, destroyed in 1954, long before many of us had the chance to see it. But the views remain—paradise to hikers! In this open country you can see other ridges and peaks that look obtainable and fun to visit. Save the cross-country adventures for another day. Instead, head down from Noble Knob to the north and follow the primitive bootpath off the peak, dropping into the lake basin below. Watch your ankles and tread lightly since these trails are steep and rocky.

In 1.2 miles from leaving the Knob, arrive at turquoise George Lake. If time and weather permit, jump in! Your teeth might chatter, but what a treat! After you've dried off or simply enjoyed the shoreline, climb out of the basin on the same bootpath you came in on. In 0.3 mile, go right, heading north and reconnecting with Trail No. 1184 again, which takes you back to your waiting vehicle.

You'll likely be alone with your thoughts as you look out from the lofty summit of Norse Peak.

39 Norse Peak Loop

RATING/ DIFFICULTY	LOOP	ELEV GAIN/ HIGH POINT	SEASON
★★★/4	11 miles	3150 feet/ 6856 feet	late July– Oct

Maps: Green Trails Mount Rainier Wonderland No. 269SX, Crystal Mountain Smartphone Trail App (Google Play and iTunes); **Contact:** Mount Baker–Snoqualmie National Forest, Snoqualmie Ranger District, Enumclaw Office; **Permit:** None; **Notes:** Norse Peak's summit is exposed and dry, so bring plenty of water on hot days. Wilderness regulations apply. In the summer of 2017, the Norse Peak Fire burned nearly 56,000 acres, and parts of this hike were affected. Contact the Forest Service before setting out to ensure the trail is open for use. Dogs permitted; **GPS:** N 46 57.753 W 121 28.791

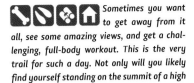 Sometimes you want to get away from it all, see some amazing views, and get a challenging, full-body workout. This is the very trail for such a day. Not only will you likely find yourself standing on the summit of a high barren peak without crowds, but you will be graced with views across the Crystal Mountain basin and beyond to Mount Rainier in the distance. A decent climb gets your heart pumping as you explore a landscape filled with herds of mountain goats and sweeping, open hillsides.

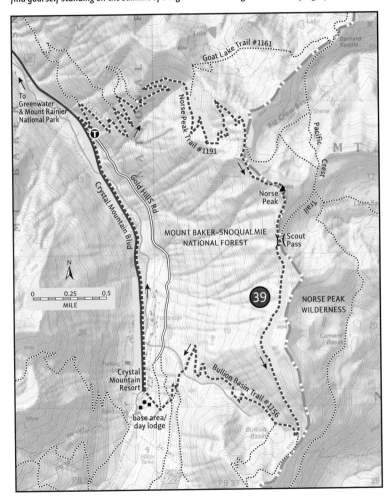

FIRE!

On August 11, 2017, lightning caused a wildfire that burned hot and fast, wiping out nearly 56,000 acres of timberlands in this area. Norse Peak was at the beating heart of the blaze, so much so that the fire was officially called the "Norse Peak Fire." As I write this guide, in October of 2017, the area is still smoldering and will likely continue to do so until the first heavy snowfall calms Mother Nature's wrath. Thankfully, the peak was home mostly to grasses, but unquestionably, nearby timberlands will be visibly damaged and it will take some time for the landscape to rebound. When it does, the views will still be there, along with lessons and wisdom that can only come from loamy soils and creaking, charred wood of fire zones.

GETTING THERE

From Enumclaw, drive southeast on State Route 410 for 31.5 miles and turn left onto Crystal Mountain Boulevard. Proceed for 4.2 miles on until you see an unsigned gravel road, called Gold Hills Road on most maps, heading to the left. This road is often gated. If so, park on the shoulders of Crystal Mountain Boulevard. Parking is very limited on the road's edges. If Gold Hills Road is open, proceed for 0.1 mile, then park along its shoulders, again using caution as the road is narrow. The trailhead is located a short distance up the road to the left. Services and bathrooms available in Crystal Mountain Village, where Crystal Mountain Boulevard dead-ends 2 miles to the south.

ON THE TRAIL

Follow Gold Hills Road for roughly 0.2 mile from its intersection with Crystal Mountain Boulevard and locate the signed trailhead for Norse Peak to the left. On the way there, you'll pass a trail coming in from the right that leads down toward Crystal Mountain Boulevard and provides equestrian access.

Once your feet are firmly on Norse Peak Trail No. 1191, prepare your calves and your lungs for the exertion you're about to undergo. Not to worry, though, in just shy of 2 miles you'll find your eyes completely entertained with vistas, and somehow the pain eases.

The Norse Peak Trail has been rerouted over the years and has plenty of old, closed trail sections that you should avoid. Pay attention so you don't accidentally follow one and ramble into the brambles.

In 0.4 mile from Crystal Mountain Boulevard, the Norse Peak Trail intersects the Half Camp Trail, a spur trail to a horse camp during summer months. Stay on the main trail and continue switchbacking on long, consistently steep zigzags until, at 1.8 miles from where you started, you stop to catch your breath and enjoy a very pleasant view of Crystal Mountain Resort and the basin. The spring in your steps gets more energy as you hoof it higher. Former trails can be confusing along this stretch, so when in doubt, just keep switchbacking uphill and you'll be on the right path.

More great views show up, including the tippy-top of Mount Rainier's ice-cream-cone summit, broader views of Crystal Mountain's eastern high ridge, and Green Valley, Campbell, and Silver basins.

In 2.8 miles from where you started, pass a signed junction with Goat Lake Trail No. 1161, coming in from the left. Your trail goes south here and pops in a few more switchbacks until it gains the ridge and does a little dancing with the east and west slopes. Look for the large herds of mountain goats that frequently visit this area.

Continue along the ridgeline, gazing at the sweeping panoramas until, at 4.9 miles from where you started, you arrive at an unsigned trail spur heading to the right. This is it! Follow the short spur until you are standing on the top of Norse Peak and a makeshift windbreak made with a horseshoe-shaped stone pile. From here, views are outstanding, and you'll want to spend some time playing with your camera.

When you've enjoyed the summit, continue heading down the ridgeline on an unofficial, somewhat scruffy, boot-beaten path to the south, connecting with the Pacific Crest Trail (PCT) and the area known as Scout Pass 0.4 mile from the top of Norse Peak. Follow the PCT southbound for 1.4 miles until you arrive at an unsigned but fairly well-used steep trail heading to the right. Use extreme caution on this trail as it's often dusty and loose and can be challenging in dry summer months. Eventually, this trail becomes Bullion Basin Trail No. 1156 and drops you down the slopes, passing a nice camp near a small lake. A creek playfully bounces near the trail in this area, so if your water bottle is empty, stop, filter, and drink.

In 1.7 miles from leaving the PCT, the trail crosses a service road and continues on the other side. This area is rather confusing as service roads and trails, mostly unsigned, all seem to merge. Just keep following the Bullion Basin Trail, which, to add even more befuddlement, was a former service road at this junction. If you are dropping steeply, you are going the right way.

In 9 miles, arrive at Crystal Mountain Resort. During summer months, a gift shop offers beverages, candy, and other snacks for hungry hikers to purchase.

After you've enjoyed the resort, follow Crystal Mountain Boulevard to the north,

walking the shoulder cautiously back to your car to complete the loop.

40 Palisades Trail

RATING/ DIFFICULTY	ROUNDTRIP	ELEV GAIN/ HIGH POINT	SEASON
★★★/4	8.4 miles	2200 feet/ 4375 feet	June–Oct

Map: Green Trails Greenwater No. 238; **Contact:** Mount Baker–Snoqualmie National Forest, Snoqualmie Ranger District, Enumclaw Office; **Permit:** None; **Notes:** Mountain bikers frequently use this trail, so keep your wits about you when hiking. There are two trails in this book with the name Palisades; this one is a forested hike outside park boundaries and leads to various vistas, while the other (Hike 12) is inside the park and leads to lakes. Mountain bikers and dogs permitted. Stock prohibited; **GPS:** N 47 02.949 W 121 34.199

Look up the word palisade and you'll find it means "a fence or barricade." As you walk among large old-growth conifers and pop out along cliff faces, you might feel as if you are safely barricaded from the world of hustle and bustle. What's more, great views of neighboring peaks from quiet stone perches encourage you to spread out a picnic and spend an afternoon. Mountain bikers use this trail frequently, so be aware of those on two wheels as you enjoy your two feet.

GETTING THERE

From Enumclaw, head east on State Route 410 for 25.9 miles, passing the town of Greenwater and the Skookum Falls viewpoint. Just 0.3 mile beyond the viewpoint, keep your eyes open for a large pullout on the left (east) as it's easy to miss. The trailhead parking area fits about six cars. The trailhead is to the parking area's north, tucked tightly into the evergreens.

ON THE TRAIL

The trail begins ascending on moderate switchbacks and reaches a junction with White River Trail No. 1199 in just 0.2 mile. Palisades Trail No. 1198 bears left at the junction and continues climbing through thick conifers. The trail wraps around a couple of creek drainages before it really starts switchbacking, arriving at a spur trail in 0.9 mile from the trailhead that heads to a waterfall. Turn right and walk roughly 200 feet to check out the seasonally wide waterfall, which cascades over textured stone. Don't forget to look up; it's so high you can barely see where it starts!

After the waterfall, return to the main trail where the grade continues with very tight, crazy-short switchbacks, making you marvel how folks actually bike this trail. Most walk this small section, but even walking a bike through this stretch seems like a superhero feat. In 1.1 miles from the trailhead, arrive at masterfully constructed stairs cut from a giant log that lead you up a very vertical stretch of trail. Hold on to the handrails and walk gingerly, using care not to take a tumble. A couple more steep switchbacks lead to a much gentler grade where your calves breathe a sigh of relief.

Well-crafted trail stairs aid your ascent along a steep section of the Palisades Trail.

From here, the trail crosses a couple of creeks, one by rock hopping, one by a small bridge, before it arrives at the first of three viewpoints, 1.5 miles from the trailhead. The exposed cliff-band edges open up sweeping views of the White River valley below and Suntop Mountain to the west. Those who have had enough climbing may want to break out lunch and call this the top, while others may want to keep rolling to check out the other two vistas.

Onward you go, cruising through a mixture of spindly forest and mature conifers before arriving at the next viewpoint, 1.4 miles from the first and 2.9 miles from the trailhead. This one is higher than the last and has even better views of the surrounding peaks and is naturally landscaped with penstemon, paintbrush, and lupine, a nice foreground for some fine photos.

Reach the final viewpoint by traveling under more evergreens, through a brushy, clear-cut area, and over a bridge across a creek before popping back out onto the cliff band and resuming your views. Bird nerds should keep their eyes out for olive-sided flycatchers, gray jays, and winter wrens enjoying the abundance of nearby food. As with the other vistas, use care near cliff edges and beware of loose, rocky soil. When you've found a solid perch, see if you can spy the fire-lookout tower across the valley to the west on neighboring Suntop Mountain. The lookout, a classic L4-style tower, was built in 1934 and has been standing guard over the valley ever since. This is a great turnaround point since it is the last spot for panoramic views.

EXTENDING YOUR HIKE

For a longer day, duck back into the forest and continue climbing for roughly another 2.4 miles to a junction with Ranger Creek Trail No. 1197, where a classic three-sided shelter built by the Boy Scouts years ago still stands, happily in condition.

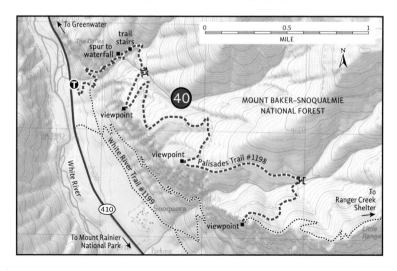

41 Snoquera Falls Loop

RATING/ DIFFICULTY	LOOP	ELEV GAIN/ HIGH POINT	SEASON
★★★/3	3.8 miles	+760 feet/ 3200 feet	late Apr– early Nov

Map: Green Trails Greenwater No. 238; **Contact:** Mount Baker–Snoqualmie National Forest, Snoqualmie Ranger District, Enumclaw Office; **Permit:** Northwest Forest Pass; **Notes:** Use caution on slippery rocks near falls. Dogs permitted; **GPS:** N 46 39.986 W 121 53.487

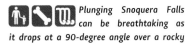 *Plunging Snoquera Falls can be breathtaking as it drops at a 90-degree angle over a rocky* talus, or it can leave you scratching your head wondering if you took the right trail. Hike here after wet weather or during times of high snowmelt and you'll be gobsmacked, but it can dry up entirely during dry summer months—save this one for a rainy day.

GETTING THERE
From Enumclaw, head southeast on State Route 410 for roughly 28 miles, then turn left at the sign for Camp Sheppard, just past Dalles Campground. The trailhead is to the right in 0.1 mile. Privy available.

ON THE TRAIL
The trail kicks off with a lush forest of conifers, including western red cedar, bending their big boughs as if to say "welcome,"

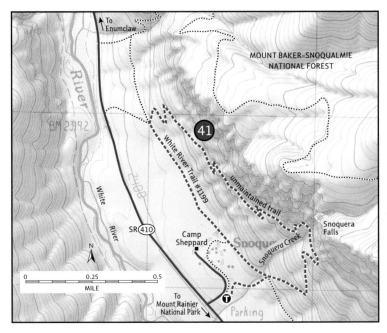

Visit in springtime or during rainy periods to see Snoquera Falls in all its cascading glory; in the summer, it's just a trickle.

and continues through a so-green-it-hurts understory. Parts of the Boy Scout camp, Camp Sheppard, are in this area, including an amphitheater and a nature trail, which may be a fun diversion if you have time for the extra 0.6-mile loop.

For now, stay on the main trail, which crosses Snoquera Creek and reaches a junction with the White River Trail. You will use White River Trail No. 1199 as the return portion of the loop and, should you choose to do the whole hike, you will return on it from the west (left). But for now, continue forward on the main trail, following signs for Snoquera Falls Trail No. 1167 and ascending through forest groves laden with devil's club, Oregon grape, and vanilla leaf.

If you find yourself here on a quiet day lost in thought, keep your eyes peeled for elk. They tend to stop and stare, often unseen in the forest until the very last minute, when they take off in a rush and scare the living liver out of you. And to think some people pay good money for adrenaline rushes!

Continue your climb, hitting a couple of long switchbacks and passing some giant old-growth conifers before the trail spits you out at the base of Snoquera Falls.

Snoquera Falls, at 449 feet, is one of the tallest waterfalls in the state but is not visible all the way to the top due to the steepness of the slope. From this viewpoint, you often see a 162-foot drop spread roughly 60 feet wide over a talus field, which is still impressive.

The waterfall gets its name from a blend of "Snoqualmie" and "ERA," the Emergency Relief Appropriation Act of 1935. Camp Sheppard, located in the basin below, and now a Boy Scout camp, was originally used by the Civilian Conservation Corps (CCC), which helped build roads, bridges, and park structures. The CCC had come from the Snoqualmie area and was supportive of the ERA's public works program, which attempted to pull the country out of the Great Depression.

At this point on the trail, you have options. If you aren't very sure-footed, if the trail is muddy, or if the water is extremely high, you'll likely want to snap a few pictures and then head back the way you came. Completing the loop can be a hazardous proposition as loose soil, scree, and talus can cause those with questionable balance to tumble hiney over teakettle. But if you are confident in your abilities and you have more coordination than an elephant on ice skates, follow the rough trail as it skirts the base of the falls and then switchbacks haphazardly down a steep incline until the grade eases up.

At 2.6 miles, arrive at the junction with White River Trail No. 1199 and follow it to the left and back toward Camp Sheppard and your waiting car.

High meadowland awaits hikers who wander near Tatoosh Lakes and Tatoosh Peak (Hike 47).

cayuse pass/sr 123/
packwood

When you just need to get away from it all, look no further than this historic, water-rich landscape. The physical remoteness of this area's noted trails offers a quiet place to rest the mind while your feet walk in the footsteps of both natural and human histories. Elk frequent the forested thickets, enjoying greens and cooling off under a swaying canopy of large conifers, while Douglas and golden-mantled ground squirrels flash through the verdant understory. Because of the elevation on some of the trails, early-season hiking is possible when other areas are buried under a stubborn carpet of leftover winter snow.

42 Eastside Trail Waterfalls

RATING/ DIFFICULTY	ONE-WAY	ELEV GAIN/ HIGH POINT	SEASON
★★★/3	7 miles	620 feet/ 3300 feet	late July– Oct

Maps: Green Trails Mount Rainier East No. 270, Mount Rainier Wonderland No. 269SX; **Contact:** Mount Rainier National Park or White River or Longmire Wilderness Information Centers, Ohanapecosh Visitors Center; **Permit:** Mount Rainier National Park Pass or America the Beautiful Pass; **Notes:** Bridges occasionally wash out, so contact the park before you set out; **GPS:** N 46 50.037 W 121 32.127

If you fancy waterfalls, riparian areas, and rushing waterways, this hike is a great choice for you! There are several ways to enjoy this hike but the best, if you can swing it, is to use two cars, leaving one at the Grove of the Patriarchs parking area off Stevens Canyon Road and driving the other to the Deer Creek trailhead off State Route 123. Hiking from the Deer Park trailhead to the Grove of the Patriarchs trailhead allows you to hike primarily on a gentle descent, passing water feature after water feature without your quads shouting about difficulty. If only one car is in your fleet, you can start at either trailhead and go as far as your legs can carry you before turning back. No matter whether you head north or south, shooting for the small canyon on the Ohanapecosh River is a good goal and a great place to snap some pictures before heading back.

GETTING THERE
Grove of the Patriarchs Trailhead
From the last stoplight **in Enumclaw** on State Route 410 eastbound (284th Avenue SE/Farman and Roosevelt), proceed on SR 410 for 40.2 miles, passing the park boundary and White River/Sunrise Road, to a junction with SR 123. At the fork, stay straight and proceed on SR 123/Cayuse Pass for 11 miles to Stevens Canyon Road. Turn right (northwest) and enter the park via the entrance booth. In 0.2 mile beyond the entrance booth find the large parking area to the right (east).

From Packwood, drive roughly 7.5 miles north on US Highway 12 and then turn left (northwest) on SR 123. Proceed for 5.4 miles and turn left (northwest) at Stevens Canyon Road. Enter the park through the entrance booth and find the large parking area to the right (east) in 0.2 mile.

From Ashford, drive 6.3 miles to the Nisqually Entrance of Mount Rainier National Park. Enter the park through the entrance booth and proceed for roughly 15.5 miles, passing the Longmire area, to a junction with Stevens Canyon Road. Follow Stevens Canyon Road for 18.9 miles to the large parking area to the left (east) just before the exit booths. Toilets available.

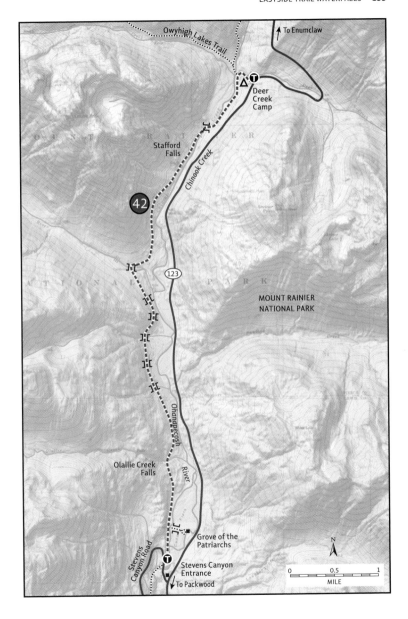

↑ To Enumclaw

Owyhigh Lakes Trail

Deer Creek Camp

Stafford Falls

Chinook Creek

42

123

MOUNT RAINIER NATIONAL PARK

Ohanapecosh

River

Olallie Creek Falls

Grove of the Patriarchs

Stevens Canyon Entrance

Stevens Canyon Road

↓ To Packwood

N

0   0.5   1

MILE

Deer Park Trailhead

From Enumclaw, follow SR 410 east-southeast for roughly 47 miles to Cayuse Pass and a junction with SR 123. Head southbound on SR 123 for just shy of 5 miles. Parking is limited to two to three cars on the right near a small, easy-to-miss sign pointing to Owyhigh Lakes/Deer Creek.

From Packwood, follow US Highway 12 north roughly 7 miles and turn left (west) onto SR 123. Continue for 16.9 miles, passing the Stevens Canyon Entrance. Parking is limited to two to three cars on the left near a small, easy-to-miss sign pointing to Owyhigh Lakes/Deer Creek.

From Ashford, drive 6.3 miles to the Nisqually Entrance of Mount Rainier National Park. Enter the park through the entrance booth, then proceed for roughly 15.5 miles, passing the Longmire area, to a junction with Stevens Canyon Road. Follow Stevens Canyon Road for 19 miles and exit past the entrance booths. Turn left on SR 123 just after the park exit and proceed for 11.5 miles. Parking is limited to two to three cars on the left near a small, easy-to-miss sign pointing to Owyhigh Lakes/Deer Creek.

ON THE TRAIL

From the Deer Creek trailhead, duck into the forest and follow the trail for approximately 0.4 mile to a somewhat poorly signed junction with the Owyhigh Lakes Trail. The park seems slightly conflicted about the spelling of the Eastside Trail, as it's variously one word or two. However you choose to spell it, be sure to follow it as it cruises left (south) at this junction and passes by Deer Creek Camp in just 0.1 mile. If nature calls, a primitive toilet perched on a hillside awaits. If a potty break is not in the cards, continue southbound on the Eastside Trail through thick

Sturdy bridges like this one are key for crossing rushing waterways along the Eastside Trail.

riparian forest with a white-noise soundtrack of rushing Chinook Creek to the right (west). In 1.1 miles from where you started, cross Chinook Creek on a glad-it's-there sturdy wooden bridge as the water flows through a rocky canyon far below. From the creek's western banks, continue southbound and reach pretty Stafford Falls to the right, just 0.7 mile from crossing Chinook Creek and 1.8 miles from the trailhead.

Water is everywhere in this canyon, and the mossy green stones surrounding the streams and creeks make picturesque places to point a camera and practice your slow-shutter waterfall pictures. Onward you go, doing the dance of the evergreens until you reach another beautiful waterfall over a majestic small canyon located 3.2 miles from the trailhead. Here, the Ohanapecosh River thunders toward the valley, making you shake in your boots and glad for the bridge over the whole kit and caboodle. If you don't have two cars, this makes a good turnaround spot. If the other car is parked at the Grove of the Patriarchs trailhead or if gumption allows, keep on rolling. Cross five more bridges over beautiful waterways before arriving at dramatic Olallie Creek Falls, 5.7 miles from the trailhead. You may forget which falls are which since there are so many and they aren't signed, but each is impressive in its own right!

Onward you go, and just shy of 1 mile beyond Olallie Creek Falls (6.6 miles from the Deer Creek trailhead), come to a junction with the Grove of the Patriarchs Trail and its suspension bridge crossing the Ohanapecosh River. Visit this awesome feature that leads to massive old-growth trees if time permits (Hike 56). If not, it's only a short 0.4 mile to the Grove of the Patriarchs trailhead, where restrooms and the comings and goings of park visitors make for a busy scene.

43 Laughingwater Creek and Three Lakes

RATING/ DIFFICULTY	ROUNDTRIP	ELEV GAIN/ HIGH POINT	SEASON
★★★/4	12.2 miles	2815 feet/ 4850 feet	July–Oct

Maps: Green Trails Mount Rainier East No. 270, Bumping Lake No. 271, Mount Rainier Wonderland No. 269SX; **Contact:** Mount Rainier National Park or Longmire or Ohanapecosh Wilderness Information Centers; **Permit:** Mount Rainier Park Pass or America the Beautiful Pass, available at Stevens Canyon entrance booth or self-service payment booth. **Notes:** Park pass not required for parking but should be available to show if you are asked to do so. Laughingwater Creek Trail leads to Pacific Crest Trail so is the only trail in the park that allows stock. Pets prohibited; **GPS:** N 46 45.105 W 121 33.436

Laughingwater Creek seems to maniacally laugh when you are straining on the steep parts of the trail. Other times, it laughs jovially, guiding you gently through deep forest, tarns, and the occasional meadow. For most folks, the true destination of this hike is a series of three forested, peaceful lakes where waterfowl gracefully glide and dragonflies buzz overhead. Hikers also delight in the rustic patrol cabin built in 1934 that stands guard over this area and gives the landscape a homey feel.

GETTING THERE

From Enumclaw, head southeast on State Route 410 for 39.9 miles, passing the town of Greenwater and the White River Entrance of Mount Rainier National Park, until you reach Cayuse Pass. Stay straight at Cayuse

Pass and follow SR 123 south to the Stevens Canyon Entrance, 10.9 miles beyond Cayuse Pass. Proceed another 0.2 mile south on SR 123 to the tough-to-see trailhead darting into the forest on the left (east). Parking is available for roughly three cars on the right (west) immediately after the trailhead.

ON THE TRAIL

The trail begins deep in the forest and immediately starts climbing. The roar of cars along SR 123 soon fades as you switchback through the mossy ground cover and the high canopy of conifers. Up, up, up you go until you reach a ridgeline at roughly 1 mile, where you hear the first cackle of Laughing-water Creek far below.

The incline eases a bit now, and the trail passes a pond on the left before guiding you through gentle ups and downs. Keep your eyes out for forest creatures, such as red fox, elk, and black-tailed deer, as you wander. If you don't see them, you might encounter their droppings as animals use this trail almost as much as humans. Huge old-growth trees, such as Douglas fir, silver fir, and even Alaska cedar, pepper the landscape as you saunter along. Snapping their picture is a hard proposition since the awe the massive trees inspire is hard to capture on camera.

A historic ranger cabin and three pretty lakes are nestled in the forest—your reward for your climbing efforts!

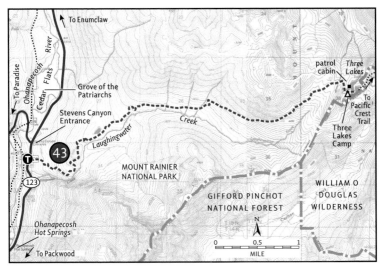

Well-crafted wooden bridges over tributaries distract you from the gradual climb as you pass ancient tree after ancient tree.

The climbing reprieve peters out, and before long the trail gives way to a final grunt up around the southern shoulders of an unnamed peak before leveling off for good.

Here, the pathway pops in and out of lupine-lined meadows alternating with thickets of conifers and delivers you to a peekaboo sight of the first of the Three Lakes to the left (north). From here, the trail gently descends to Three Lakes Camp to the right (south) and to the old patrol cabin, perched in between two of the shallow lakes to the left (north). Overnight stays require prearranged permits, but day hikers are free to wander through the sites, spread out a picnic, or use the camp privy if necessary.

The well-cared-for patrol cabin is usually locked, unless a ranger is visiting and will let you see the inside. Near the front porch, a sign-in register tempts you to share a few words and read those of others gone before you. Log "furniture" around the cabin makes a fine place to sit for a break and a snack, just be sure to use your bug goo since the mosquitoes are often hunting for a feast! If you need water, a couple of skinny bootpaths lead to the lakes' shorelines where it's possible, in most seasons, to get deep enough to sink a bottle or float a filter hose. Always treat water to keep your tummy happy.

If you want to go for a dip, the best lake for swimming is the third lake, which is located farther along the trail to the right (southeast). Just be sure to think twice about jumping in if you've covered yourself in bug spray or sunscreen. Amphibians in the park count on you to help them survive by not introducing contaminants to their home.

The trail meets up with the Pacific Crest Trail 2.1 miles beyond the cabin as it bounces back and forth over the park's boundary. Ramble along as far as you like before heading back the way you came.

44 Ohanapecosh Hot Springs

RATING/ DIFFICULTY	LOOP	ELEV GAIN/ HIGH POINT	SEASON
★★/1	0.6 mile	120 feet/ 1930 feet	early June– early Oct

Map: Green Trails Mount Rainier Wonderland No. 269SX; **Contact:** Mount Rainier National Park, Ohanapecosh Visitors Center; **Permit:** Mount Rainier Park Pass or America the Beautiful Pass; **Notes:** Open seasonally so check park website. Hot springs are very fragile so please stay on trails and walkways. Hot-springs water is unfit for human consumption so swimming and soaking prohibited; **GPS:** N 46 44.168 W 121 33.979

While you can't take a soak in the natural hot springs, seeing the hot water run over the rocks is a good reminder that the earth is very much alive with activity. As a bonus, the rich history of this location causes your mind to wander back to a time when the park was just getting traction in managing the tourism industry. This short loop is a good one for young kids or those with physical limitations. It's also a good place to stop the car and stretch the road-trip legs.

GETTING THERE

From the last stoplight **in Enumclaw** on State Route 410 eastbound (284th Avenue SE/Farman and Roosevelt), proceed on SR 410 for 40.2 miles, passing the park boundary and White River/Sunrise Road, to a junction with SR 123. At the fork, stay straight and proceed on SR 123/Cayuse Pass for 12.3 miles, passing the entrance to Stevens Canyon, and turn right (west) into Ohanapecosh Campground and Visitors Center.

From Packwood, drive roughly 7.5 miles north on US Highway 12 and then turn left (northwest) on SR 123. Proceed for 3.6 miles and turn left into Ohanapecosh Campground

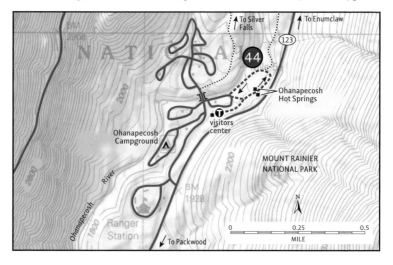

and Visitors Center. Toilets available at trailhead and campground.

ON THE TRAIL

You'll have to put on your sleuthing hat to find the trailhead as it's a little tricky. Walk to the left (north) of the visitors center and wander behind it through the self-guided interpretive trails until you arrive at a well-traveled, wide pathway on the southeast side of the Ohanapecosh River. If you get lost and end up back at the visitors center, try wandering down to Loop B of the campground and find the trailhead near the north end. Trust me, you'll find it on your own eventually, but if you don't, just put on a smile and ask someone roasting marshmallows.

The trail starts off in grand old-growth conifers that create a spectacular canopy high above you as the soundtrack of the Ohanapecosh River dances in your ears. In 0.1 mile from the campground, the Hot Springs Loop heads to the main trail's right. If you smell rotten eggs, otherwise known as sulfur, you've likely made it to the stinky educational area!

You might notice that the water in places looks oddly colorful. When you see orange, you are seeing some algae that grow beautifully at 80 degrees Fahrenheit. On the other hand, green-blue algae prefer much warmer water temperatures. Studies have shown that the water here is not actually heated by Mount Rainier as you might think, but rather

Warm water heated far beneath the earth's surface bubbles up at Ohanapecosh Hot Springs.

is heated far beneath the earth's surface and then escapes through cracks in the earth.

This area has a rich history, although when you see it now, it's hard to believe that large buildings stood here until they were demolished in 1967. As early as 1912, a small tent operation touted the therapeutic benefits of the hot springs. In 1924, some businessmen from Tacoma constructed a health spa that subsequent owners developed into quite an impressive operation, which at its peak included 32 cabins, a large bathhouse, a five-car garage, and several maintenance buildings.

Animals, especially in winter, enjoy coming to this area to warm up, so give the kids (or yourself) the fun activity of trying to spot some animal tracks in the muddy areas.

In 0.3 mile around the loop, arrive back at the main trail and turn left, completing the loop in another 0.1 mile. Or reach the visitors center by following a side trail 0.1 mile to the southeast near the end of the loop. If time and energy are on your side, you can prolong your hike by checking out Silver Falls (Hike 46). You can make a loop by hiking north to the falls and crossing to the other side of the river thanks to a beautiful, well-constructed bridge.

45 Shriner Peak

RATING/ DIFFICULTY	ROUNDTRIP	ELEV GAIN/ HIGH POINT	SEASON
★★★★★/5	8.4 miles	3435 feet/ 5835 feet	July–Oct

Maps: Green Trails Mount Rainier East No. 270, Mount Rainier Wonderland No. 269SX; **Contact:** Mount Rainier National Park, Longmire Wilderness Information Center; **Permit:** Mount Rainier Park Pass or America the Beautiful Pass; **Notes:** Cayuse Pass/State Route 123 closes seasonally so check park website for updates. This hike can be hot, dusty, and waterless, so bring plenty of water; **GPS:** N 46 48.135 W 121 33.302

 *Fire-lookout tower lovers, rejoice! Not only does the lookout tower, built in 1932, thrill those who are willing to climb up to its balcony, but the views afforded by the challenging effort are a treat for the eyes and a rest for the soul. The lookout tower is one of only four remaining in the park; the others are Gobblers Knob, Mount Fremont, and Tolmie Peak.*

GETTING THERE

From the last stoplight in Enumclaw on State Route 410 eastbound (284th Avenue SE/Farman and Roosevelt), proceed on SR 410 for 40.2 miles, passing the park boundary and White River/Sunrise Road, to a junction with SR 123. At the fork, stay straight and proceed on SR 123/Cayuse Pass for 7.4 miles to the pullout on the right (west). The trailhead, marked by a large sign, is across the road roughly 250 feet to the southeast.

ON THE TRAIL

The trail starts off climbing and continues doing so nearly the whole way to the top. Thankfully, the grade isn't super steep, but it does keep the ticker ticking and gives your calves a good burn. Up you go, through maples, conifers, and forest understory until the trail breaks into a more open landscape, thanks to a long-ago fire, and reaches the first switchback at 1.7 miles. On a warm day, this area can be cookin' so bring lots of water to chugalug as you motor along. Lupine, wild strawberry, beargrass, and huckleberry bushes line the trail. At 2.6 miles, reach a viewpoint among some boulders perfect for perching and breath catching. Gaze across the valley for stellar views of Mount Rainier and the Indian Bar basin along the Wonderland Trail.

From here the trail climbs through open, rocky slopes laden with vegetation that turns brilliant red in the fall. Glance behind you for views of Mount Rainier.

At last, the trail traverses the shoulders of Shriner Peak before a few switchbacks finally deliver you to the large, flat summit and the lookout tower with commanding views of Mount Rainier to the northwest. If nature is calling, you are in luck! A two-campsite wilderness camping area (by permit only) is nearby and has a primitive backcountry privy. It's no flush toilet, but when you've gotta go. . . .

The Shriner Peak Lookout, along with most of the others in the Pacific Northwest, was built by the Civilian Conservation Corps in the 1930s and boasts the rustic architecture standard for national parks at the time. The lower level is a storage area while the top offers a perimeter balcony and lots of windows for fire spotting. As with many of these structures, the weathered wood could use some TLC, so use extra caution when enjoying the lookout.

Autumn foliage entices hikers to continue climbing up to the lookout at Shriner Peak.

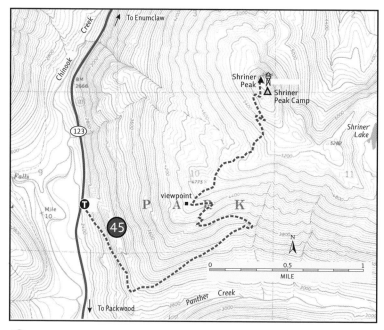

46 Silver Falls Loop

RATING/ DIFFICULTY	LOOP	ELEV GAIN/ HIGH POINT	SEASON
★★★★/2	3 miles	415 feet/ 2280 feet	early June– early Oct

Map: Green Trails Mount Rainier Wonderland No. 269SX; **Contact:** Mount Rainier National Park, Ohanapecosh Visitors Center; **Permit:** Mount Rainier Park Pass or America the Beautiful Pass; **Notes:** Open seasonally so check park website. Hot springs are very fragile so please stay on trails and walkways. Hot-springs water is unfit for human consumption, and swimming and soaking are prohibited; **GPS:** N 46 44.168 W 121 33.979

This hike is a gem in so many ways! When early-season hikes are still snowbound, this one is usually ready for your footprints. What's more, the combination of deep old-growth forest and a wide, rushing waterfall are treats for the eyes and white-noise harmony for the ears.

GETTING THERE

From the last stoplight in Enumclaw on State Route 410 eastbound (284th Avenue SE/Farman and Roosevelt), proceed on SR 410 for 40.2 miles, passing the park boundary and White River/Sunrise Road, to a junction with SR 123. At the fork, stay straight and proceed on SR 123/Cayuse Pass for another 12.3 miles, passing the entrance to Stevens Canyon, and

Experience Mount Rainier's water chisel first hand as you watch Silver Falls.

turn right (west) into Ohanapecosh Campground and Visitors Center.

From Packwood, drive roughly 7.5 miles north on US Highway 12 and then turn left (northwest) on SR 123. Proceed for 3.6 miles and turn left into Ohanapecosh Campground and Visitors Center. Toilets available at trailhead and campground.

ON THE TRAIL

From the visitors center, follow the sidewalk into the campground and across the car bridge over the Ohanapecosh River. Once across, keep your eyes peeled to the right for the trail, which ducks into the forest.

Begin climbing on a gradual grade that steepens in places, making you question the rumor you may have heard about this hike being easy. Consider the little ups and downs a bonus workout and distract your mind with the large, swaying old-growth western cedar and Douglas fir as the forest welcomes you with big branch-y hugs. The copious quantities of moss on nearly every available surface are a reminder of the amount of rainfall this valley gets each year, an average of 75 inches.

The trail follows the ridgeline that drops east and west in deep forest with an occasional sighting of swampy marshes through the conifers. In 1.3 miles from where you

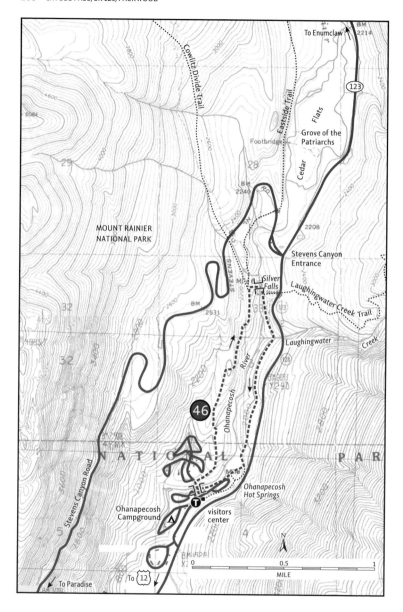

started, arrive at a signed junction with the Cowlitz Divide Trail that darts up to the left toward Stevens Canyon Road. Continue hiking on the Silver Falls Loop Trail for 0.1 mile to reach a signed junction with the Eastside Trail. This is the top of the loop! Take a right here on a hairpin turn and make your way closer to the river. In 0.1 mile, several overlooks provide views of the falls and the rushing (and sometimes spraying) water below. Barricade fences are there for your safety, although some heedless folks have made some small side trails. Don't fall in the drink or you might be introduced to the grim reaper.

At 1.6 miles from where you started, arrive at a sturdy wooden bridge over the river. This beautiful bridge, a work of art in its own right, was badly damaged by the floods of 2006, but has been lovingly restored by trail crews. Silver Falls, named for the rush of white water that crashes from a height of roughly 40 feet over layers of stone, is an impressive sight to hear and see, as is the canyon below. Get the best view by crossing the bridge and standing at its eastern edge. Take your time and take your pictures before climbing up and away from the bridge and back into the so-green-it-hurts forest.

In just 0.1 mile, pass a signed junction for the Laughingwater Creek Trail to the left. The Laughingwater Creek Trail has something of an identity crisis and is also know as the Three Lakes Trail, depending on which sign, map, or literature you happen to see. Rest assured that you are on the correct forested walk here. Continue onward, crossing several smaller bridges over creeks, as Douglas squirrels chatter and scold from their evergreen perches. In 1.1 miles from Silver Falls, 2.7 miles from where you started, arrive at a signed junction with the Ohanapecosh Hot Springs Trail (Hike 44)

to the left. Check out the hot springs if time permits or simply continue onward, reaching the visitors center in 0.3 mile. Some folks have a tricky time finding the visitors center as it's not really well marked in this area. If you take a wrong turn, you'll likely end up in Loop B of the campground, which works out fine too. Simply keep walking through the campground and you'll locate the main road, which will deliver you to the visitors center. If all else fails, pull up a camp chair and eat a s'more.

47 Tatoosh Lakes and Tatoosh Peak

RATING/ DIFFICULTY	ROUNDTRIP	ELEV GAIN/ HIGH POINT	SEASON
★★★★★/5	11.7 miles	4750 feet/ 6310 feet	late July– Oct

Map: Green Trails Packwood No. 302; **Contact:** Gifford Pinchot National Forest, Cowlitz Valley Ranger District; **Permit:** Free wilderness use permits available at trailhead; **Notes:** Steep, exposed trail in places so use extra care with footing. Forest Road 5270 is rough and is one lane in places so high-clearance vehicles recommended but passenger cars will make it by going slowly. Overnight camping is challenging due to sloping landscape. Pack and saddle stock prohibited on Tatoosh Lakes Trail and in Tatoosh Lakes basin. Dogs permitted; **GPS:** N 46 42.802 W 121 42.973

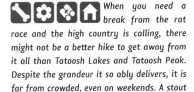 *When you need a break from the rat race and the high country is calling, there might not be a better hike to get away from it all than Tatoosh Lakes and Tatoosh Peak. Despite the grandeur it so ably delivers, it is far from crowded, even on weekends. A stout*

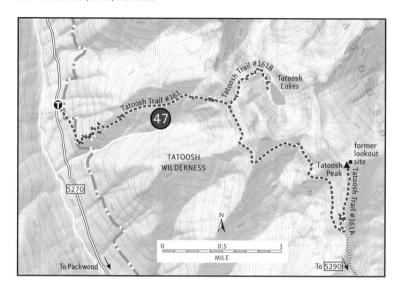

climb reveals meadows bursting with wildflowers, exhibiting all the colors in the crayon
box. What's more, Mount Rainier reveals
itself high above the pristine ridgeline, and
two azure lakes twinkle in the valley below.
This place is truly a soul tonic with a twist of
solitude.

GETTING THERE

From Packwood, turn north onto paved
Skate Creek Road (Forest Road 52) near
the Shell gas station. Proceed for roughly 4
miles and then turn right (northeast) onto
gravel FR 5270. Stay on FR 5270 for 7.1 miles,
bear right at the Y, and look for the sign for
Tatoosh Trail No. 161. Park on the right
shoulder. No facilities available.

ON THE TRAIL

The trail enters the Tatoosh Wilderness
and traverses south among mixed conifers
and an understory that includes beargrass,

Oregon grape, and various mosses, before it
enters a series of tight switchbacks. Up you
go, wanting, waiting, and wishing for views,
until at 1.3 miles you reach the first vista and
you feel like you are finally getting somewhere. Views of grassy, seasonal-wildflower
meadows start to show themselves along
with several unnamed peaks to the southwest. At last, the high country!

The trail hugs the southern shoulders of
a large grassy cirque until it reaches a couple of boot-beaten, unsigned, unofficial trails
heading to the west, 2.2 miles from where
you started. These trails appear to provide
access to Rainier views by eventually heading
northwest. In years past, this area was used
by Native Americans for hunting and gather-
ing and some of their pathways remain.

But for now, follow Tatoosh Trail No. 161, the
main trail, as it curves to the right (southeast)
and, 2.5 miles from the trailhead, reaches a
signed junction with Tatoosh Lakes Trail No.

An imaginary mountain band plays along to nature's soundtrack on top of Tatoosh Peak.

161B to the left. Follow this trail as it crests the ridgeline and then drops over the other side while Mount Rainier keeps a watchful eye.

Switchbacks guide you through huckleberries, lupine, Lewis's monkeyflower, aster, bistort, heather, mountain daisy, and so many others that you'll want to have your wildflower guide at your fingertips to ID them all. What a vision!

In 3.2 miles from where you started, arrive at the smallest of the Tatoosh Lakes and then a little farther, the largest. The shorelines here are often marshy and lack adequate places to sit, and plenty of bitty bug biters wait for a meal. Still, the lakes are simply stunning, tucked away in a subalpine cirque with grassy meadowed hillsides. From

the basin, the very top of Mount Rainier's summit is visible, but the bulk of it is hidden. You may want to just snap a few pictures and continue on your way as there is much more to see.

Head back out of the lake basin the way you came and turn left (southeast) when you arrive back at Tatoosh Trail No. 161. The open meadows and mountain views are endless as you walk around not one, not two, but three separate wildflower-laden cirques to the west of the ridgeline.

In 2 miles from reaching Tatoosh Trail No. 161, arrive at an easy-to-miss signed junction for Tatoosh Peak Trail No. 161A. Turn left (north) here and climb the steep, open ridgeline toward the peak, gaining 550 feet in 0.7 mile. At the top, park yourself for a break and marinate in backcountry magic. The area you are enjoying was once the site of a classic L4-style fire-lookout tower that stood guard over these hills from the 1930s to the mid-1960s when it was removed. Today, concrete pillars and a benchmark reading "Tatoosh L O" are the only remnants. Sweeping panoramic views in all directions reveal Mount Rainier in all its glory, along with countless other jagged peaks. You'll want to stay forever, but since all good things must end, head back the way you came, or mix it up. If you've done a two-car shuttle, follow Tatoosh Trail No. 161 to the south past Butter Peak and down to FR 5290. This is a very steep descent, however, and might make your quads cry. For directions and information on the southern approach, please check out my *Day Hiking Mount Adams and Goat Rocks* guidebook.

Stick around for sunset and wait for the colorful views from Tipsoo Lake to take your breath away (Hike 51).

chinook pass/sr 410

The high and stunning Chinook Pass area is one of my favorites in the vicinity of Mount Rainier National Park. Not only does the region around Tipsoo Lake offer a carpet of fragrant, multicolored wildflowers (in season), but the proximity to the road also makes the area accessible for those with physical disabilities. Explore the backcountry further, and you'll be treated to quiet lakes and brilliant meadows where wildlife peacefully carries on its business of finding food. Just be forewarned, you might not want to go home!

Maps: Green Trails Mount Rainier East No. 270, Bumping Lake No. 271; **Contact:** Okanogan-Wenatchee National Forest; **Permit:** Northwest Forest Pass or Inter-agency Pass; **Notes:** Chinook Pass closes during winter months and may take a long time to melt out completely during high snow years, so check with rangers for current trail conditions before you go. Dogs and stock permitted; **GPS:** N 46 52.522 W 121 31.084

48 Anderson and American Lakes

RATING/ DIFFICULTY	ROUNDTRIP	ELEV GAIN/ HIGH POINT	SEASON
★★★★/4	14 miles	2870 feet/ 5890 feet	July–Oct

While this hike is lengthy, the ups and downs are mixed throughout the trek, making it less of a direct climb and more of a gradual grade. Three beautiful lakes and a few tarns are also in the mix, as well as huckleberry brambles that provide delicious fruit in the summer months and showy red foliage in the fall.

It's a long day to reach American Lake, but you'll likely have the whole place to yourself.

GETTING THERE

From Enumclaw, follow State Route 410 east for roughly 50 miles to Chinook Pass. Once at the pass, near Tipsoo Lake, drive 0.3 mile farther and locate a large parking area on the left-hand side (west). Privy and trash cans available at trailhead.

From Naches, follow US Highway 12 westbound for nearly 4.5 miles to a junction with SR 410. Follow SR 410 west for just over 47 miles to the large parking area to the right (west). A signed trailhead connects the parking area with the trail at the lot's northern end.

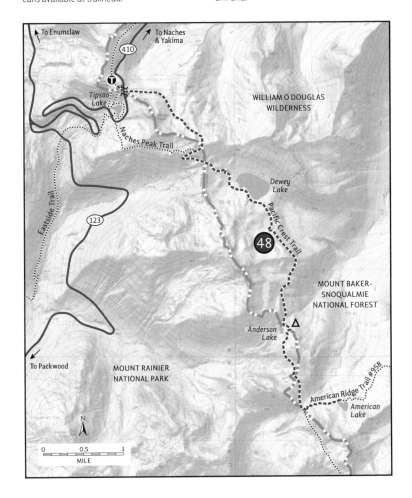

ON THE TRAIL

Find the Pacific Crest Trail (PCT) by heading west (the opposite direction from SR 410) via a small spur trail from the parking lot. Once on the main trail, go left (southbound) for 0.2 mile and cross over SR 410 on a pedestrian bridge. A sign announces that you are on the PCT in 0.1 mile from the crossing.

The trail passes through the William O. Douglas Wilderness and traverses a subalpine hillside until it reaches a slate-colored tarn, 1.1 miles from the parking area. This is a great place to stop for a break or at least a picture.

Gentle ups and downs follow until you reach a viewpoint of the Dewey Lake basin and a junction with the Tipsoo Lake and Naches Peak trails and the Mount Rainier park boundary. If you don't have the pup in tow (they aren't allowed on the Naches Peak Trail), you could follow the arrow here toward Tipsoo Lake and enjoy going through the park to make a loop. Instead, continue on the PCT, following the arrow toward Dewey Lake. In 3.3 miles from where you started, arrive at the serene shores of Dewey Lake and enjoy a few camera snaps before continuing on your journey.

More ups and downs follow as the trail winds its way around brushy meadows, tripping streams, and forest glens to deliver you to quiet conifer-lined Anderson Lake, 1.9 miles from Dewey Lake and just inside the boundary of Mount Rainier National Park. Although the lake is inside the park, dogs and stock are permitted along this particular stretch of the PCT, provided you keep them on the trail. A signed designated camping area is located a few steps beyond the lake as you continue onward with your romp. Next, a small climb leads past grassy meadows and several tarns and, 1.3 miles from Anderson Lake, you reach a signed junction

for American Ridge Trail No. 958, American Lake, Cougar Lakes Trail No. 9584, and a few other destinations. Turn left (east) here and follow the arrows toward American Lake. In 0.5 mile, arrive at the restful banks of American Lake with views of surrounding unnamed craggy peaks. Sit and suck in the grand ambiance before heading back.

49 Dewey Lake

RATING/ DIFFICULTY	ROUNDTRIP	ELEV GAIN/ HIGH POINT	SEASON
★★★★/2	6.6 miles	1320 feet/ 5890 feet	July–Oct

Maps: Green Trails Mount Rainier East No. 270, Bumping Lake No. 271; **Contact:** Okanogan-Wenatchee National Forest, Naches Ranger District; **Permit:** Northwest Forest Pass or Interagency Pass; **Notes:** Chinook Pass closes during winter months and may take a long time to melt out completely during high snow years, so check with rangers for current trail conditions before you go. Dogs and stock permitted; **GPS:** N 46 52.522 W 121 31.084

 Large azure Dewey Lake is tucked into a forested basin and is a rewarding place to visit on a warm summer's day to spread out a picnic or simply splash your feet at the water's edge.

GETTING THERE

From Enumclaw, follow State Route 410 east for roughly 50 miles to Chinook Pass. Once at the pass, near Tipsoo Lake, drive 0.3 mile farther and locate a large parking area on the left-hand side (west). A signed trailhead connects the parking area with the trail at the lot's northern end.

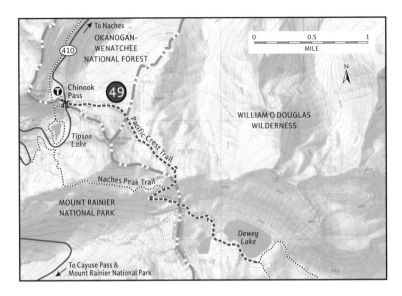

From Naches, follow US Highway 12 westbound for nearly 4.5 miles to a junction with SR 410. Follow SR 410 west for just over 47 miles to the parking area to the right (west). Privies and trash cans available.

ON THE TRAIL

From the parking lot, head west (the opposite direction from SR 410) and locate a small spur trail going uphill that connects with the unsigned Pacific Crest Trail (PCT). From there, walk left (south) for 0.2 mile and then cross the Mount Rainier park boundary to the left (east) on a sturdy pedestrian bridge above the road. Once across, 0.3 mile from your car, arrive at a signed trailhead and begin hiking eastbound on the PCT.

In 0.5 mile, arrive at a sign announcing the arrival of the William O. Douglas Wilderness and listing all the dos and don'ts. Traverse a beautiful hillside with gentle ups and down amid seasonal flowers and the occasional grazing deer and arrive at a scenic trailside tarn, 1.1 miles from where you started. If the lighting is right, this tarn can be a brilliant azure color and makes for a postcard-perfect picture. Practice your best Leave-No-Trace ethics if you decide to explore its shoreline as this area is fragile and the growing season is short. If mobility is limited or you have the wee ones along, you may want to make this your destination for the day and head back once you've snapped some memories with the family.

Otherwise, onward you go, winding your way through subalpine landscape until, 0.7 mile from the tarn and 1.7 miles from the parking lot, you reach a viewpoint showing the Dewey Lake basin, where you are headed, as well as the high country of the Goat Rocks Wilderness in the far distance.

A high-country jaunt gives way to a large, peaceful lake with plenty of picnicking opportunities on the shorelines of Dewey Lake.

A signed junction for Tipsoo Lake (via the Naches Peak Trail) and Dewey Lake are just around the corner from the viewpoint. If you don't have the pooch along (dogs are not permitted on park trails), consider making a loop by following the Naches Peak Trail toward Tipsoo at this junction on your return (Hike 51). Mount Rainier National Park flirts with the PCT here, but you are still in the William O. Douglas Wilderness. Stop to pick up a free wilderness permit at the wooden box as you begin your descent toward Dewey Lake.

In 3.3 miles from the parking area, arrive at the tranquil shoreline of Dewey Lake. Dig your lunch out of your pack and enjoy the ambiance of the area or simply snap a few pics and head back the way you came.

50 Sheep Lake and Sourdough Gap

RATING/ DIFFICULTY	ROUNDTRIP	ELEV GAIN/ HIGH POINT	SEASON
★★★★/3	6 miles	1570 feet/ 6415 feet	mid-July– Oct

Map: Green Trails Mount Rainier Wonderland No. 269SX; **Contact:** Mount Baker–Snoqualmie National Forest, Snoqualmie Ranger District, Enumclaw Office; **Permit:** Northwest Forest Pass or Interagency Pass; **Notes:** State Route 410 at Chinook Pass is often slow to open during years of heavy winter snow, so check road status before you set out. Use only established rings for campfires. During dry summers, campfires may be

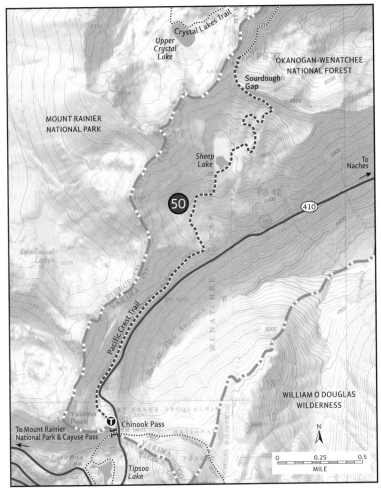

prohibited. Leashed dogs permitted; **GPS:** N 46 52.522 W 121 31.084

 This hike is a vision! Not only does it lead to a beautiful turquoise mountain lake in a subalpine setting, but getting there is usually doable for kids or for those who aren't up for longer jaunts. Those interested in going beyond the lake will be treated, on a clear day, to views of distant Goat Rocks and Mount Adams. Mountain goats, elk, deer, and the occasional black bear wander around these parts.

GETTING THERE

From Enumclaw, follow State Route 410 east for roughly 50 miles to Chinook Pass. Once at the pass, near Tipsoo Lake, drive 0.3 mile farther and locate a large parking area on the left-hand side (west). A signed trailhead connects the parking area with the trail at the lot's northern end.

From Naches, follow US Highway 12 westbound for nearly 4.5 miles to a junction with SR 410. Follow SR 410 west for just over 47 miles to the large parking area on the right (west). Privy and trash cans available at trailhead.

ON THE TRAIL

Hop onto the trail above SR 410 and begin heading northeast, traversing a steep hillside on rocky-at-times tread. The grade is rather gentle in this stretch, and brushy swales containing fauna such as Cascade ash, aster, and corn lily entertain your eyes.

Cars whirling along the highway below are quickly forgotten as the trail turns northwest and ducks into evergreen groves of cedar and Douglas fir. Back and forth you go, alternating between tree thickets and wildflower pocket meadows and climbing rather steeply at times, until you arrive at Sheep Lake, which almost startles you since you pop out of the forest and BOOM!—there it is, 1.8 miles from the trailhead. Around the lake, lush grassy hillsides dotted with emerald evergreens and high stone buttresses make this basin a place you'll want to sit and soak up. From every angle there are landscapes worthy of camera snaps. The greenish-blue lake is somewhat shallow and perfectly nestled into this quiet basin, as if an artist painted it. Around the edges are several well-used camping spots that make good picnic places if you brought the kiddos or if

The landscape near Sheep Lake offers a wonderland of autumn colors as the seasons change.

your time is limited. Those who have more time and gumption will want to keep rolling after they've snapped some memories and grabbed a snack; Sourdough Gap awaits!

For fun—and without cheating by looking at a map—try to figure out where the trail goes! There are so many beautiful subalpine grassy hillsides that you could probably climb them all. Only one pathway climbs out of this valley, though, so follow the well-worn trail and see if your guess is right.

From Sheep Lake the trail wanders up through wildflower meadows showing off various viewpoints that beg you to stop and gawk. The views are timed perfectly with the huffs and puffs so when you need to stop and catch your breath, conveniently, the landscape beckons. In the distance, cars continue buzzing along SR 410 near Chinook Pass while Naches Peak looks on. The various peaks of Goat Rocks show off their distinct profiles to the south, and Mount Adams comes to the "pretty party" with its flat snowy summit. It's hard not to stop, but now you are excited to get to the top of the ridge, so onward you go! Most of Mount Rainier is hidden behind large cliff bands, but its tippy-top peeks over one of the ridges almost as if it's playfully spying on you as you climb higher and higher.

At 3 miles from the trailhead and 1.2 miles from Sheep Lake, crest the ridge known as Sourdough Gap and enjoy the scenery in all directions—wondrous peaks, grassy meadows, rocky outcroppings, and, hopefully, a mountain goat or two!

Sourdough Gap is named for the gold prospectors who staked mining claims near this area. The "sourdoughs," as they were nicknamed, always carried a small amount of sourdough bread starter with them as they roamed from claim to claim. Foodies were around even way back then!

Those who have had enough can turn back here, but if the clock and the quads allow you to go farther, walk just shy of 0.1 mile north of Sourdough Gap to locate a boot-beaten, unsigned spur trail that crosses a scree field and leads to a ridgeline above Crystal Lakes on the eastern edge of Mount Rainier National Park. The Crystal Lakes Trail, an established park trail, connects at the top of this ridge and drops into Crystal Lakes basin. If you follow the Crystal Lakes Trail to the west here, you'll reach a junction with the Crystal Peak Trail and eventually

find yourself near SR 410. Are you thinking what I'm thinking? If you want to make a full, fun day of it and have two cars, leave one car at the Crystal Lakes/Crystal Peak trailhead (Hikes 3 and 4) off SR 410 for a perfect return shuttle without seeing the same scenery twice. Then again, seeing that beautiful scenery twice is not so bad either. Do what you do and enjoy it to pieces!

51 Tipsoo Lake and Naches Peak Loop

RATING/ DIFFICULTY	LOOP	ELEV GAIN/ HIGH POINT	SEASON
★★★★★/2	3.7 miles	685 feet/ 5890 feet	mid-July– Oct

Map: Green Trails Mount Rainier Wonderland No. 269SX; **Contact:** Okanogan-Wenatchee National Forest, Naches Ranger District, Mount Rainier National Park, White River Wilderness Information Center; **Permit:** No permit required to park at Tipsoo Lake; **Notes:** State Route 410 at Chinook Pass is often slow to open during years of heavy winter snow, so check road and trail status before you set out. Wildflower areas are fragile and growing season is short, so stay on established trails. Parking limited in Tipsoo Lake area on busy summer weekends. For more parking, continue 0.3 mile east on SR 410 to large parking area to the left (west), which requires Northwest Forest or Interagency Pass. If you park there, cross the highway to the east and begin Naches Peak Loop along the Pacific Crest Trail. This loop crosses both National Forest land and Mount Rainier National Park. Pets and stock prohibited on all park trails, including Tipsoo Lake Trail and southern side of Naches Peak Loop; **GPS:** N 46 52.040 W 121 31.108

During the height of flower season (which can be anytime between early July and mid-August, depending on snowpack), there may be no place dreamier than the colorful, fragrant shoreline of Tipsoo Lake and the high subalpine meadows of the Naches Peak Loop. Some of the vistas are postcard-worthy landscapes, filled with rainbow carpets of wildflowers, grassy meadows, jagged peaks, and small twinkling tarns. In late summer, the berry bushes turn a brilliant shade of red, elk bugle from nearby valleys, and the hills empty of people. Because it's so accessible and popular during summer months, it's likely you won't be alone, but those you pass will have the same amazed smiles on their faces as you. Visit on weekdays, if possible, to bump shoulders with solitude.

GETTING THERE

From Enumclaw, follow State Route 410 east for roughly 49.5 miles to just before the Chinook Pass. Once at the pass, locate the parking area to the left (northeast). Restrooms and picnic tables available.

From Naches, follow US Highway 12 westbound for nearly 4.5 miles to a junction with SR 410. Follow SR 410 west for just over 47 miles. Pass Tipsoo Lake and locate the parking area on the lake's far western side. Restrooms and picnic tables available.

ON THE TRAIL

There are several ways to approach this hike, and you can hike it either clockwise or counterclockwise. Clockwise is ultimately the best because it gives you the best views of Rainier, and somehow it feels a little easier.

One of my favorite things to do is take a 0.5-mile lap around Tipsoo Lake on the various trails to get warmed up. If Mount Rainier is visible, the eastern side of the lake provides a peekaboo view and, on quiet mornings, will even offer a reflection. Western anemone,

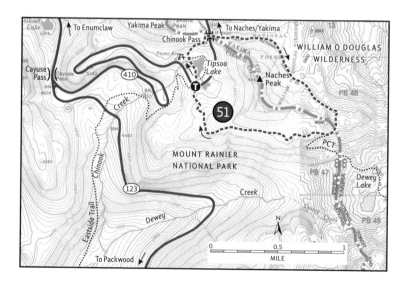

lupine, paintbrush, mountain bistort, Sitka valerian, and mountain daisy are just a few of the colorful, fragrant wildflowers you'll see during peak season. Take your time; this is a special place. You can hike Tipsoo Lake either clockwise or counterclockwise on any number of unnamed spur trails, but they will all eventually take you back to the parking lot. With wide-open views and the purring highway nearby to serve as a compass, it's hard to get lost. Those with tiny tots or physical disabilities will be very pleased to find a place where they can hike in the high country with small elevation gains and losses and may be content counting their loop around

Tipsoo, and perhaps a picnic, as their goal for the day.

Back at the parking area, follow the signed trail climbing northeast under the castle-like shoulders of Yakima Peak for 0.3 mile to reach a bridge that crosses over SR 410. Cross the highway and continue on the trek, following the Pacific Crest Trail (PCT) eastbound and leaving the park for the William O. Douglas Wilderness. Meadowed, open hillsides greet you as you wander, so enjoy the fresh breezes and expansive views. In 0.8 mile from crossing the highway, note a twinkling, unnamed pond set in a grassy meadow to the left (north). Explore

On a clear day when the wildflowers are blooming, there's no better place for a short ramble than Tipsoo Lake and Naches Peak Loop.

it if you wish or keep rolling for even more beauty up ahead.

In 0.4 mile from the pond, reach a couple of viewpoints to scenic Dewey Lake, which is tucked in a valley far below the trail. Grab a few snapshots of this marvelous countryside! In 0.2 mile beyond the viewpoints (0.6 mile beyond the pond), reach a signed trail junction. The PCT makes a hard left (south) here toward Dewey Lake, while your trail continues onward, now going west. If you are confused, just follow the arrowed sign that says "Tipsoo Lake." A smaller sign reminds you that no pets or horses are permitted along the next stretch.

From here, the trail climbs some and then levels off in expansive meadows underneath knobby Naches Peak. A tarn tucked into the green meadows appears to the right (north), 0.2 mile from the signed junction, a worthy place to pull out the camera once more if time permits.

Keep your eyes out for bear, elk, deer, and sooty grouse in this area, as it's very popular with a large variety of wildlife. Sooty grouse, in particular, are not very smart but have a great sense of humor. They enjoy sitting quietly, hidden in bushes, until an unsuspecting hiker walks close by, at which point they take off in a fit of flapping and clucking, causing adrenaline-fueled pandemonium and a soaring heart rate in those who were enjoying the peaceful hillsides. The one that scared me is still laughing!

After the tarn, the trail rolls gently onward, popping out for a couple of grand viewpoints that highlight Mount Rainier in all its glory. Then it begins to descend through huckleberry bushes and sparse conifers back to Tipsoo Lake.

In 1.2 miles from the signed junction with the PCT and Dewey Lake, arrive at another signed junction with the Eastside Trail, which turns left (west) here. You might miss this junction because at this point, immediately ahead of you, the highway and Tipsoo Lake are clearly visible. Cross the highway and make your way back to the parking area via one of the many trails near Tipsoo Lake.

Postcards and picture books are made of visions such as these as the sun sets over Pinnacle Peak (Hike 57).

stevens canyon road

Taking a scenic drive on Stevens Canyon Road is a treat for all visitors, but getting out of your car and exploring the breathtaking backcountry as it winds through riparian valleys and high verdant meadows is truly a delight! Completed in 1952, Stevens Canyon Road was the last road constructed in the park. It was designed to be an essential link between the east and west sides, allowing visitors to stay inside park boundaries and strategically visit natural features, such as Box Canyon and Reflection Lakes. Visitors can still enjoy the features along the roadway, but those who take the time to wander through the trails of Stevens Canyon will enjoy Mount Rainier in all of its raw, untamed beauty through a much different lens.

52 Bench and Snow Lakes

RATING/ DIFFICULTY	ROUNDTRIP	ELEV GAIN/ HIGH POINT	SEASON
★★★★★/2	2.8 miles	600 feet/ 4735 feet	July–early Oct

Maps: Green Trails Mount Rainier Wonderland No. 269SX, Mount Rainier East No. 270; **Contact:** Mount Rainier National Park, Longmire Wilderness Information Center; **Permit:** Mount Rainier National Park Pass or America the Beautiful Pass; **Notes:** Stevens Canyon Road closes during winter months, so check park website for up-to-date information. Stock and pets prohibited; **GPS:** N 46 46.060 W 121 42.488

A gentle, accessible trail leads to two scenic subalpine lakes where tranquility awaits on the Bench and Snow Lakes Trail.

 *This gently graded trail leads to one of the most picturesque lakes in the park. It's a great hike for kids or for those who aren't up for longer, more challenging hikes but still want to get a taste of the backcountry.*

GETTING THERE

From the last stoplight **in Enumclaw** on State Route 410 eastbound (284th Avenue SE/Farman and Roosevelt), proceed on SR 410 for 40.2 miles, passing the park boundary and White River/Sunrise Road, to a junction with SR 123. At the fork, stay straight and proceed on SR 123/Cayuse Pass for 11 miles to Stevens Canyon Road. Turn right (northwest) and enter the park via the entrance booth and then drive for 16.2 miles to the parking area for Snow and Bench lakes to the left (south).

From Packwood, drive roughly 7.5 miles north on US Highway 12 and then turn left (northwest) on SR 123. Proceed for 5.4 miles and turn left (northwest) at Stevens Canyon Road. Enter the park through the entrance booth and drive for 16.2 miles to the parking area for Snow and Bench lakes to the left (south).

From Ashford, drive 6.3 miles to the Nisqually Entrance of Mount Rainier National Park. Enter the park through the entrance booth, then proceed for roughly 15.5 miles, passing the Longmire area, to a junction with Stevens Canyon Road. Follow Stevens Canyon Road for 2.9 miles, past Reflection Lakes, to the parking area for Snow and Bench lakes to the right (south). Parking can be tight on weekends, so arrive early. No facilities available.

ON THE TRAIL

The trailhead is to the parking area's east and is found easily thanks to a couple of well-marked signs. Off you go, climbing up a few trail stairs before leveling off and passing some scenic meadows laden with huckleberry bushes and small evergreens. Keep your eyes peeled for the bears that frequent these meadows, dining on greens and delighting hikers as they munch.

Gentle ups and downs follow and in 0.5 mile, you arrive at an unsigned overlook, also known as The Bench, of Bench Lake, in the shallow basin below the trail. On clear days, this spot is picture worthy, but if fog or mist has moved in, you may want to just keep rolling.

In another 0.2 mile, the trail delivers you to a signed junction with a spur trail leading to Bench Lake on the left. Due to erosion, the often-muddy spur has some large drops, or naturally created giant stairs, which may be hard for older folks or those with balance issues. Additionally, the lake's shoreline is brushy and not very easy to access, so taking pictures and sitting around can prove challenging. This isn't the lake you came for, but you are here, so you may as well check it out. Every lake has beauty and purpose in its own right.

After the spur to Bench Lake, the trail drops slightly to rock hop its way across a creek and then roller coasters up and down to another striking meadow, which if you visit in fall, displays brilliant burgundies, oranges, and reds.

Finally, the climbing really starts. In just a mere 0.2 mile, your ticker will be pumping up 165 feet! Pace yourself on your way to the top, drop a little, and then climb some more. You'll feel like you are walking on a teeter-totter with so many rises and falls, but the good news is that Snow Lake comes up quickly, and when it does, the treat for the eyes will make you forget all about your heaving lungs.

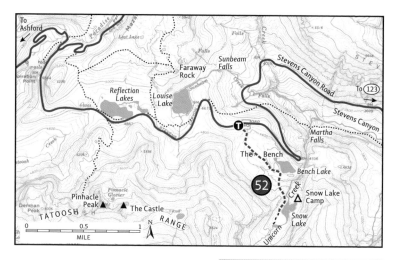

In 1.1 miles from the trailhead, arrive at a signed junction just before the lake. Arrows to the left go toward Snow Lake Camp (permit required) and a backcountry toilet, while the arrow to the right points to Snow Lake. For views from all angles, you'll want to check out both. Start by heading left and descend to a log-bridge crossing of Unicorn Creek at the lake's outlet. Climb a small hill and reach the camp, perched on a mini knoll above the lake. What views! From here, the jagged outline of Unicorn Peak is a beautiful contrast with the azure water.

When you've seen the views from the camp, head back toward the junction and this time go right, or from this direction, straight ahead. Several boot-beaten trails lead to the lake for peekaboo lake views. Those with time to spare may want to keep hiking to the lake's southern end where a large talus field tempts you to explore. When your soul is fulfilled, check this one off your list and return to your waiting car.

53 Box Canyon and Nickel Creek

RATING/ DIFFICULTY	ROUNDTRIP	ELEV GAIN/ HIGH POINT	SEASON
★★/2	2.2 miles	400 feet/ 3400 feet	July–early Oct

Maps: Green Trails Mount Rainier Wonderland No. 269SX, Mount Rainier East No. 270; **Contact:** Mount Rainier National Park, Longmire Wilderness Information Center; **Permit:** Mount Rainier National Park Pass or America the Beautiful Pass; **Notes:** Stevens Canyon Road closes during winter months, so check park website for up-to-date information. Stock and pets prohibited; **GPS:** N 46 45.949 W 121 38.125

The highlight of this hike is attractive Nickel Creek, which playfully trips and cascades into small pools from lofty heights above the trail. On a hot summer day, kids and adults will enjoy spreading out a blanket and cooling off by splashing around at the water's rocky edges. As a bonus, the hike starts and ends at Box Canyon, an interesting natural feature worthy of a visit.

GETTING THERE

From the last stoplight **in Enumclaw** on State Route 410 eastbound (284th Avenue SE/Farman and Roosevelt), proceed on SR 410 for 40.2 miles, passing the park boundary and White River/Sunrise Road, to a junction with SR 123. At the fork, stay straight, and proceed on SR 123/Cayuse Pass for 11 miles to Stevens Canyon Road. Turn right (northwest) and enter the park via the entrance booth. In 10.3 miles find the parking area for Box Canyon to the left (south).

From Packwood, drive roughly 7.5 miles north on US Highway 12 and then turn left (northwest) on SR 123. Proceed for 5.4 miles and turn left (northwest) at Stevens Canyon Road. Enter the park through the entrance booth. In 10.3 miles find the parking area for Box Canyon to the left (south).

From Ashford, drive 6.3 miles to the Nisqually Entrance of Mount Rainier National Park. Enter the park through the entrance booth, then proceed for roughly 15.5 miles, passing the Longmire area, to a junction with Stevens Canyon Road. Follow Stevens Canyon Road for 8.8 miles to the parking area for Box Canyon to the right (south). Outhouses are usually available at trailhead, although it's been hit or miss. The original restrooms

A mix of deciduous and evergreen trees line the picturesque trail near Box Canyon.

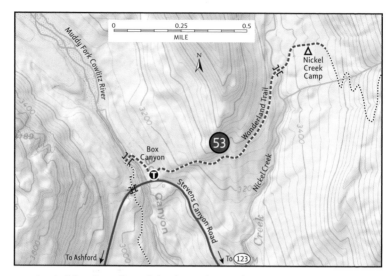

were in a building that still stands but has been out of service for years.

ON THE TRAIL

Cross busy Stevens Canyon Road while channeling your mother's advice to look both ways. The Box Canyon natural feature walkway makes a loop, but the best way to hit it and the trail is to follow the paved sidewalk east of the river for 0.2 mile until you reach the main feature, the bridge over Box Canyon. The Muddy Fork Cowlitz River enters a narrow slot canyon here, which funnels the water through a tight space with furious speed. Just the sound is impressive, not to mention the sight. The natural feature contains a sign mentioning that the depth of the canyon from where you are standing to the water's surface far below is 180 feet. Shudder! When you've seen it, walk back the way you came and locate the easy-to-miss signed junction with the Wonderland Trail near Stevens Canyon Road.

The Wonderland heads east at this spot and begs you to follow it as it begins wrapping around the shoulders of an unnamed peak. As you ascend, the forest thickens and familiar woodland creatures, such as Douglas squirrels and Townsend's chipmunks, hop from branch to branch, sometimes silently, sometimes scolding anyone who passes by. In 0.8 mile from Box Canyon, arrive at the log bridge that crosses Nickel Creek. Play in the water, snap a few pictures, or just enjoy the white noise. Nickel Creek Camp is 0.1 mile beyond the creek to the right and has a rustic privy for those needing a potty break. If extra energy is flowing through your bones, consider continuing your hike all the way to Cowlitz Divide or Indian Bar (Hike 54), but be forewarned, it's a doozy of a climb!

54 Cowlitz Divide and Indian Bar

RATING/ DIFFICULTY	ROUNDTRIP	ELEV GAIN/ HIGH POINT	SEASON
★★★★★/5	14.6 miles	4270 feet/ 5930 feet	July–early Oct

Maps: Green Trails Mount Rainier Wonderland No. 269SX, Mount Rainier East No. 270; **Contact:** Mount Rainier National Park, Longmire Wilderness Information Center; **Permit:** Mount Rainier National Park Pass or America the Beautiful Pass; **Notes:** Stevens Canyon Road closes during winter months so check park website for up-to-date information. Stock and pets prohibited; **GPS:** N 46 45.949 W 121 38.125

If you are up for this very challenging hike, you'll be rewarded with some of the most scenic landscapes in the entire park. Visions of mountain magnificence with panoramic views of lush green meadows and carpets of wildflowers in all directions await you!

GETTING THERE

From the last stoplight **in Enumclaw** on State Route 410 eastbound (284th Avenue SE/Farman and Roosevelt), proceed on SR 410 for 40.2 miles, passing the park boundary and White River/Sunrise Road, to a junction with SR 123. At the fork, stay straight, and proceed on SR 123/Cayuse Pass for 11 miles to Stevens Canyon Road. Turn right (northwest) and enter the park via the entrance booth. In 10.3 miles find the parking area for Box Canyon to the left (south).

From Packwood, drive roughly 7.5 miles north on US Highway 12 and then turn left (northwest) on SR 123. Proceed for 5.4 miles and turn left (northwest) at Stevens Canyon Road. Enter the park through the entrance booth. In 10.3 miles, find the parking area for Box Canyon to the left (south).

From Ashford, drive 6.3 miles to the Nisqually Entrance of Mount Rainier National Park. Enter the park through the entrance booth, then proceed for roughly 15.5 miles, passing the Longmire area, to a junction with Stevens Canyon Road. Follow Stevens Canyon Road for 8.8 miles to the parking area for Box Canyon to the right (south). Outhouses are usually available at trailhead, although it's been hit or miss. The original restrooms were in a building that still stands but has been out of service for years.

ON THE TRAIL

This hike heads north on the Wonderland Trail, so cross Stevens Canyon Road and walk to the northeast side of the Box Canyon natural feature walkway. Once you're on your way, the trail gently ascends through mixed conifers for 0.8 mile to a log bridge that crosses Nickel Creek. If you didn't bring much water, you should stop here and fill up everything you have as there won't be much for nearly 6.5 miles, and you'll be sweating like a yeti in a snowsuit.

In 0.1 mile, the Wonderland Trail comes to a junction with Nickel Creek Camp, where a backcountry privy awaits those who've gotta go. Give your heart and lungs a pep talk here because you are about to embark on a climb, climb, climb-ity climb that will make you pine for anything resembling level ground. Thankfully, the sustained climbing eventually breaks out into views that take your breath away for a different reason. Up, up, up you go into deep, beautiful forest, switchbacking this way and that until you reach a junction with the Cowlitz Divide Trail, an alternative and longer approach from Stevens Canyon to where you are standing, 2.7 miles from where you started. Bear left here, remaining on the Wonderland, and, you guessed it, keep climbing.

In roughly a mile, the landscape opens up to views of neighboring peaks, and the vegetation shows off huckleberry brambles that offer nibbles in late summer. Keep your eyes, ears, and wits about you as these slopes are popular with bruins that cruise around dining on delectable vegetation and teaching their young how to forage.

Higher and higher you go, heart pumping, skin glowing, muscles bursting, until you reach the top of the Cowlitz Divide, which is arguably one of the most beautiful spots on the entire Wonderland Trail. Hollywood has never animated such grandeur! Wildflower meadows erupt with color, fragrance, and splendor in all directions while Mount Rainier towers above the landscape. Cowlitz Park to the northwest and Double Peak to the northeast all pop out, with green meadows and rocky buttresses adding to the vision. It's tempting to stay here all day, scanning the area for wildlife and popping off snaps from the camera, but more beauty lies ahead!

Continue onward with gentle rolling ups and downs until down finally wins and your quads thank you. A series of trail stairs delivers you to Indian Bar Camp on the banks of the Ohanapecosh River, your first reliable water since Nickel Creek. A rustic stone shelter built by the Civilian Conservation Corps

The lush meadow-laden vistas of the Cowlitz Divide area are drop-dead gorgeous.

in 1940 serves as the camp's group site and is worth a visit. If your bladder is dancing, the hill behind the shelter offers a primitive loo, with one of the best views from a toilet in the Northwest. Since you're here, you may also want to check out Wauhaukaupauken (pronounced "Wow-How-Cow-Pow-Ken") Falls, as fun to say as it is to see. Use caution when crossing the falls as the wooden bridge seems a little rickety these days and in need

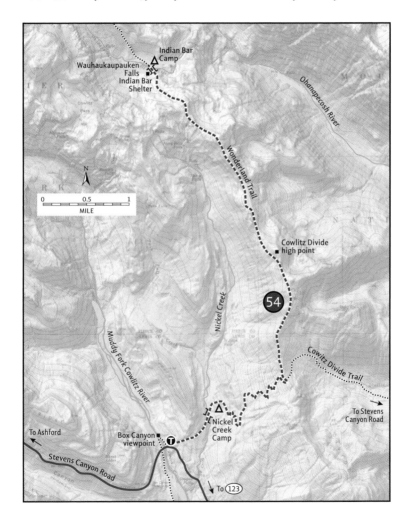

of some TLC. Once across, the individual campsites of Indian Bar Camp are located up an adjacent hill.

After you've explored the place and let your body take a much needed break to refresh and refuel, head back the way you came, which, thankfully, has a lot more downhill than up.

55 Faraway Rock and Lakes High Trail Loop

RATING/ DIFFICULTY	LOOP	ELEV GAIN/ HIGH POINT	SEASON
★★★/2	3 miles	600 feet/ 5380 feet	July–early Oct

Maps: Green Trails Mount Rainier Wonderland No. 269SX, Mount Rainier East No. 270; **Contact:** Mount Rainier National Park, Longmire Wilderness Information Center;

Permit: Mount Rainier Park Pass or America the Beautiful Pass; **Notes:** Stevens Canyon Road closes during winter months so check park website for up-to-date information. Stock and pets prohibited; **GPS:** N 46 46.060 W 121 42.488

Reflection Lakes and the environs are sights to behold on a clear day. Folks limited by time or abilities will appreciate this rather short loop that wanders through meadows with low-growing huckleberry bushes to a viewpoint of Stevens Canyon and Louise Lake from the perch of Faraway Rock.

GETTING THERE

From the last stoplight **in Enumclaw** on State Route 410 eastbound (284th Avenue SE/Farman and Roosevelt), proceed on SR 410 for 40.2 miles, passing the park boundary and

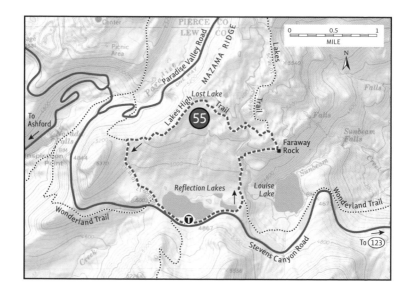

White River/Sunrise Road, to a junction with SR 123. At the fork, stay straight, and proceed on SR 123/Cayuse Pass for 11 miles to Stevens Canyon Road. Turn right (northwest) and enter the park via the entrance booth. In 17.6 miles, find the parking area for Reflection Lakes to the right (north).

From Packwood, drive roughly 7.5 miles north on US Highway 12 and then turn left (northwest) on SR 123. Proceed for 5.4 miles and turn left (northwest) at Stevens Canyon Road. Enter the park through the entrance booth. In 17.6 miles, find the parking area for Reflection Lakes to the right (north).

From Ashford, drive 6.3 miles to the Nisqually Entrance of Mount Rainier National Park. Enter the park through the entrance booth, then proceed for roughly 15.5 miles, passing the Longmire area, to a junction

with Stevens Canyon Road. Follow Stevens Canyon Road for 1.5 miles to Reflection Lakes and the parking area to the left (north). Parking can be tight on weekends, so arrive early. No facilities at trailhead. Use extra caution in this area as the parking lot is extremely close to the busy roadway.

ON THE TRAIL

Start off by following the path around Reflection Lakes to the right (east). Pass the larger of the two lakes and pop out on the road's shoulder for a short distance before ducking back onto an actual trail (signed the Wonderland Trail) to the left (northeast), 0.5 mile from where you started. In 0.1 mile, bear left (north) at a fork with the Lakes Trail. A gentle climb begins through huckleberry brambles, conifers, and seasonal wildflowers as

Leftover winter snow lingers near Reflection Lakes on the way to Faraway Rock.

the trail meanders eastbound. In 1 mile from your car, arrive at a rocky overlook called Faraway Rock. From this lofty perch, Louise Lake twinkles in the valley below and you can see the ribbon of Stevens Canyon Road. Behind the lake to the south, Unicorn and Stevens peaks show their craggy ridgelines and pockets of lingering snowfields. This is quite a sight for such little effort!

Onward you go, leaving Faraway Rock and moseying just 0.2 mile to arrive at a junction with the Lakes High Trail (also called the High Lakes Trail, depending on who you talk to or which map you follow) that scoots off to the left (northwest) to complete the loop. Head left here, or, if you have plenty of time, stay straight and follow the Lakes Trail toward the shoulder of Mazama Ridge, a mind-blowingly grand series of subalpine meadows. When you return, head back this way.

The Lakes High Trail is a wandering one that crosses dry creek beds and brushy bilberry meadows while providing occasional pastoral views, seasonal wildflowers, and tasty berries. The bears like them too, so keep your wits about you when cruising through this landscape and don't startle a mama or her sweet little cubs.

In 1.3 miles from the Lakes High Trail junction, 2.5 miles from where you started, turn left at the next signed junction and head south again toward Reflection Lakes. In another 0.5 mile, bear left and continue following the pathway around Reflection Lakes until you reach your waiting vehicle.

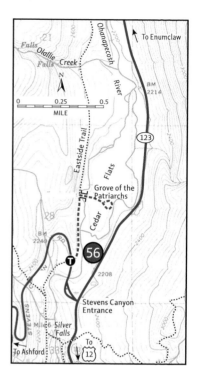

56 Grove of the Patriarchs

RATING/ DIFFICULTY	ROUNDTRIP	ELEV GAIN/ HIGH POINT	SEASON
★★★/1	1.3 miles	120 feet/ 2220 feet	early June– early Oct

Maps: Green Trails Mount Rainier Wonderland No. 269SX, Mount Rainier East No. 270; **Contact:** Mount Rainier National Park, Ohanapecosh Visitors Center; **Permit:** Mount Rainier National Park Pass or America the Beautiful Pass; **Notes:** Stevens Canyon Road closes during winter months so check park website for up-to-date information. Stock and pets prohibited; **GPS:** N 46 45.504 W 121 33.456

 *Calling all huge-tree lovers: don't miss this feature! The peaceful "stand of the behemoth daddies" is a perfect place to tip your head skyward and stand in awe of the goli-*

Large "papa" trees, protected by boardwalks, are a sight to behold in the Grove of the Patriarchs.

ath conifers that have grown happily on this shoreline for hundreds of years. And, because the grove is on an island, kids and adults alike will enjoy testing their courage on the suspension bridge that takes them over the Ohanapecosh River.

GETTING THERE

From the last stoplight **in Enumclaw** on State Route 410 eastbound (284th Avenue SE/Farman and Roosevelt), proceed on SR 410 for 40.2 miles, passing the park boundary and White River/Sunrise Road, to a junction with SR 123. At the fork, stay straight, and proceed on SR 123/Cayuse Pass for 11 miles to Stevens Canyon Road. Turn right (northwest) and enter the park via the entrance booth. In 0.2 mile, find the large parking area for the trail to the right (east).

From Packwood, drive roughly 7.5 miles north on US Highway 12 and then turn left (northwest) on SR 123. Proceed for 5.4 miles and turn left (northwest) at Stevens Canyon Road. Enter the park through the entrance booth. In 0.2 mile, find the large parking area to the right (east).

From Ashford, drive 6.3 miles to the Nisqually Entrance of Mount Rainier National Park. Enter the park through the entrance booth, then proceed for roughly 15.5 miles, passing the Longmire area, to a junction with Stevens Canyon Road. Follow Stevens Canyon Road for 18.9 miles to a large parking area to the left (east) just before the exit booths. Toilets available at trailhead.

ON THE TRAIL

This well-used, well-loved trail guides you through the conifers and cruises through primeval-feeling forest, filled with ancient evergreens, as it plays peekaboo with the tranquil Ohanapecosh River to the right. In

0.3 mile, reach a signed trail junction with the Eastside Trail, which heads straight. Go right here and begin a short descent to the slightly wobbly suspension bridge that crosses the river.

In the historic storm of 2006, this area sustained some terrible damage. Between the high winds and the massive rainfall, the bridge twisted and turned, bending its heavy metal side bars, flexing its cables, and ripping off wooden boards. On the island, many interpretive signs were destroyed, portions of the wooden boardwalks were missing, and debris covered the roots of the large trees. Thanks to volunteers and park crews, today everything is back to normal and hikers can enjoy this area to the fullest.

Sway and balance your way across the bridge to arrive at the grove on the other side. Interpretive signs guide you through the giant trees, some 800 to 1000 years old; oh, the things they've seen! Western red cedar, Douglas fir, and western hemlock reach their massive tops upward in an ongoing search for light as chickadees, juncos, and Steller's jays

flit about. Nurse logs decorate the trail's edges in places, teaching the value of an ecosystem that provides nutrients to the forest floor.

Follow the boardwalk in either direction to make a loop and return to your starting point.

57 Pinnacle Peak

RATING/ DIFFICULTY	ROUNDTRIP	ELEV GAIN/ HIGH POINT	SEASON
★★★★★/3	2.6 miles	1050 feet/ 6000 feet	mid-late July–early Oct

Map: Green Trails Mount Rainier East No. 270; **Contact:** Mount Rainier National Park, Longmire Wilderness Information Center; **Permit:** Mount Rainier National Park Pass or America the Beautiful Pass; **Notes:** Stevens Canyon Road closes during winter months, so check park website for up-to-date information. Avalanche hazards possible if trail is hiked too early or too late in the season so check park website for up-to-date trail conditions. Stock and pets prohibited; **GPS:** N 46 46.096 W 121 43.869

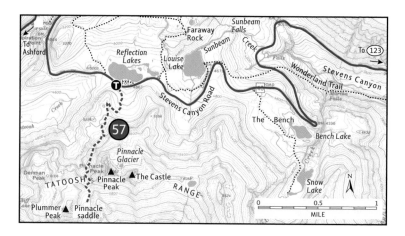

When the lighting is just perfect, the evening sky from the Pinnacle Peak area is unbeatable.

🌸 ❄️ This trail climbs its way steeply up open slopes to grand views of Mount Rainier. Sunsets can be brilliant, so if you time it right, your camera will be busy and your soul's cookie jar will be filled to the top.

GETTING THERE

From the last stoplight in Enumclaw on State Route 410 eastbound (284th Avenue SE/ Farman and Roosevelt), proceed on SR 410 for 40.2 miles, passing the park boundary and White River/Sunrise Road, to a junction with SR 123. At the fork, stay straight, and proceed on SR 123/Cayuse Pass for 11 miles to Stevens Canyon Road. Turn right (northwest) and enter the park via the entrance booth. In 17.6 miles find the parking area for Reflection Lakes to the right (north).

From Packwood, drive roughly 7.5 miles north on US Highway 12 and then turn left (northwest) on SR 123. Proceed for 5.4 miles and turn left (northwest) at Stevens Canyon Road. Enter the park through the entrance booth. In 17.6 miles find the parking area for Reflection Lakes to the right (north).

From Ashford, drive 6.3 miles to the Nisqually Entrance of Mount Rainier National Park. Enter the park through the entrance booth, then proceed for roughly 15.5 miles, passing the Longmire area, to a junction with Stevens Canyon Road. Follow Stevens Canyon Road for 1.5 miles to Reflection Lakes and the parking area to the left (north). Parking can be tight on weekends, so arrive early. No facilities at trailhead. Use extra caution in this area as the parking lot is extremely close to the busy roadway. Trail is across the highway to the south.

ON THE TRAIL

The trail begins by moderately climbing through scant conifers intermixed with open huckleberry meadows. In 0.4 mile, the trail nears the top of a ridgeline and makes a hairpin turn to the northwest before heading south again. Now the fun begins!

Chug your way up the slopes, which begin to open up views as they get steeper and steeper. Slopeside meadows steal the show with stunning wildflower displays, including mountain bistort, lupine, and heather, while Mount Rainier watches over things to the north.

The last push throws in a switchback to really get those quads and ticker talking and crosses steeply pitched slopes underneath craggy, grand Pinnacle Peak.

In 1.3 miles, with little fanfare, arrive at the end of the maintained trail, Pinnacle saddle. The saddle doesn't have much room for sitting without feeling you are on the trail itself and, in places, it's quite precarious to hang out due to the steep hillsides. Still, it's well worth the effort to get there and beautiful in all directions.

If you are about as coordinated as a walrus on Rollerblades, don't go farther than the official trail's end. However, those with scrambling skills may want to continue—at their own risk—and bushwhack up Plummer Peak, found by heading right (southwest) at the end of the Pinnacle Peak Trail.

58 Reflection Lakes and Paradise Loop

RATING/ DIFFICULTY	LOOP	ELEV GAIN/ HIGH POINT	SEASON
★★★★★/3	5.8 miles	1420 feet/ 5800 feet	July–early Oct

Maps: Green Trails Mount Rainier Wonderland No. 269SX, Mount Rainier East No. 270; **Contact:** Mount Rainier National Park, Longmire Wilderness Information Center; **Permit:** Mount Rainier National Park Pass or America the Beautiful Pass; **Notes:** Stevens Canyon Road closes during winter months so check park website for up-to-date information. Stock and pets prohibited; **GPS:** N 46 46.060 W 121 42.488

 *With meadows, wildflowers, lakes, and even a waterfall, this loop is a marvelous way to sample all the best features of the park. What's more, it passes the Henry M. Jackson Visitors Center, which sells ice cream . . . just sayin'!*

GETTING THERE

From the last stoplight **in Enumclaw** on State Route 410 eastbound (284th Avenue SE/Farman and Roosevelt), proceed on SR 410 for 40.2 miles, passing the park boundary and White River/Sunrise Road, to a junction with SR 123. At the fork, stay straight, and proceed on SR 123/Cayuse Pass for 11 miles to Stevens Canyon Road. Turn right (northwest) and enter the park via the entrance booth. In 17.6 miles find the parking area for Reflection Lakes to the right (north).

From Packwood, drive roughly 7.5 miles north on US Highway 12 and then turn left (northwest) on SR 123. Proceed for 5.4 miles and turn left (northwest) at Stevens Canyon Road. Enter the park through the entrance booth. In 17.6 miles find the parking area for Reflection Lakes to the right (north).

From Ashford, drive 6.3 miles to the Nisqually Entrance of Mount Rainier National Park. Enter the park through the entrance

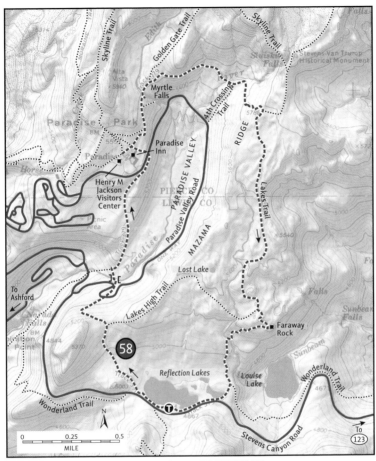

booth, then proceed for roughly 15.5 miles, passing the Longmire area, to a junction with Stevens Canyon Road. Follow Stevens Canyon Road for 1.5 miles to Reflection Lakes and the parking area to the left (north). Parking can be tight on weekends, so arrive early. No facilities at trailhead. Use extra caution in this area as the parking lot is extremely close to the busy roadway.

ON THE TRAIL

From the parking area, walk toward the lake and then take a left (west) on a pathway that is technically, although not signed as such, the Wonderland Trail around the lake's southern shoreline. In 0.2 mile, arrive at a signed trail junction with the Lakes Trail and go right (north). Low-growing huckleberry brambles decorate the trail's edges as you climb gently at first and then more steeply. In 0.5 mile, arrive at another signed trail junction, this one for the Lakes High Trail, which heads to the right. Save that one (Hike 55) for another day and continue onward until the trail makes a hairpin turn and spits you out at a crossing with Paradise Valley Road, 1 mile from where you started.

Look both ways to avoid becoming a hood ornament, then cross the road and find the trail again on the other side. In 0.1 mile from the road, cross the Paradise River on a rustic little bridge with views of mini waterfalls created by rushing water dropping into quiet pockets. In 0.1 mile from the bridge, arrive at another signed trail junction pointing you toward Paradise to the right. Turn right here and start climbing rather steeply, breathing a little heavily as you trudge along

until you pop out just behind the Paradise Inn and your feet hit blacktop, 0.5 mile from the last trail junction, 1.7 miles from where you started.

If this is your first visit to Paradise, you'll want to visit the historic inn and check out the grand antique timber building. Perhaps a visit to the gift shop, dining room, or snack bar is also in order. Once you've seen that, be sure to swing by the Henry M. Jackson Visitors Center to the southwest across the parking lot from the inn. Exhibits and another gift shop and snack bar (with ice-cream cones) beckon! Picnic tables and toilets are also here—what luck!

When you've seen it all, locate a small spur trail (to the northeast) that delivers you to the paved-at-first Skyline Trail adjacent to the Paradise Inn. Follow the Skyline Trail as

Stopping frequently to take in the sublime beauty is essential as you wander near the eastern shoulders of Mazama Ridge.

it climbs gently up toward Myrtle Falls in 0.5 mile. Be sure to take the short, signed spur trail that drops to a viewpoint of breathtaking, 72-foot, horsetail-shaped Myrtle Falls, coming off Edith Creek.

Views of Rainier abound as you continue on the Skyline Trail, passing a trail junction with the Golden Gate Trail and dropping into a small valley with a babbling brook and pops of seasonal wildflowers. Since what goes down must come up, begin climbing again and in 1 mile from the Paradise Inn, pass a trail junction with the 4th Crossing Trail. Up, up, up you go on a few switchbacks that are steep and seemingly endless, until *bam!*, the signed Lakes Trail junction nearly hits you in your sweaty face.

The lovely Lakes Trail now descends happily through wildflower meadows, occasionally dotted with small tarns and peaceful vistas as it cruises along the eastern shoulder of Mazama Ridge. Keep your eyes out for bear and deer, as they often use this area for foraging, and look for ravens clacking in the trees above. In 1.2 miles from turning onto the Lakes Trail from the Skyline Trail, pass a signed junction with the Lakes High Trail and continue heading south to complete your loop. Be sure to stop and check out Faraway Rock and its views of Stevens Canyon and Louise Lake just 0.2 mile from the Lakes High Trail.

Next, a forked, signed trail junction drops you onto the Wonderland Trail 0.5 mile from Faraway Rock. Bear right on the Wonderland, where you pop out to Stevens Canyon Road for a brief stretch while walking past the smaller of the Reflection Lakes before following the shoreline trail near the larger lake. In just 1 mile from Faraway Rock, arrive back at your car where you can rest your legs, get a sip of water, and reminisce about your busy day on the trail.

59 Stevens Canyon Waterfalls

RATING/ DIFFICULTY	ROUNDTRIP	ELEV GAIN/ HIGH POINT	SEASON
★★★/3	8 miles	1935 feet/ 4085 feet	July–early Oct

Maps: Green Trails Mount Rainier Wonderland No. 269SX, Mount Rainier East No. 270; **Contact:** Mount Rainier National Park, Longmire Wilderness Information Center; **Permit:** Mount Rainier National Park Pass or America the Beautiful Pass; **Notes:** Stevens Canyon Road closes during winter months so check park website for up-to-date information. Stock and pets prohibited; **GPS:** N 46 45.623 W 121 38.372

While this hike doesn't offer Rainier views, it does a great job of ambling through pleasant emerald riparian landscapes filled with chattering brooks and dancing waterfalls, proving that some of the wonders along the Wonderland Trail can be wondrously enjoyed on a day hike.

GETTING THERE

From the last stoplight **in Enumclaw** on State Route 410 eastbound (284th Avenue SE/Farman and Roosevelt), proceed on SR 410 for 40.2 miles, passing the park boundary and White River/Sunrise Road, to a junction with SR 123. At the fork, stay straight, and proceed on SR 123/Cayuse Pass for 11 miles to Stevens Canyon Road. Turn right (northwest) and enter the park via the entrance booth. In 10.9 miles find the parking area for Stevens Creek Trail to the left (south).

From Packwood, drive roughly 7.5 miles north on US Highway 12 and then turn left (northwest) on SR123. Proceed for 5.4 miles and turn left (northwest) at Stevens Canyon

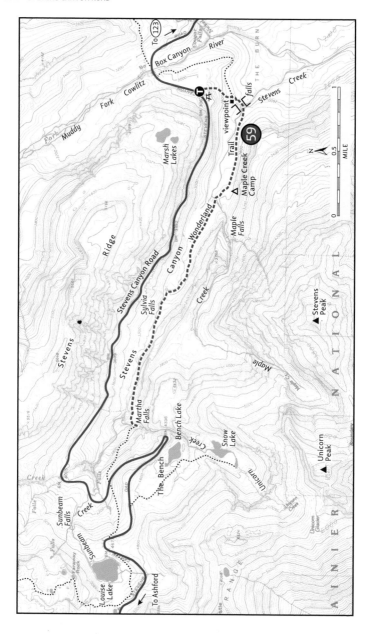

Road. Enter the park through the entrance booth. In 10.9 miles, find the parking area for Stevens Creek Trail to the left (south).

From Ashford, drive 6.3 miles to the Nisqually Entrance of Mount Rainier National Park. Enter the park through the entrance booth, then proceed for roughly 15.5 miles, passing the Longmire area, to a junction with Stevens Canyon Road. Follow Stevens Canyon Road for 8.2 miles to the parking area for the Stevens Creek Trail to the right (south). Toilets and picnic areas available.

ON THE TRAIL

Start off by gettin' on down! The trail warms you up with a beautiful descent through familiar forest conifers, like Douglas fir and western hemlock, as well as some of their deciduous cousins like alder and big-leaf and vine maples. Down, down, down you go

until you reach a viewpoint in 0.5 mile with a sneak peek of the coming attractions of Stevens Creek. Over the years, the prospect has been slightly compromised by fallen trees, "disrespecting" us hikers who want to see the sights! Still, there is usually enough of a glimpse to make it worthwhile, although every year things change and shift.

In 0.2 mile beyond the viewpoint, 0.7 mile beyond where you started, arrive at a signed junction with the Wonderland Trail. Make a sharp right and cross the sturdy wooden bridge over rushing Stevens Creek. Mini waterfalls ebb and flow with the seasons into smaller pools and pockets, a lovely sight to behold against the background of evergreens.

Onward you go as the trail grade levels off; the very gentle ups and downs almost feel flat at times. Stevens Creek continues to

A wooden bridge crosses the giggling Stevens Creek.

make an appearance here and there to the right as you saunter along, taking it all in.

In 1.8 miles from where you started, arrive at Maple Creek Camp to the left. The group site and composting toilets are to the left, while the individual sites are just a little farther. Stop if you want to check it out or need to piddle; otherwise, keep going and cross Maple Creek on a log bridge just beyond the camp. In 2006, this area was badly flooded, and the silty debris still conceals Maple Creek Falls, located upstream.

The trail begins a gradual climb up Stevens Creek Canyon, displaying brilliant apple-green foliage, such as maidenhair and bracken ferns, vanilla leaf, thimbleberry, and vine maple, until it reaches Sylvia Falls, 3 miles from the trailhead. Beautiful Sylvia Falls, found by stepping off the trail to the right and looking through the conifers, drops 43 feet at almost a 90-degree angle, making a grand white-water veil. The falls seem to beg you to get closer for better photographs, but use extreme caution as the mossy embankment slopes downward toward the edge of a cliff band.

Continue climbing on a somewhat brushy hillside until you arrive at a washed-out trail area where you should exercise caution with your fancy footwork. In 2006, the Wonderland simply disappeared here until the Park Service creatively cut it back into this loose hillside.

Once across, it's only 0.4 mile until you reach the final waterfall of this hike, Martha Falls. Named after Ben Longmire's mother, Martha Falls can either impress you or disappoint you from this angle, depending on its water flow. When flowing well, it cascades down Unicorn Creek over mossy stones and plunges roughly 50 feet into a shimmering pool. What you can't see from here is that this waterfall is one of the tallest in the state. As it comes out of Snow Lake, it drops 12 different times, and the longest drop is 151 feet! Cross the log bridge over the creek for better views, and when you've snapped enough pictures, head back the way you came, or—if you've planned ahead—you can make a car shuttle by continuing onward to a junction with Stevens Canyon Road.

The rewarding views make you forget the huff and puff required to reach Eagle Peak saddle (Hike 62).

ashford/nisqually entrance/ westside road/longmire

Located in the southwest corner of the park, Longmire and the surrounding areas contain some of the oldest and most interesting history since Mount Rainier first became a park. The park entrance here, officially called the Nisqually Entrance, has been observing visitors' comings and goings since the late 1880s, after James Longmire, an immigrant explorer, first laid claim to the area. Today, guests are still able to enjoy a peek back in time through the Longmire museum, the transportation exhibit, the historic wilderness information center, and the historic National Park Inn. Creature comforts include the dining room of the National Park Inn, where huckleberry cobbler awaits; a gift store for picking up sundries and the quintessential T-shirt; and, of course, the opportunity to spend the night in the National Park Inn, where you can see Mount Rainier from the front porch on a clear day. The wilderness information center is a great place to get up-to-date trail information, the latest weather information, and hiking suggestions from friendly park staff. Once you've seen the Longmire area up close and personal, lace up those boots for an outdoor adventure where you can get even closer to the essence of Mount Rainier as you meander through often historic and always charming backcountry trails.

60 Carter and Madcap Falls

RATING/ DIFFICULTY	ROUNDTRIP	ELEV GAIN/ HIGH POINT	SEASON
★★★★/2	2.5 miles	500 feet/ 3680 feet	late June– Oct

Maps: Green Trails Mount Rainier Wonderland No. 269SX, Mount Rainier West No. 269; **Contact:** Mount Rainier National Park, Longmire Wilderness Information Center; **Permit:** Mount Rainier National Park Pass or America the Beautiful Pass; **Notes:** Parking fills up quickly, especially on weekends. If roadside parking is full, head back to Longmire and park behind National Park Inn, then head east on the Wonderland Trail and follow signs toward Paradise River Wilderness Camp. From this trailhead, you reach Carter and Madcap falls in 3.1 miles with roughly 875 feet elevation gain. Check trail conditions to ensure bridge over Nisqually River is in place. Stock and pets prohibited; **GPS:** N 46 45.991 W 121 47.465

Those who love the soothing sounds and exhilarating sights of water cascading over stone will appreciate this short and sweet hike. As a bonus, the trail cruises through welcoming western red cedar and Douglas fir, tucking you into the forest and providing some welcome shade in hot summer heat.

Madcap Falls purrs gently down 34 feet of mossy stone.

GETTING THERE

From Ashford, drive 6.3 miles to the Nisqually Entrance of Mount Rainier National Park. Enter the park through the entrance booth, then proceed for 8.8 miles, passing Longmire. Park along the road to the right (southeast) near the sign that says "Carter Falls Trailhead." The nearest privies are at Cougar Rock Campground, 0.1 mile north along the road.

ON THE TRAIL

Once you've jockeyed for position to get a parking spot, the fun begins! The trail drops rather steadily to cross the purring, milky-colored Nisqually River on a half-log bridge, complete with a handrail, just 0.1 mile from the trailhead sign. The wide, rocky riverbed has grand views of Mount Rainier on clear days, and the bridge offers a great location for fun photos of you and your hiking partners crossing the river. The river is actually meltwater coming off Nisqually Glacier high on the mountain and gets its cloudy color from glacial flour, which is silty particles of ground-up rock.

Leave the riverbed and continue hiking east on a very wide trail landscaped with deciduous trees and evergreens. As the trail gets narrower, a curious large wooden penstock pipe shows up on the left, 0.9 mile from where you started. The pipe is evidence of the park's history and is one of the few signs left of a power plant that was located where the Paradise and Nisqually rivers converge. Years ago, it provided water pressure to the plant's generator.

In 1.1 miles from the trailhead, arrive at a signed viewpoint for Carter Falls. Despite the sign, this baby is hard to see! Use extra caution when executing your moves to snap a picture, and respect the wooden safety barriers or you might just put an end to a perfect day. Carter Falls was named after Henry Carter, a mountain guide and trail builder who was employed by James Longmire to build trails back in the early days of the park.

Just shy of 0.2 mile farther east, arrive at Madcap Falls, which is much easier to see! For some reason, this waterfall seems less popular, but in my opinion, it's the best. While Carter Falls offers a higher drop, Madcap Falls holds its own by gently cascading down 34 feet of mossy stone. If your camera has a slow shutter, you can usually get some wonderful white-water, motion-blur pictures even on bright days, thanks to the shadowy evergreens.

Enjoy the soundtrack of the white noise as you make your way back the way you came.

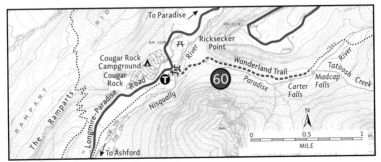

61 Comet Falls

RATING/ DIFFICULTY	ROUNDTRIP	ELEV GAIN/ HIGH POINT	SEASON
★★★★★/4	4 miles	1245 feet/ 4875 feet	July–Oct

Maps: Green Trails Mount Rainier Wonderland No. 269SX, Mount Rainier West No. 269; **Contact:** Mount Rainier National Park, Longmire Wilderness Information Center; **Permit:** Mount Rainier National Park Pass or America the Beautiful Pass; **Notes:** Snow can linger in high country until Aug. Slick rocks and embankments are present due to the spray of falls. Watch for rockfall around the base of falls. Parking is limited and is usually full by 8:00 AM on summer weekends so arrive early to avoid traffic congestion. If possible, hike weekdays when less crowded. Stock and pets prohibited; **GPS:** N 46 46.714 W 121 47.013

 *If you love waterfalls, you are in for a treat! Comet Falls, coming off Van Trump Creek at a 90-degree angle, cascades 462 feet in a series of tiered plunges. In other words, it's a treat for the eyes and a banquet for the soul. What's more, you can extend your day and see even more grandeur by visiting the subalpine meadows of Van Trump Park and/or see Mount Rainier in all its glory from Mildred Point. With a giant waterfall, subalpine wildflower meadows, and a panoramic volcano view, visiting all three destinations might just be the best hike in the whole park—and the crowds show it. Greet your hiking compadres with a smile as you wander, and don't expect solitude until you reach the upper portions of Van Trump Park; at that point, it's game on.*

GETTING THERE
From Ashford, drive 6.3 miles to the Nisqually Entrance of Mount Rainier National Park. Enter the park through the entrance booth and proceed for 10.9 miles, passing the Longmire area, to the trailhead and parking area on the left side of the road. Use restrooms at Longmire before you arrive as there are none at trailhead.

ON THE TRAIL
The trail wastes no time getting you to magnificent views. In 0.3 mile from the trailhead, *boom!* A sturdy wooden bridge crosses dreamy Van Trump Creek, which rushes through a mini slot canyon and makes you want to spend half the day with your camera in this spot. Those with mobility issues or tiny kids practicing their toddle might be able to get to this spot and feel like they have the world by the tail. If you can, however, keep going; this is just the appetizer!

The soundtrack to your journey is the ever-present white noise of Van Trump Creek that creates tempos for your trail runners. Up you go, crossing rooty and rocky trail tread and passing pockets of cedar and fir with boughs reaching down to curtsy at your arrival. Talus slopes with brushy swales of riparian brush pop up as you pick your way northbound.

In 1.2 miles from the trailhead, notice the beautifully placed trail staircase, known to trail builders as a crib ladder. In the winter of 2011–12, avalanches ripped down these hillsides, leaving massive piles of debris behind, a real buzzkill for hikers who found the trail closed the following summer. The Washington Trails Association stepped up to the plate to help repair this stretch, which is once again a safe passage. Tip your beanie to them as you crawl up the stairs, or even better, when

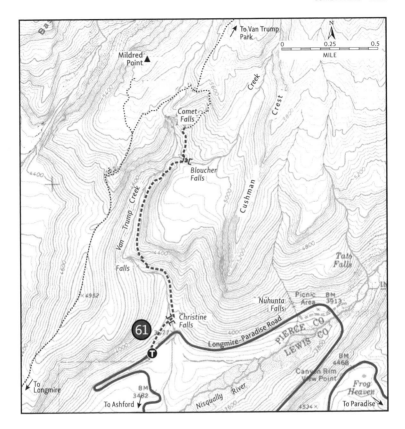

you return home, tip your wallet in apprecia-
tion of this volunteer-based nonprofit.

Several smaller waterfalls tease you into
thinking they are Comet Falls, but trust me,
you'll know Comet when you see it! In 1.6
miles from the trailhead is one such teaser,
Bloucher Falls, a tiered series of plunging
white water, where the East Fork of Van
Trump Creek teams up with its big brother,
Van Trump Creek. A log footbridge provides
a safe crossing of the waterway.

Just beyond Bloucher Falls, a sign notes
the first view of Comet Falls, which gets you
excited but is far from the delicious main
course. For that, you need to keep rolling
another 0.4 mile. Comet Falls got its name
because it looks like the tail of a comet,
which today might be somewhat hard to
imagine since the volume of water is less
due to the ever-receding Van Trump Glacier. It's almost as if your camera wants to
snap its own shutter over and over again; it

seems impossible to get enough shots. The riverbank below the falls is often wet and slippery, so use extra caution if you decide to attempt some funky camera fun and leave the trail. If this is it for you today, turn back the way you came.

EXTENDING YOUR HIKE

If zip and stamina are your friends, keep promenading into the high country. Beyond the falls, the trail gets its more serious climb on to reach a signed junction with Van Trump Park, 3.3 miles from the trailhead and 1.3 miles from the falls. Follow this trail north for roughly 0.3 mile to the end of the maintained trail. Around you, carpets

Comet Falls is one of the most iconic waterfalls in Mount Rainier National Park.

of wildflowers make a stunning visual with colors that match the setting sun. On clear days, the mountain views are breathtaking and swoon-inducing. Wander to your heart's delight in these brilliant meadows, named after P. B. (no, not peanut butter but Philemon Beecher) Van Trump, who along with Hazard Stevens, was the first to reach the summit of Mount Rainier in 1870.

Head back to the signed junction when you are done and, if time permits, turn right (west) and follow Van Trump Park Trail 0.7 mile with ups and downs to a signed junction with Mildred Point. Turn right here and begin an ascent of a steep hillside with rough trail tread. Stick with it as you wheeze; it's well worth the effort! In 0.5 mile find yourself staring at Mount Rainier, Kautz Glacier, and the cavernous valley below. Hillsides decorated with grassy meadows and evergreen thickets provide a stark contrast to the gray stone. Use extreme caution in your footing as one slip will ruin your day if not your life.

When you've sucked it all in, retrace your steps to your waiting car with a full camera and memories to last a lifetime.

62 Eagle Peak Saddle

RATING/ DIFFICULTY	ROUNDTRIP	ELEV GAIN/ HIGH POINT	SEASON
★★★/5	7.4 miles	2820 feet/ 5740 feet	late July– early Oct

Map: Green Trails Mount Rainier Wonderland No. 269SX; **Contact:** Mount Rainier National Park, Longmire Wilderness Information Center; **Permit:** Mount Rainier National Park Pass or America the Beautiful Pass; **Notes:** If snow and ice are present near the top, hike can be extremely hazardous due to corniced ridges and avalanche conditions. Do not attempt in snowy conditions as even lower slopes can be dangerous and cause navigational challenges. This hike leads to Eagle Peak saddle; attempting to climb to true summit is not recommended due to loose rock and fall hazards. Even in summer months, use extreme caution near the saddle as the ridge is narrow and falls could be deadly. As with all trails, check conditions before heading out. Stock and pets prohibited; **GPS:** N 46 44.896 W 121 48.485

Eagle Peak is a challenging hike, but it offers partial views of Mount Rainier and can sometimes provide a respite from the crowds that flock to the park in the summer months. What's more, the meadows near the top often entice wildlife looking for a quiet place to graze. Keep your eyes open!

GETTING THERE

From Ashford, drive 6.3 miles to the Nisqually Entrance of Mount Rainier National Park. Enter the park through the entrance booth, then proceed 6.5 miles to the Longmire area. After passing the National Park Inn, turn right (southeast). Drive past the wilderness information center (distinguished by the flagpole) and the employee housing and cross the one-lane suspension bridge. In 300 feet, find roadside parking and the trailhead to the left (southeast).

ON THE TRAIL

The trail starts off climbing steadily in mixed conifers and reaches a side spur for some park water tanks in 0.2 mile. There isn't much to see on the spur, so continue heading west on the main trail until, roughly 0.8 mile from where you started, the trail gets serious and heads up some fairly steep switchbacks. Grumble, groan, and grunt your way along them, stopping to catch your

Eagle Peak saddle gives hikers a clear view of all but the very western corner of Mount Rainier.

breath occasionally and enjoy the cool forest. In early summer, you might hear the delicate song of a hermit thrush, which almost sounds like someone is playing a soft piccolo. There is no sweeter sound resonating from the canopy!

As you move along, the trail crosses a couple of seasonal babbling brooks, bringing some playful running water to your hiking soundtrack. In 2.2 miles from where you started, cross a small bridge over a tributary of the Nisqually River, which is far below you

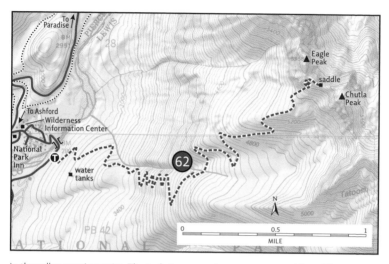

in the valley near Longmire. The trail gives you a break from the switchbacks for now and takes a slight turn to the northeast.

In roughly 3 miles, conifer pockets alternate with flowered meadows, and you start to feel like you are nearing your destination. Wildflowers of so many different varieties are present in this wonderfully fertile soil! If you brought your flower guide, now is the time to pull it out. Look for lupine, anemone, paintbrush, spirea, bistort, tiger lily, columbine, lousewort, and so many others. Also, keep your eyes open for the critters, such as hoary marmots, golden-mantled ground squirrels, and yellow-pine chipmunks, that call these meadows home. Impress your friends and know the difference between a ground squirrel and a chipmunk. Here's a hint: ground squirrels are larger and have no stripes on their face. Look for pikas in the rocky areas; they often announce your arrival with one loud "eeep"!

The top is visible now and so are the smaller, steeper, exposed switchbacks that lead you

and your camera toward the saddle. Up, up, up you go, back and forth, watching your step and enjoying views of Chutla Peak and Wahpenayo Peak to the east, part of the mighty Tatoosh Range. The best is yet to come!

Reach the saddle and check it out; isnt't that Mount Rainier? The farther right (southeast) you go along the ridge, the better the view; just watch your feet because it's a long way down from this perch and nothing would kill your euphoric vibe faster than unintentionally setting sail. When you've nibbled on the bounty from your pack and exhausted your camera battery, head on back.

63 Glacier View

RATING/ DIFFICULTY	ROUNDTRIP	ELEV GAIN/ HIGH POINT	SEASON
★★★★/3	4.2 miles	1000 feet/ 5450 feet	July–Oct

Map: Green Trails Mount Rainier West No. 269; **Contact:** Gifford Pinchot National Forest,

Cowlitz Valley Ranger District, Randle Office; **Permit:** Free wilderness use permit at trailhead; **Notes:** Road to trailhead can be rough but passenger cars will make it by going slowly. Use caution on rocky summit. Wilderness regulations apply. Stock and pets permitted; **GPS:** N 46 47.772 W 121 56.855

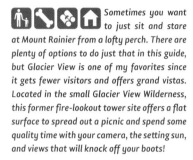 *Sometimes you want to just sit and stare at Mount Rainier from a lofty perch. There are plenty of options to do just that in this guide, but Glacier View is one of my favorites since it gets fewer visitors and offers grand vistas. Located in the small Glacier View Wilderness, this former fire-lookout tower site offers a flat surface to spread out a picnic and spend some quality time with your camera, the setting sun, and views that will knock off your boots!*

GETTING THERE

From Elbe, drive eastbound on State Route 706 for roughly 10.8 miles, passing the town of Ashford. At unpaved, poorly signed Copper Creek Road (Forest Road 59), turn left (north) and drive for 8.6 miles until the road peters out. Park in the roadside pullouts. No facilities at trailhead.

ON THE TRAIL

From where you parked, follow the obvious spur trail for a short distance to enter the Glacier View Wilderness and arrive at an intersection with Glacier View Trail No. 267. Going right leads you toward a plethora of other wonderful hiking options, including Mount Beljica (Hike 68), which you'll want to come visit for sure another day, or even this afternoon, if time permits. To see Glacier

Glacier View shows off her namesake: a picturesque view of glaciers on Mount Rainier!

View in all its grandeur, turn left here and begin your amble along a ridgeline through beargrass, huckleberry brambles, and other seasonal wildflowers interwoven with small firs and towering hemlocks.

In 1984, the Glacier View Wilderness, a 3073-acre parcel of land, was created, saving it from the threat of logging and offering a spectacular place to rest the eyes on the glaciated shoulders of Mount Rainier to the east.

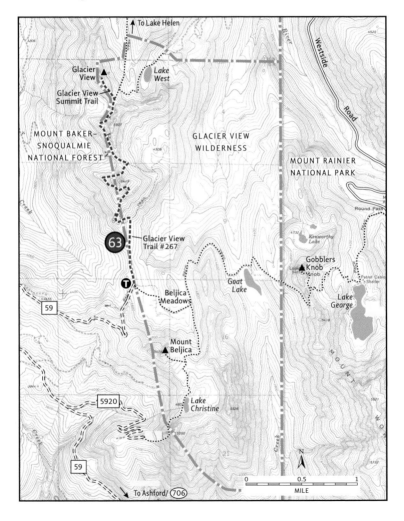

As you continue along the ridgeline, keep your eyes open for the deer, golden-mantled ground squirrels, and conifer-loving birds, such as varied thrush, that spend their time foraging for sustenance in this sublime landscape.

A couple of ups and downs guide you to the west of a rocky knoll before the climb commences and you find yourself working up a sweat until you reach the easy-to-miss junction with the Glacier View Summit Trail, 1.8 miles from where you started. Your path goes left to the top at this junction, but if you feel energetic, go right here on your return and drop into the Lake West and Lake Helen basins.

For now, climb, climb, climb until your breath is completely taken away by the scenery and you are standing on the tippy-top of the site that once contained a fire-lookout tower. On this rocky summit, a classic four-sided, L4-style cabin, built in 1934, stood tall for 26 years. Boarded up for protection in the winter and staffed with folks who dutifully watched for smoke in the summer, the cabin was one of several on these neighboring peaks that, save for a few such as Puyallup Ridge and Gobblers Knob (visible from this perch), are now gone.

The sweeping views in all directions will keep your camera busy and build memories to cherish after you eventually turn back and retrace your steps to where you started.

64 High Rock Lookout

RATING/ DIFFICULTY	ROUNDTRIP	ELEV GAIN/ HIGH POINT	SEASON
★★★★★/3	3.2 miles	1400 feet/ 5665 feet	late July– Oct

Map: Green Trails Randle No. 301; **Contact:** Gifford Pinchot National Forest, Cowlitz Valley Ranger District, Randle Office; **Permit:** None; **Notes:** Road to trailhead is rough, so high-clearance vehicles recommended. Use extreme caution around lookout as steep cliffs abound and lookout needs repairs. Off-road vehicles and bicycles prohibited. Dogs and horses permitted; **GPS:** N 46 39.986 W 121 53.487

This hike has it all and is one of the most scenic in this guide, provided you don't mind the rough, potholed road to get there. Not only does it offer a beautiful walk through the woods, but the ending is perhaps the greatest crescendo of all the music of the mountains! Unbeatable panoramic views of Mount Rainier and one of the last fire-lookout towers in the vicinity greet you. Get there!

GETTING THERE

From Packwood, turn north onto Skate Creek Road (Forest Road 52) near the Shell gas station. In approximately 18 miles, turn left onto FR 84. Proceed for 6.7 miles and stay right at the Y, putting you on FR 8440. Continue another 2.6 miles to the flat area known as Towhead Gap.

From Elbe, head east on State Route 706 for 10.1 miles and turn right (south) onto Skate Creek Road (FR 52). In 4.7 miles, turn right onto FR 84. Proceed for 6.7 miles and stay right at the Y, putting you on FR 8440. Continue another 2.6 miles to the flat area known as Towhead Gap. The trailhead is on the right. **Note:** While it's possible to drive to the trailhead using FR 85 from Ashford, it's extremely rough to the point of possible car damage and not recommended.

Perched on a large rocky knoll, the weathered lookout on High Rock has charmed hikers for years.

ON THE TRAIL

Even before you leave the car, you'll know this place is special. Towhead Gap is located up a high, sunny divide between Allen Mountain and High Rock and offers enjoyable views of the surrounding hillsides. The secret is out and this hike can be popular on weekends, so get there early or go on weekdays if you wish for solitude. But those tough souls who battled the potholed road deserve a prize as well, so enjoy the hike in harmony with others.

Hop onto the trail and start a gentle climb accompanied by beargrass near your feet and Cascade blueberries conveniently near your fingers. As the trail gets steeper, grunt and groan your way along the west side of the ridgeline until, just when you need one,

the first of two trail benches appears, 0.7 mile from where you started.

The path wanders around exposed rocky outcroppings with a couple of views of Mount Rainier, Mount Adams, and Mount St. Helens before it enters the forest again and plays peekaboo with conifer thickets.

The trail begins to switchback and delivers you to a steep ledge with a memorial to a gentleman named Johnnie T. Peters, who helped construct High Rock and 10 other local towers, using mules to haul materials.

Next, the trail makes a hard right and traverses rock slabs toward the lookout and the remains of an old shed. In no time at all, you find yourself standing at the lookout with jaw-dropping views in all directions. In summer months, the warm, welcoming rocks

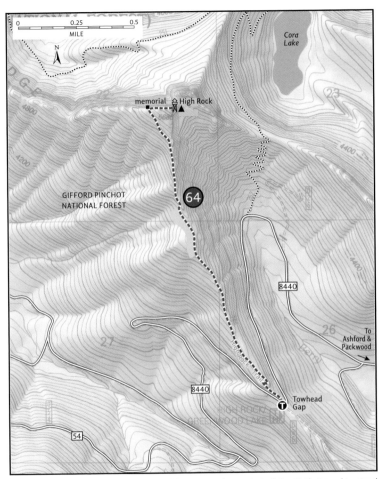

invite hoary marmots to sun themselves like the Hollywood elite.

On a clear day, you can see four volcanoes: Mount Rainier, Mount Adams, Mount Hood, and Mount St. Helens—as well as smaller peaks in nearly every direction.

Not only are the views inspiring, but the lookout tower itself is a living legend and stands as only 1 of the 62 that used to stand tall in this region. The construction of this proud little gem took place in 1929, with mule trains delivering each piece of the four-sided, gable-roof, L4 structure. It was assembled and secured in 31 days by drilling steel pillars deep into the rock and fastening four strong guide wires to hold it firmly in place. In 1980, when Mount St. Helens blew its top, the force of the ash and steam thoroughly rocked the building, which was still boarded up for the winter. Thankfully, the deep snowpack prevented too much damage.

Today, the tower needs repairs and can be downright rickety in places. It is no longer staffed because of inadequate lightning protection. Use extreme caution as losing your footing would be a real buzzkill. Enjoy the sweeping panoramas and the historic structure for as long as you can, then force yourself to head back.

65 Indian Henrys Hunting Ground

RATING/ DIFFICULTY	ROUNDTRIP	ELEV GAIN/ HIGH POINT	SEASON
★★★★★/5	14 miles	3285 feet/ 5300 feet	July–Oct

Maps: Green Trails Mount Rainier Wonderland No. 269SX, Mount Rainier West No. 269; **Contact:** Mount Rainier National Park, Longmire Wilderness Information Center; **Permit:** Mount Rainier National Park Pass or America the Beautiful Pass; **Notes:** Mosquitoes can be voracious during early summer so bring plenty of insect repellent. Lahars (volcanic mudflows) may occur on Kautz Creek; know the signs and take action if you smell, see, or hear one. Stock and pets prohibited; **GPS:** N 46 45.012 W 121 48.713

�★ ✿ ❁ ⌂ *Indian Henrys Hunting Ground is home to one of the most breathtaking subalpine meadows in the park as well as the park's oldest patrol cabin. The sweeping views of Mount Rainier make this hike an unforgettable treat*

for the eyes and the up-and-down terrain make it a challenging workout for the legs.

GETTING THERE
From Ashford, drive 6.3 miles to the Nisqually Entrance of Mount Rainier National Park. Enter the park through the entrance booth, then proceed 6.5 miles to the Longmire area and park behind the National Park Inn. Privies, restaurant, general store, and wilderness information center available.

ON THE TRAIL
The trailhead is northwest of the Wilderness Information Center at Longmire and is marked by a sign with an image of a figure wearing a backpack, a large arrow, and the words "Wonderland Trail." Head north and begin your romp on a wide, well-used cruising lane through the conifers. In 0.1 mile, turn left at a signed trail junction for a number of different landmarks, among them Indian Henrys.

Cross Nisqually–Longmire Road in 0.2 mile from the junction; keep your head on a swivel as cars zip by here on a semi-blind corner. Once across, locate the trail on the other side and begin your ascent. Gentle climbing leads you to a boardwalk through brilliant green foliage in 0.5 mile from the road. After that the trail gets serious about climbing.

Water is abundant from trailside sources all the way to Indian Henrys, so if you need to filter some, you have plenty of options. In 1.8 strenuous miles from where you started, pass a trail junction for the Van Trump Park Trail and in 0.2 mile, one for the Rampart Ridge Trail.

In 3 miles from the trailhead, cross the washed-out Kautz Creek basin on a series of half-log bridges, and enjoy the brief but grand view of Mount Rainier in the distance. Kautz Creek is a moody little rascal that is prone to

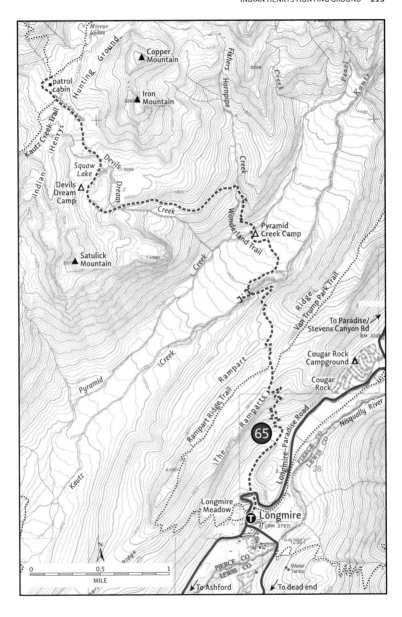

The exquisite meadows of Indian Henrys Hunting Ground contain a rich history.

volcanic outbursts, so keep your eyes, nose, and ears open as you cross this stretch.

In just 0.3 mile from Kautz Creek, pass Pyramid Creek Camp, the first of two wilderness camps on this stretch. If you have to use the facilities, you are in luck! A primitive backcountry privy is located within this camp and, although it's no flush toilet, it will do quite well in times of desperation.

Cross silty Pyramid Creek on a log bridge just past the camp and then, in 1 mile, cross melodic Fishers Hornpipe Creek. Ben Longmire, grandson of James Longmire, had a creative imagination and gave this waterway its name after he claimed it sang a fisher's hornpipe to him and his group when they camped nearby.

After the creek, the trail takes a jog to the west and passes a few more water sources, including Devils Dream Creek, before it arrives, rather suddenly, right in the middle of Devils Dream Camp, 5.6 miles from the trailhead. A rustic outhouse to the right offers a better toilet option than Pyramid Creek Camp if you have the luxury of picking one or the other. The mosquitoes here have a reputation for carrying people away, so foxtrot with your insect repellent or button up!

Thankfully, the climbing grade abates after Devils Dream Camp and you transition from forest to pockets of subalpine meadows. In 0.5 mile from Devils Dream, the trail delivers you to spectacular Squaw Lake with views of Iron Mountain, trailside right. You might be tempted to stay here with your camera all day, but there's more ahead!

The huffing and puffing continue as you wander through a meadow and up erosion-preventing trail stairs that seem to go on and on and up and up. In 0.7 mile from Squaw Lake (6.8 miles from where you started), you officially arrive at Indian Henrys Hunting Ground and also a junction with the Kautz Creek Trail, which heads to the left. Wide-open meadows in all directions fill your eyes with colorful carpets of seasonal wildflowers while grandiose views of Mount Rainier make you purr.

If you like history, you'll especially appreciate this area. Indian Henry was a Native American guide who became legendary thanks to his guiding skills and extensive knowledge of the mountain's backcountry. When he first met pioneers James Packwood and Henry Windsor, he introduced himself with what sounded like the name "Sotolick," but finding that name too hard to articulate, the men renamed him Henry and it stuck. Since he was often seen with his horses in these meadows hunting and collecting berries, the area was named in his honor. In fact, Satulick Mountain, located near this area, is named (phonetically) after Sotolick. Another fun historical fact is that these meadows used to house the Wigwam Hotel. It wasn't a hotel at all but rather a primitive campground where, in the early 1900s, folks paid to stay in rustic conditions. Poor sanitation from human waste and deplorable cooking facilities quickly drove the operation out of business, and today, no signs of such activity remain. Nature has graciously forgiven and forgotten.

Just when you think you can't handle any more beauty, there is a rustic little cabin tucked into the trees. This patrol cabin, built in the early 1900s, was the first such structure in the park and is now on the National Register of Historic Places. When you visit, be sure to walk around the cabin's southern side to check out a small pond teeming with aquatic life and with a plethora of muddy pawprints on the fragile shoreline. Stick to the trails as this area has a short growing season and is adversely impacted by too many visitors. Head back the way you came or, if you have two cars, you can do a shuttle and follow the Kautz Creek Trail (Hike 66) to its trailhead. It's a full day no matter which way you return.

66 Kautz Creek

RATING/ DIFFICULTY	ROUNDTRIP	ELEV GAIN/ HIGH POINT	SEASON
★★★★/4	11.4 miles	3830 feet/ 5600 feet	late July– Oct

Map: Green Trails Mount Rainier Wonderland No. 269SX; **Contact:** Mount Rainier National Park, Longmire Wilderness Information Center; **Permit:** Mount Rainier National Park Pass or America the Beautiful Pass; **Notes:** Check trail conditions to ensure footbridge over Kautz Creek is in place before setting out. Stock and pets prohibited; **GPS:** N 46 44.195 W 121 51.413

 *Excitable Kautz Creek has thrown some serious volcanic tantrums, resulting in damage to park roads and trails recorded as far back as 1947 and as recently as 2006. Today, the mostly quiet Kautz Creek Trail heads north over hills and vales and reaches the lovely subalpine meadows of Indian Henrys Hunting Ground, where the oldest remaining park patrol cabin stands. You'll get an eyeful with views of Mount Rainier and seasonal wildflowers near the cabin.*

GETTING THERE

From Ashford, drive 6.3 miles to the Nisqually Entrance of Mount Rainier National Park. Enter the park through the entrance booth, then proceed 3.5 miles to the parking area for Kautz Creek to the right (south). The trailhead is across the road to the north. Toilets and picnic tables available at trailhead.

ON THE TRAIL

Cross the road from the parking area and locate the trailhead to the right (east) of the educational sign exhibit. Once happily on your way, note that the trail surface is a mix of sand and stone left here by the creek when it changed course. Through the alders, you can glimpse the eroded banks along with stands of evergreens still holding their ground. In less than a mile, arrive at a log bridge spanning a branch of Kautz Creek and delivering you to the other side. The trail is obvious but if you have trouble, look for rocky cairns along the bank to ensure you stay your course.

Conifers add a cozy feeling to the trail as they invite you to walk through them, climbing steeply and steadily north. Eventually, trees give way to small meadows bursting with beargrass, a treat for all senses when it's blooming.

In roughly 2.3 miles from where you started, the trail guides you up a small series of switchbacks with wonderful views of rocky ridgelines where mountain goats often linger, clicking and clacking along the vertical inclines. Bears love these meadows too, and since the trail occasionally has blind corners, practice good bear smarts to avoid startling

It's challenging, but the Kautz Creek Trail offers grand views and is a great place to escape the crowds on busy summer weekends.

them. Up, up, up you go, climbing higher and higher and steeper and steeper, until finally, at nearly 4 miles from where you started, the trail reaches the top of a hummock covered with brilliant white beargrass, dwarf huckleberries, and sparse subalpine firs. Stop here, first to breathe, then to swoon at the meadows and peekaboo Rainier views. This place

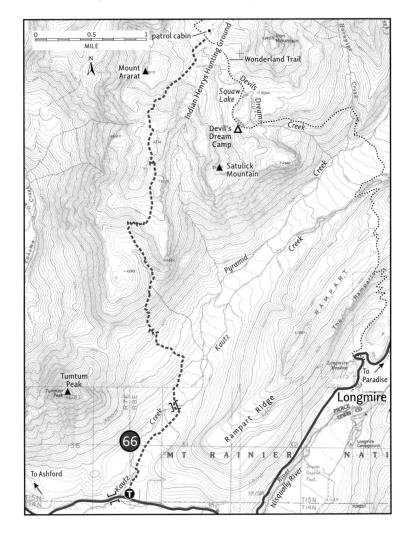

is truly a gift and our forefathers knew it when they created this park! Onward you go, the trail dipping down and then back up several times until you start to wonder if you will ever reach your goal. Persistence pays off, however, and the views continue to improve as you find yourself near a seasonal creek that provides some white noise as a soundtrack. In 5.7 miles, find yourself in Indian Henrys Hunting Ground, staring at magical views of Mount Rainier and the rustic little patrol cabin. The Kautz Creek Trail dead-ends at a junction with the signed Wonderland Trail. To see the cabin, head left on the Wonderland, then take the small spur trail to the right. A small pond teeming with frogs and other aquatic life is to the cabin's east, offering some photo opportunities and a chance to check out the animal tracks near its muddy edges. Head back the way you came when you've tucked all the wonderful memories safely into your medial temporal lobe.

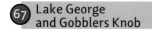

67 Lake George and Gobblers Knob

RATING/ DIFFICULTY	ROUNDTRIP	ELEV GAIN/ HIGH POINT	SEASON
★★★★★/4	12.6 miles	2640 feet/ 5465 feet	July–Oct

Maps: Green Trails Mount Rainier Wonderland No. 269SX, Mount Rainier West No. 269; **Contact:** Mount Rainier National Park, Longmire Wilderness Information Center; **Permit:** Mount Rainier National Park Pass or America the Beautiful Pass; **Notes:** Bicycles permitted on washed-out Westside Road but not on park trails. Area subject to geohazards so check trail conditions and be aware of your surroundings when hiking. Westside Road closes in winter months; check park website

before you go. Stock and pets prohibited; **GPS:** N 46 46.742 W 121 53.067

 A quiet hike up decommissioned Westside Road leads to grand views of Mount Rainier from one of the four remaining fire-lookout towers in the park. As a bonus, the peaceful shoreline of Lake George, tucked under the shoulders of Mount Wow, brings a tranquil sense of solitude and an opportunity to explore a historic patrol cabin near its edges.

GETTING THERE

From Ashford, drive 6.3 miles to the Nisqually Entrance of Mount Rainier National Park. Enter the park through the entrance booth and then proceed east for 1 mile to the easy-to-miss Westside Road to the left (north). Follow the gravel road for just shy of 3 miles, to the road's end, and park along the shoulders. Walk roughly 500 feet from where you parked to find the fixed gate.

ON THE TRAIL

There are a couple of ways to access Gobblers Knob. You can either take Puyallup Trail No. 248 from outside the park (see Hike 68) or you can take Westside Road as described here, my personal favorite. Not only is it easier on your car, but walking up Westside Road and seeing the battered road signs is an interesting experience. It feels like you are one of the only humans left on Earth and nature is trying to reclaim the landscape. Years ago, cars buzzed up this road, delivering throngs of eager backpack-wearing trail traipsers to the various trailhead parking areas. However, glacial outbursts, one after the next, caused the Park Service to close the road to vehicle traffic in the late 1980s. Today, the trailheads off the road are accessible either by foot or by bicycle, although you may still see an occasional high-clearance, park-sanctioned vehicle making its way along the gravel surface. Park staffers get a hall pass and a high five for their patrols.

After walking around the gate, begin your trek up the gravel road to the car bridge over Fish Creek.

Views of Tahoma Creek and the devastation around its edges are evidence of the power of volcanic tantrums and will make you shudder, while the occasional views of the mountain will make you swoon. In 1.4 miles from where you started, the road takes a hairpin turn to the left where the Tahoma

Creek Trail used to commence before it was wiped off the map a few years back.

Onward you go, climbing slightly until you reach a former parking area for the Tahoma Vista picnic area. Mount Tahoma, the Native American name for Mount Rainier, is no longer visible from this spot as the trees have grown too tall. An old comfort station is located here through the trees, although it is locked and inaccessible.

Saunter along the road for another 1.6 miles past Tahoma Vista and arrive at an area known as Round Pass, a fairly level divide between Mount Wow and Emerald Ridge. Here are your trails! To the left, adjacent to an old parking area, is the official

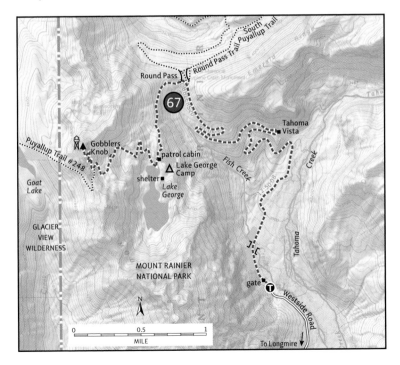

Built in 1933, the patrol cabin on Gobblers Knob is a rustic structure worth exploring.

trailhead for Lake George and Gobblers Knob. The trail is used enough that it's still obvious and finding it shouldn't give you any problems when you search the forest edges. If you brought your bike, you need to lock it here as bicycles are permitted on the road only.

Once you are officially on the Lake George Trail, begin by climbing through the conifers and then the trail has a gentler grade as it winds south to Lake George on the left in 0.8 mile. Shaped like a large spoon, the lake is much longer than you can see from its northern shore, but access by Lake George

Camp allows tranquil views. The patrol cabin here, built in 1934, was originally intended to be a horse barn but was later converted into ranger accommodations. The rustic architecture earned this and many structures in the park spots on the National Register of Historic Places. Nearby, a three-sided shelter, also built back in the day, is a good place to set down your pack and hang out, especially if the weather isn't cooperating. Luckily for us day hikers, the wilderness camp (permit required for overnight stays) here has a rustic outhouse for those that gotta go.

After you've enjoyed Lake George as much as you wish, follow the trail away from the lake and climb to the west, the incline causing you to work a bit! In 1.2 miles from the lake, after passing a small pond to the right, arrive at a signed junction for Gobblers Knob. Follow this short, crazy-steep trail to the right for 0.4 mile until the hallelujah choir sings and there it is—the Gobblers Knob lookout tower! There isn't a lot of room at the top, so use care, especially if the whole scout troop came along.

This rustic lookout, built in 1933, has one of the most breathtaking views of Mount Rainier. Also visible to the southwest is the sunken crater of Mount St. Helens. If luck is with you, you may even catch a glimpse of mountain goats on the rocky southern slopes of the unnamed peak to the south. In the massive storm of 2006, high winds ripped off the roof and collapsed two walls of this historic structure; such is the life of an exposed mountain cabin. Thankfully, repairs put it back to its old self.

When you're ready to head back, retrace your steps to Westside Road, or make a shuttle out of things and follow Puyallup Trail No. 248 west toward Goat Lake and use one of the trailheads near Lake Christine (Hike 68).

68 Mount Beljica

Southern Trailhead

RATING/ DIFFICULTY	ROUNDTRIP	ELEV GAIN/ HIGH POINT	SEASON
★★★★/3	3 miles	1065 feet/ 5475	July–early Oct

Northern Trailhead

RATING/ DIFFICULTY	ROUNDTRIP	ELEV GAIN/ HIGH POINT	SEASON
★★★★/3	5.4 miles	1160 feet/ 5475	July–early Oct

Maps: Green Trails Mount Rainier West No. 269, Mount Rainier Wonderland No. 269SX; **Contact:** Gifford Pinchot National Forest, Cowlitz Valley Ranger Station, Randle Office; **Permit:** Free wilderness use permit at trailhead; **Notes:** Road to southern trailhead is rough, and a high-clearance vehicle, all-wheel, or four-wheel drive is recommended. Road to northern trailhead is longer but less rough and better for passenger cars. Dogs permitted in all areas except where trail crosses into Mount Rainier National Park 0.9 mile east of Goat Lake; **GPS:** N 46 46.418 W 121 56.670

   Jagged Mount Beljica makes a lovely perch to pass the afternoon marveling at wondrous views of Mount Rainier to the east. The shallow, forested shoreline of Lake Christine adds even more enjoyment to the adventure as you trace its western edges.

GETTING THERE

To reach the southern trailhead from Elbe, drive eastbound on State Route 706 for roughly 10.8 miles, passing the town of Ashford. At unpaved Copper Creek Road (Forest Road 59), turn left (north) and proceed for 4.3 miles. Turn right (east) onto FR 5920 and continue for 1.5 miles to the trailhead. No facilities at trailhead.

To reach the northern trailhead from Elbe, drive eastbound on SR 706 for roughly 10.8 miles, passing the town of Ashford. At unpaved Copper Creek Road (FR 59), turn left (north) and proceed for 8.6 miles until the road peters out. Park in the pullouts. No facilities at trailhead.

ON THE TRAIL
Southern Trailhead

From the parking area, Lake Christine Trail No. 249 climbs steeply eastbound up the shoulders of an unnamed ridgeline before it turns sharply back to the west. It finally agrees to a northern trajectory and reaches the Glacier View Wilderness boundary in 0.7 mile from the trailhead. Just beyond the boundary, and exactly when you need a climbing reprieve, emerald Lake Christine shows up to the left with Mount Beljica reflected in its waters. If you want a break, and the biting battalions of the mosquito variety aren't feasting, a couple of campsites in the area provide a pleasant pack-off break option.

In 0.4 mile from Lake Christine, arrive at an unsigned trail junction that heads left (west, then northwest). There is talk of this being signed in the near future, but for the time being, it's easy to miss. Pat yourself on the back for taking the correct trail when you finally discover yourself climbing. Up you go for 0.4 mile until you are standing tall on the ledge-y summit of the rocky peak of Mount Beljica. The views will make you want to stay all day. Look around; you are in volcano country and at least three should catch your eyes—Mount St. Helens, Mount Adams, and of course, front and center, Mount Rainier.

Fellow Mountaineers Books author Craig Romano stares out into the vast open landscapes from the summit of Mount Beljica.

This peak has some fun history. In the 1930s a tent cabin facility was set up here for fire watchers during the summer months. It was later determined that the better perch was Glacier View (Hike 63), and a classic L4-style lookout tower was built there in 1934. Despite that, the tent cabin and its fixtures remained here seasonally in the summer until 1958.

Don't feel bad if you can't place the name "Beljica"; it's a made-up term. This peak was first climbed by two families and their friends in 1897, the Meslers and the LaWalls. This creative group named the peak by using the first letter of each of their names, B for Burgon Mesler; E for Elizabeth Drake, Elizabeth Sharp,

and Elizabeth Mesler; L for Lucy LaWall; J for Jesse LaWall; I for Isabel Mesler; C for Clara Mesler; and A for Alexander Mesler. Perhaps they had a mean game of rock, paper, scissors to see who got to be the first letter!

Northern Trailhead

From the parking area, follow the obvious spur trail a short distance to enter the Glacier View Wilderness and arrive at an intersection with Glacier View Trail No. 267, a larger trail. Go right (south) and follow the trail for 0.5 mile to rock hop across a small stream. In 0.2 mile, arrive at verdant Beljica Meadows, a series of grassy wetlands and pockets of

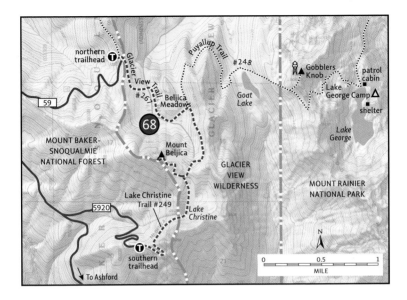

small ponds that offer colorful seasonal displays of Jeffrey's shooting star and cinquefoil. If the bitty biters are biting, you'll want to channel your inner Usain Bolt and move through these meadows like a rocket. If not, count your blessings and enjoy the ambiance!

In 1.1 miles from where you started, arrive at a signed trail junction with Puyallup Trail No. 248, which goes left toward Goat Lake, and Lake Christine Trail No. 249, which goes right toward Mount Beljica. Take the latter and follow the moderate ups and downs for 0.7 mile to another trail junction, this one unsigned. This is the Mount Beljica Trail and the one you want. Go right at this junction and follow the forest for a bit before you start huffing and puffing up to the rocky summit, 2.3 miles from where you started. Be sure to read the fun history in the southern trailhead section above to make your mind wander back in time.

EXTENDING YOUR HIKE

Options abound for making this hike longer after you've exhausted the attractions of Mount Beljica. Descend from the summit and head north at the unsigned trail junction. After 0.7 mile, arrive at the signed junction with Puyallup Trail No. 248. This trail goes straight ahead while the Lake Christine Trail turns left. Follow Puyallup Trail No. 248 for 1.4 miles as it descends slightly to deliver you to the twinkling shores of Goat Lake.

If the pooch isn't with you and time and stamina are on your side, keep hiking eastbound for 0.4 mile to the park boundary, then another 0.5 mile to reach a signed spur trail that climbs very steeply for 0.4 mile to the summit of Gobblers Knob. A two-story frame cabin built in 1933 still graces the boulder-laden peak and offers outstanding views of Mount Rainier.

69 Narada Falls

RATING/ DIFFICULTY	ROUNDTRIP	ELEV GAIN/ HIGH POINT	SEASON
★★★/1	0.4 mile	170 feet/ 4525 feet	July–Oct

Maps: Green Trails Mount Rainier Wonderland No. 269SX, Mount Rainier East No. 270; **Contact:** Mount Rainier National Park, Longmire Wilderness Information Center; **Permit:** Mount Rainier National Park Pass or America the Beautiful Pass; **Notes:** Rocks and walkways near falls can be slippery so use caution. Be prepared to get wet, especially during high-runoff periods. Stock and pets prohibited; **GPS:** N 46 46.515 W 121 44.785

A must-see for all visitors, Narada Falls offers a quick, leg-stretching stroll for families who wish to check out one of the most classic roadside waterfalls in Mount Rainier National Park.

A short, stretch-your-legs walk leads to the rushing Narada Falls.

GETTING THERE
From Ashford, drive 6.3 miles to the Nisqually Entrance of Mount Rainier National Park. Enter the park through the entrance booth, then proceed for 15.4 miles, passing the Longmire area, to a signed pullout and a very large parking area to the right (southeast). Cross the car bridge over the top of the falls and locate the trailhead to the right. Continue past the trailhead to find restrooms in a building to the left.

ON THE TRAIL
When the park is busy, the parking lot for Narada Falls is a zoo, but don't let that deter you, it's worth it. The trailhead starts down a fairly steep slope to the east of the falls, showing off the rushing water.

Views get better the farther down you go, and a few unofficial stop-n-gawk spots over a wooden railing keep your camera busy. An official viewpoint with an interpretive sign arrives just 0.1 mile from the trailhead and helps visitors understand the geologic history behind this large curtain of falling water.

This beautiful horsetail-shaped falls plunges a total of 176 feet in two tiered drops over basalt. Years ago, the falls were called Cushman, but in 1893 the name was changed to Narada (meaning "uncontaminated" in Hindu) in honor of the Narada branch of the Theosophical Society of Tacoma.

Continue hiking down for better views, or extend your trip by hiking another 0.1 mile to a junction with the Wonderland Trail and then heading either right toward Longmire

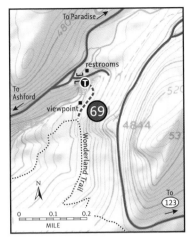

and Carter and Madcap Falls (Hike 60) or left toward Reflection Lakes (Hike 58) and Faraway Rock and Lakes High Trail Loop (Hike 55). The world is your oyster!

70 Rampart Ridge Loop

RATING/ DIFFICULTY	LOOP	ELEV GAIN/ HIGH POINT	SEASON
★★★/3	5.2 miles	1355 feet/ 4080 feet	late June– early Nov

Map: Green Trails Mount Rainier Wonderland No. 269SX; **Contact:** Mount Rainier National Park, Longmire Wilderness Information Center; **Permit:** Mount Rainier National Park Pass and America the Beautiful Pass; **Notes:** Mosquitoes near Rampart Ridge and Wonderland Trail junction can be vicious so bring plenty of insect repellent. Stock and pets prohibited; **GPS:** N 46 44.986 W 121 48.827

Those looking for a decent workout, a stately conifer forest, and a couple of pleasant viewpoints will enjoy this trek along Rampart Ridge. On a sunny summer day, when bright yellow rays fan through the evergreens in the afternoon, you'll feel like you've been dropped into the pages of a fairy tale.

GETTING THERE

From Ashford, drive 6.3 miles to the Nisqually Entrance of Mount Rainier National Park. Enter the park through the entrance booth, then proceed 6.5 miles to the Longmire area and park behind the National Park Inn. Privies, restaurant, general store, and wilderness information center available.

ON THE TRAIL

You can hike this loop in either direction from Longmire, but I generally prefer the clockwise direction. Cross the Nisqually–Longmire Road and locate the Trail of the Shadows Loop directly across from the National Park Inn. Turn left (west) and walk the Trail of the Shadows Loop for 0.2 mile until you arrive at a signed junction for the Rampart Ridge Trail.

Turn left at the trail junction and begin your ascent toward the top of the ridge. Switchbacks begin almost immediately and get tighter and steeper as you climb. Thankfully, swaying Douglas fir and western hemlock give you plenty of shade if the summer sunshine is hot. In early summer, look for plentiful, pinkish western coral root, a member of the orchid family, that gets nutrients from decaying organic matter in the soil and not from photosynthesis.

In 0.9 mile from Longmire, a view through the trees shows the Nisqually River valley far below you. Beyond that, in just 0.2 mile, pass one of nature's finest pieces of art, a spectacular old-growth hardwood in the shape of an arch. This piece of trailside sculpture is a fascinating feast for the eyes!

A stony outcropping 1.5 miles from where you started makes a good place to flop down for a break and scare up a snack if the climb has left your tummy's fuel tank empty.

Next, a signed viewpoint spur 1.9 miles from the start of your hike points the way to the main trail's right and, in 200 feet, carries you to a picturesque view of the Nisqually River basin. Years ago, Rainier was clearly visible to the left, but the thriving evergreens have made seeing the mountain here nearly impossible.

Back on the main trail, your body starts to breathe a sigh of relief as the incline levels off and you reach the top of the ridge. Views of Rainier pop in and out through the conifers and in at least one spot are quite clear, a good opportunity for a picture, but the best view is just ahead. Roughly 0.3 mile beyond the signed viewpoint, an unsigned spur trail

heads to the right and ends at a stony patch of rocks, perfect for sitting, thinking, and dreaming. Views of the mountain are pleasant here, with only a couple of rascal trees to impede the view. It's a good place to spread out lunch and enjoy the sunshine of the afternoon. Beware of the beautiful gray jays, also known as camp robbers, that will steal a sandwich from your very hands. Resist their sweet faces and don't feed them: they need to learn to forage for themselves since people won't be here year-round.

In 3.1 miles from Longmire, arrive at a signed junction with the Wonderland Trail, the return portion of your loop. Turn right at the sign and fire up the quads for the downhill portion of the hike. Down, down, down you go, through more magnificent evergreens and past a signed junction for the Van Trump Park Trail. It's only 1.6 miles

An interesting trailside sculpture along the Rampart Ridge Trail calls out for a photo.

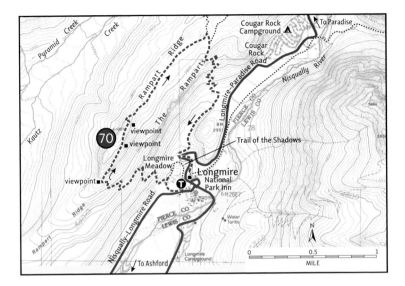

of walking on the Wonderland before you arrive back at the Nisqually–Longmire Road, but it feels longer. Hear the words of your mother in your head as you look both ways before crossing the road as it can be hard to see the cars zipping around these corners.

Find the trail on the other side of the road and duck back into the trees. In 0.2 mile, the Wonderland turns to the left, but you turn to the right and make your way back to the Longmire area and the National Park Inn. Perhaps some huckleberry cobbler from the inn's dining room is in order before you hop back in your waiting vehicle and call it a great day.

Maps: Green Trails Mount Rainier Wonderland No. 269SX, Mount Rainier West No. 269; **Contact:** Mount Rainier National Park, Longmire Wilderness Information Center; **Permit:** Mount Rainier National Park Pass or America the Beautiful Pass; **Notes:** Bicycles permitted on the washed-out Westside Road but not on park trails. Area subject to geohazards so check trail conditions and be aware of your surroundings when hiking. Westside Road closes in winter months so check park website before you go; **GPS:** N 46 46.742 W 121 53.067

71 South Puyallup Trail

RATING/ DIFFICULTY	ROUNDTRIP	ELEV GAIN/ HIGH POINT	SEASON
★★★/4	12 miles	2175 feet/ 4200 feet	July–Oct

Westside Road is closed to vehicles so only hikers who make the effort to walk the road will reap the benefits of the adjacent peaceful and often-forgotten trails. Along this route, a forested trail leads you to a backcountry Wonderland Trail camp and some interesting andesite columns called the Colonnade. During your journey, you may also want to stop at Round Pass and pay your respects to the US Marines who perished in a 1946 plane crash on South Tahoma Glacier. A somber memorial along tranquil former West-side Road is the perfect place for a moment of silence in their honor.

GETTING THERE

From Ashford, drive 6.3 miles to the Nisqually Entrance of Mount Rainier National Park. Enter the park through the entrance booth and then proceed for 1 mile east to the easy-to-miss Westside Road to the left (north). Follow the gravel road for just shy of 3 miles to the road's end, and park along the shoulders. Walk roughly 500 feet to find the gate.

ON THE TRAIL

Head up the abandoned roadway and notice that people are scarce and the neglected speed-limit and trail signs are worn and for-saken. With limited access, this area takes on an air of solitude, and you can easily find quiet for thoughts as you walk or pedal your bike to the trailhead.

Hike or bike the washed-out roadway for 3.8 miles, passing the abandoned Tahoma

Andesite columns, called the Colonnade, along the South Puyallup Trail are a compelling wayside stop.

Vista parking lot, and arrive at a moderately level area known as Round Pass. This area was fairly busy before the road was closed and is home to a couple of trailheads and also a sobering memorial. On December 10, 1946, bad weather caused an aircraft carrying 32 US Marines to vanish. Winter weather complicated the search, which was called off after two weeks. In July 1947, a ranger spotted the wreckage on South Tahoma Glacier, but hazardous conditions prevented recovery of the bodies. On August

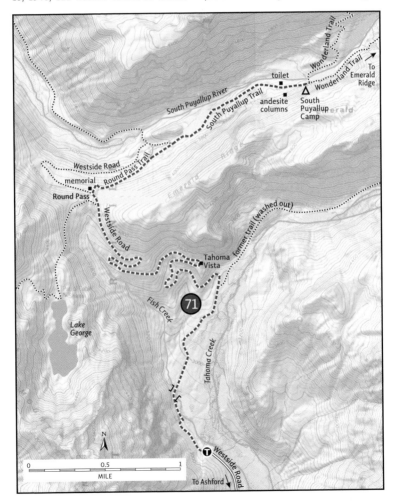

24, 1947, with South Tahoma Glacier in the background, the Navy and the Park Service held a memorial service, attended by roughly 200 people. A folded American flag was presented to each family and the ceremony concluded with the playing of "Taps" and a 21-gun salute. Today, the memorial is a reminder of the tragedy that took place over 70 years ago.

With history floating in your head, look to the right, to the memorial's south, and locate the signed Round Pass Trail darting off into the forest. If you brought your bike, you'll need to lock it at this point and use only your feet for transportation. Follow the Round Pass Trail as it bobs and weaves through conifers and delivers you to the South Puyallup Trail, just 0.6 mile beyond. Go right.

The South Puyallup Trail ducks into the forest and wanders through shrubs and thimbleberries on a gentle grade as it carries you to the northeast. In 0.4 mile, find yourself at a sandy washout where the river decided to make things a little challenging for all who pass. Thankfully, navigation is still rather easy, although you may have to stop and shake some sand out of your shoes.

In 1.4 miles from where the Round Pass Trail met up with the South Puyallup Trail, arrive at a couple of important landmarks. The first is the backcountry toilet for South Puyallup Camp, located down a short signed spur to the left. This is a day-hikers' dream if nature is calling, although since the spur trail is short, it's easy to surprise a potty squatter; give a holler if you aren't sure if it's in use. To the right are some amazing andesite columns, called the Colonnade, worthy of digging out the camera. These unique hexagonal cliffside formations are the result of a volcanic eruption several thousand years ago. The columns look like a giant comb was run through the stone as it cooled, forming long stone strands. Andesite is most commonly found in composite volcanoes, like the ones in the Pacific Northwest, and during eruptions it flows slowly and has high viscosity, forming steep and often jagged structures.

Continue up the trail and find the South Puyallup Camp on the right-hand side with seasonal water available from a small trickling stream to the trail's north. Just a little farther, arrive at a junction with the Wonderland Trail and admire the beautiful, strong bridge over the South Puyallup River to the north. When the clock says it's time, head back the way you came or mix things up. Instead of taking a left-hand turn at the junction with the Round Pass Trail, make a longer day of things and follow the South Puyallup Trail all the way to Westside Road, following it back to your car. This adds another 1.2 miles to your day and buys you at least another scoop of ice cream on your way home.

72 Trail of the Shadows Loop

RATING/DIFFICULTY	LOOP	ELEV GAIN/HIGH POINT	SEASON
★★★/1	0.8 mile	75 feet/2850 feet	Mar–Oct

Map: Green Trails Mount Rainier Wonderland No. 269SX; **Contact:** Mount Rainier National Park, Longmire Wilderness Information Center; **Permit:** Mount Rainier National Park Pass or America the Beautiful Pass; **Notes:** May be muddy during wet spells. Do not drink water along trail as it may contain toxins. Stock and pets prohibited; **GPS:** N 46 44.989 W 121 48.824

This short hike has so many wonderful perks! It is one of the easiest hikes in the park but still showcases park history and several interesting natural features. Walk back in time by visiting the Longmire cabin, the oldest structure in the park; discover colorful mineral springs; learn about the old Longmire Springs Hotel; and challenge the kids to find evidence of beavers by finding teetering trees sitting precariously on hourglass stumps carved by strong front teeth.

GETTING THERE

From Ashford, drive 6.3 miles to the Nisqually Entrance of Mount Rainier National Park. Enter the park through the entrance booth, then proceed 6.5 miles to the Longmire area and park behind the National Park Inn. Privies, restaurant, general store, and wilderness information center available.

ON THE TRAIL

The trail begins directly across the road from the front porch of the National Park Inn. Cross the Nisqually–Longmire Road to the north and locate the loop trail. You can hike it in either direction, as both ways exhibit the same sights, but the most common direction, and the one I prefer, goes clockwise.

Head left and enjoy the metal educational signs noting the various area flora, a good way to learn what is what, especially during peak bloom season. As you continue to walk, interpretive signs pop up, including one on the

It's a treat to explore the last remaining Longmire family cabin along the Trail of the Shadows.

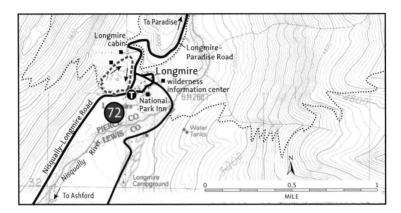

history of the Longmire area and another on the history of the former annex of the National Park Inn, which was located on this spot.

Small wooden bridges guide you over skunk-cabbage-filled wetlands, an olfactory wake-up call during springtime for sure. Western red cedar droop down with graceful limbs, inviting you to continue your stroll or to simply sit under their boughs on one of the many log benches located along this loop.

In 0.2 mile, arrive at a signed junction for the Rampart Ridge Trail that heads to the left (northwest). Make a mental note to come back and check it out (Hike 70), but for now continue wandering clockwise around the loop. Not far past the trail junction, a small viewpoint leads to the right with another interpretive sign noting the various mineral colors in the soil layers. Challenge the kids to remember one or two facts along the trail and then quiz them at the car and reward their smarts with an ice-cream sandwich from the general store!

A serene forest pathway follows, providing a wide, fir-needle-cushioned cruising lane through the dense conifers. More educational signs are displayed in the center of

the loop and you can get a peekaboo view of the top of Mount Rainier with a beautiful grassy meadow in the foreground. There is so much to see and learn!

In 0.5 mile, arrive at the most anticipated highlights of the hike, the Longmire cabin and the reddish-colored mineral spring known as Iron Mike. Surrounded by man-made river-rock walls, the rust-colored water trickles into a catch basin. The Longmire family promoted the springs by claiming the waters had healing powers. They even took out newspaper ads in the early 1890s that claimed the springs cured rheumatic pains and other afflictions. Whether or not it did, it certainly drew folks to visit the Longmire Springs Hotel.

Next to the springs stands the only remaining cabin of several that stood along this trail. James Longmire's oldest son, Elcaine, built it in 1888 as a summertime retreat for the Longmire family.

Interpretive signs continue to educate you as you continue around the loop. Keep your eyes open for the finely carved wood shapes cunningly crafted by talented beavers. The little bucktoothed critters have been hard at work making nearby dams, and you can't help but wonder about the headaches they must have after gnawing all that timber!

The loop finishes by cruising past another river-rock-walled water catch basin and more fascinating history of the original attempts at collecting water from what the Longmires believed was nature's finest spa.

Finally, you find yourself right where you started and, as luck would have it, not far from the general store gift shop at the National Park Inn where many treats await.

73 Twin Firs Loop

RATING/ DIFFICULTY	LOOP	ELEV GAIN/ HIGH POINT	SEASON
★★/1	0.4 mile	120 feet/ 2520 feet	May–Oct

Map: Green Trails Mount Rainier Wonderland No. 269SX; **Contact:** Mount Rainier National Park, Longmire Wilderness Information Center; **Permit:** Mount Rainier National Park Pass or America the Beautiful Pass; **Notes:** Blowdowns possible, so check trail conditions before heading out. Stock and pets prohibited; **GPS:** N 46 44.020 W 121 50.282

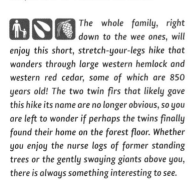 *The whole family, right down to the wee ones, will enjoy this short, stretch-your-legs hike that wanders through large western hemlock and western red cedar, some of which are 850 years old! The two twin firs that likely gave this hike its name are no longer obvious, so you are left to wonder if perhaps the twins finally found their home on the forest floor. Whether you enjoy the nurse logs of former standing trees or the gently swaying giants above you, there is always something interesting to see.*

A short loop trail takes hikers through large conifer understories complete with lush foliage.

GETTING THERE

From Ashford, drive 6.3 miles to the Nisqually Entrance of Mount Rainier National Park. Enter the park through the entrance booth, then proceed 4.2 miles to the trailhead and park at the large pullout to the left (north).

ON THE TRAIL

The trail begins by heading north past an interpretive sign that describes the extensive stands of old-growth trees in the park. Large nurse logs lie along the trail's edges, demonstrating the cycle of life as their decay provides nutrients that help seedlings grow. In late spring and early summer,

239

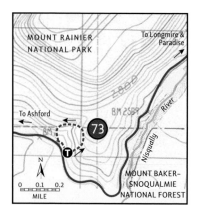

trillium, with white, pink, or burgundy flowers that have three distinct petals.

Mossy logs, stones, and tree branches are the result of the average 87 inches of rain this area receives! Ferns, such as licorice, deer, and sword, thrive in the acid soils near the conifers' edges while other plants, such as devil's club and Oregon grape, add to the plentiful pops of green. Don't forget to keep your eyes open for the avian friends who hippity-hop through the tree branches. Chickadees, juncos, winter wrens, and an occasional great horned or spotted owl thrive in the protective evergreen canopy.

keep your eyes near your feet to see if you can spot some twinflower, a creeping ground cover with slender stems that bear two pink, bell-shaped blooms. Also look for beautiful

Small half-log bridges carry you over drippy brooks as the trail loops its way west, then turns south, and finally leads you back to where you started.

The trail truly seems to meet up with the skyline as you climb higher and higher near Paradise (Hike 80).

paradise area

The Paradise area, located on Mount Rainier's southern flanks, is truly one of the most gorgeous places in the United States, if not on Earth. Because of its sublime wildflower meadows, eye-popping Rainier views, and easy access, millions of visitors flock here to see the stunning sights, and it's almost always a bustling scene. Weekdays are best if you can swing it, but even then, you likely won't be alone. Despite the crowds, the place is a bucket-list, must-see for anyone who visits the park, much like a trip to Yellowstone is not complete without seeing Old Faithful.

The Paradise area contains several features, including the historic Paradise Inn where you can hole up for the night in one of 121 rustic rooms and eat like a queen in its elegant dining room. Or maybe the cozy coffee shop where you can grab a quick snack or the well-stocked gift shop where you can do a little shopping are more your thing. Also located here is the fairly new Henry M. Jackson Visitors Center, which offers a well-staffed information booth, a cafeteria-style cafe, a gift shop, restrooms, and various mountain-inspired exhibits that educate folks about the behemoth volcano. Adjacent to the visitors center are the more historic Paradise Ranger Station, the Climbing Information Center (also called the Guide House), and a comfort station. Those wishing to climb the mountain or spend the night in a wilderness camp can obtain permits and information by visiting the Climbing Information Center, as the ranger station is no longer operational. The comfort station (aka the restroom) is open sporadically.

Even the parking lot has wonderful views of Rainier's snowy summit to the north and the jagged Tatoosh Range to the south. Just don't waste all of your camera's battery here, because if you think the parking lot views are great, just wait until you set foot into the backcountry! Be still your beating heart! Nearly every trail in the Paradise area contains scenes so beautiful you'll have to pinch yourself to see if they are real. In fact, my sister-in-law visiting from back east was jokingly convinced the whole place was a hologram (true story)! Be forewarned that once you see this area, you'll be spoiled and will compare all hiking to the trails of the Paradise area, where marmots frolic in grassy vales, fragrant breezes ruffle seasonal wildflowers, history dances through your imagination, and waterfalls roar with wild abandon.

74 Alta Vista Loop

RATING/ DIFFICULTY	ROUNDTRIP	ELEV GAIN/ HIGH POINT	SEASON
★★★★/3	1.4 miles	545 feet/ 5940 feet	July–Oct

Maps: Green Trails Mount Rainier Wonderland No. 269SX, Mount Rainier East No. 270; **Contact:** Mount Rainier National Park, Longmire Wilderness Information Center, Henry M. Jackson Visitors Center; **Permit:** Mount Rainier National Park Pass or America the Beautiful Pass; **Notes:** Watch for sudden changing weather. Arrive early as parking can be challenging, especially on weekends. Stock and pets prohibited; **GPS:** N 46 47.102 W 121 44.498

Don't let the short distance and paved walkway fool you into thinking you are just going for a relaxed ramble. The Alta Vista Trail makes you work for every second of its impressive views and blankets of colorful wildflowers. It's so steep in places that you may start thinking you've found the walkway that goes straight to the sun. But as much as it throws down in incline, it gives back in vistas that will make you feel your efforts are well rewarded.

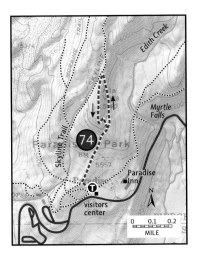

GETTING THERE

From Ashford, drive 6.3 miles to the Nisqually Entrance of Mount Rainier National Park. Enter the park through the entrance booth and proceed 18 miles, passing the Longmire area, and bear left at Stevens Canyon Road to remain on Longmire–Paradise Road. Park at one of the few parking lots or on the side of the one-way road east of the Paradise Inn. During busy summer months, arrive early as parking gets full. The Henry M. Jackson Visitors Center has restrooms, a picnic area, a snack bar, a gift shop, and many interesting exhibits.

ON THE TRAIL

The trails of Paradise can be very confusing but thankfully they are well signed. If you end up on the wrong one, don't fret, as it's likely to be breathtaking and will eventually take you where you want to go.

For the Alta Vista Loop Trail, head north from the visitors center up the concrete steps etched with the writings of John Muir and stay straight on the paved trails. In 0.2 mile, arrive at another trail junction and bear slightly left (northwest), following the signs pointing the way. At the next trail junction, just 0.1 mile from the last, make a hard right and begin a very steep climb. Sure it's paved, but nobody said it was easy!

Grunt and groan your way up the incline and in 0.4 mile, reach the start of the Alta Vista Loop. You can go in either direction, but I prefer to stay right. Continue to put

one foot in front of the other but stop a few times to breathe and take in the vast grandeur before you. To the right, the Edith Creek valley puts on a grand display in any season, bursting with rainbows of wildflowers in the summer and exhibiting an array of earth-tone colored bushes, some vibrant, some subtle, in the fall. Marmots scurry about, eating their greens and sounding alarms, while Edith Creek dances through the meadow. You might have to stop and sit on one of several benches along the route to marinate in it all.

In the early 1900s, shortly after Mount Rainier became the nation's fifth national park, a very popular camping area, called Camp of the Clouds, was in full swing near the summit of Alta Vista, not far from where you are standing. Large canvas tents were erected each summer and campers milled about trying to catch a glimpse of the massive glaciers on this side of the mountain. Mother Nature has long since erased all evidence of such primitive lodging.

The Alta Vista Loop rewards you with beautiful views—provided you are willing to crank up the steep pathways.

In 0.3 mile from the start of the loop, the trail spits you out at a large flat area off the Skyline Trail with signs pointing the way in several directions and probably some tourists looking befuddled about which way to go. Not you; you brought the guidebook!

Put your back to the mountain, and voilà! You can see the return loop to the top of Alta Vista here as it climbs the western side of the slopes. The view to the south of the Tatoosh Range is drool worthy, so keep the camera handy. Reach the top of the rise in 0.1 mile where, if need be, a bench welcomes you. Continue down the slopes until you reach the end of the loop, back where you started.

75 Camp Muir

RATING/ DIFFICULTY	ROUNDTRIP	ELEV GAIN/ HIGH POINT	SEASON
★★★★/5	9 miles	4680 feet/ 10,080 feet	Aug–late Sept

Maps: Green Trails Mount Rainier Wonderland No. 269SX, Mount Rainier East No. 270; **Contact:** Mount Rainier National Park, Longmire Wilderness Information Center, Henry M. Jackson Visitors Center; **Permit:** Mount Rainier National Park Pass or America the Beautiful Pass; **Notes:** Watch for sudden changing weather. Camp Muir is an alpine route across a snowfield with occasional

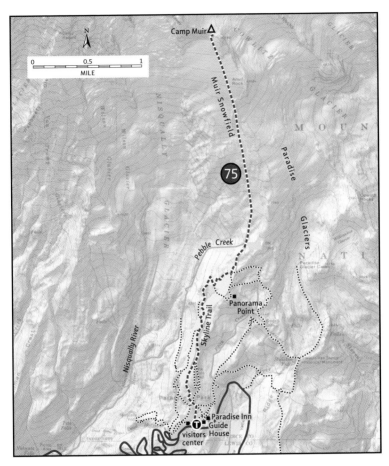

open crevasses. Only those with glacier travel experience should attempt this hike. Day hikers don't need permits if only going to Camp Muir. Blue bags (human waste bags; available at ranger stations or at Camp Muir) required if needed during high-country snow travel. Arrive early as parking can be challenging, especially on weekends. Stock and pets prohibited; **GPS:** N 46 47.102 W 121 44.498

First off, the warning: Camp Muir is a serious alpine ascent, not really a day hike. It is only for those who have experience climbing glaciers. The icy Muir Snowfield has claimed many lives but can appear deceptively easy. On sunny days, it's tempting to think "Oh, everybody's doing it, how hard can it be?" But mountain weather is fickle and can change in the blink of an eye. When bad weather moves in, routefinding becomes hazardous and challenging even for experienced climbers. If you don't have the right gear and experience, a slip in the wrong place can lead to serious injury or death. Sudden freezing fog can cause hypothermia, and blizzards can quickly move in on what started as a clear day. While we are on these serious subjects, it's also important to know that altitude-related illnesses are common above 8000 feet and some can be dangerous. Use sturdy boots, have snow traction, have the Ten Essentials with you, bring an ice ax and know how to use it, be prepared to hunker down and stay warm, know the symptoms of altitude sickness, and don't attempt anything above your skill level, even if your friends urge you to. And remember to apply sunscreen to any exposed skin—the inside of my nose got burned once! The Muir Snowfield can open up crevasses late in the season, so be sure to check conditions before you set out, and use extreme caution. Now that I've been your mother, let me be your friend. This is a spectacular climb and one that you'll never, ever forget. If you haven't experienced true snow travel, it will be one of the hardest things you'll ever do, but you will be rewarded with amazing panoramic views! The vista at Camp Muir is so vast your camera won't be able to capture it, so enjoy every minute of the high-alpine country with your own eyes.

Bring the Ten Essentials as well as snow travel know-how before setting off to Camp Muir.

GETTING THERE

From Ashford, drive 6.3 miles to the Nisqually Entrance of Mount Rainier National Park. Enter the park through the entrance booth and proceed 18 miles, passing the Longmire area, and bear left at Stevens Canyon Road to remain on Longmire–Paradise Road. Park at one of the few parking lots or on the side of the one-way road east of the Paradise Inn. During busy summer months, arrive early as parking gets full. The Henry M. Jackson Visitors Center has restrooms, a picnic area, a snack bar, a gift shop, and many interesting exhibits.

ON THE TRAIL

Access the Skyline Trail from any number of points, either up the steps etched with John Muir's writings north of the visitors center or from the spur trails north of the Guide House or Paradise Inn. Follow the Skyline Trail northwest as it climbs past a bundle of signed trail junctions toward Panorama Point. Snow can linger in the high country well into August, so be prepared to navigate snow and ice if necessary. In 1.6 miles from Paradise, arrive at the Pebble Creek Trail to the left and follow it as it climbs northeast until it reaches the Pebble Creek drainage and takes a hard northern turn. Water from Pebble Creek is the last you'll pass unless you stumble upon runoff in late season, so fill up the water bottles, especially on hot days. Shortly after Pebble Creek, the snow and the true climbing begin.

As you go up, up, up, stop and look over your shoulder. Behind you, on a clear day, the Tatoosh Range pops up to the south along with Mount Adams, Mount St. Helens (and its missing top), and Mount Hood. What a sight!

Work your way up the mountain, placing one snow-laden foot in front of the other until at 8000 feet you get a minor respite from the climb with a slightly gentler grade. Your legs thank you as you gulp the thinner air and try to catch your breath. Only a couple of thousand feet to go; no problem, right?

This is probably a good time to mention blue bags, or for the layperson, human waste bags. Yes, it's gross, but there isn't a great solution for managing the challenges of the ol' body on the snowfield! Should the need to have "a significant bio-break" arise when you are on the Muir Snowfield you'll want to ensure you have a blue bag handy. Pick one up at the Guide House before you hike. They are also available at Camp Muir if you think the urge might hit you on the way down. Blue bags are actually a kit containing a couple of twist ties and two bags, one clear and one blue. To use them, find a spot away from the trail or climbing route and do your business on the snow. Use the blue bag like a glove by turning it inside out and picking up the waste. Secure it with one of the twist ties. Put the blue bag inside the clear bag and secure it with a second twist tie. Do not throw blue bags in trash cans, but place them in specially labeled collection barrels at Camp Muir or in the tunnel outside the Paradise comfort station. Okay, enough potty talk; let's just hope you will never need to heed this paragraph!

Repeat "I got this" over and over in your head as you continue your upward push until, at 9000 feet, you see it! Camp Muir, consisting of a couple of structures, some tents, and a handful of people, comes into view. "It's just right there," you think, but your eyes are playing tricks on you. Only 1000 feet more to go; you got this, amigos!

Finally, your feet land on Camp Muir, the most popular base camp for those climbing to the top of Mount Rainier. The two permanent shelters, a public sleeping hut built in 1921 and a guide hut built in 1916, are showing signs of wear and tear but are still standing. Two stone pit toilets built in 1936 by the Civilian Conservation Corps are also still standing, although one is now used for storage. Thankfully, a solar toilet has been installed to help with human waste disposal, but it can be rather challenging to maintain. Over 10,000 people pass this way each summer, so the toilet can get rather, shall we say, aromatic. Hold your nose, be thankful it's there, and repress the memory. Most of all, keep all trash out of the crapper and tote all your garbage, even fruit peels, off the mountain.

Once you've relaxed, taken pictures, and patted yourself on your sweaty back, head on back and gloat about it on every social media channel possible. Others will want to know just how amazing you are, right?

76 Deadhorse Creek, Moraine Trail, and Glacier Vista

RATING/ DIFFICULTY	ROUNDTRIP	ELEV GAIN/ HIGH POINT	SEASON
★★★★★/4	3.8 miles	1100 feet/ 6400 feet	mid-July– Oct

Maps: Green Trails Mount Rainier Wonderland No. 269SX, Mount Rainier East No. 270; **Contact:** Mount Rainier National Park, Longmire Wilderness Information Center, Henry M. Jackson Visitors Center; **Permit:** Mount Rainier National Park Pass or America the Beautiful Pass; **Notes:** Watch for sudden changing weather. Arrive early as parking can be challenging, especially on weekends. Stock and pets prohibited; **GPS:** N 46 47.102 W 121 44.498

 Paradise is a maze of trails and there are several great ones that often get overlooked. The Deadhorse Creek Trail climbs a meadow-filled ridgeline that intersects the Moraine Trail near Nisqually Glacier and, farther up, the Glacier Vista Trail, a short side spur to sprawling Mount Rainier views. It's truly the best Mount Rainier has to offer in a short but challenging package.

GETTING THERE

From Ashford, drive 6.3 miles to the Nisqually Entrance of Mount Rainier National Park. Enter the park through the entrance booth and proceed 18 miles, passing the Longmire area, and bear left at Stevens Canyon Road to remain on Longmire–Paradise Road. Park at one of the few parking lots or on the side of the one-way road east of the Paradise Inn. During busy summer months, arrive early as parking gets full. The Henry M. Jackson Visitors Center has restrooms, a picnic area, a snack bar, a gift shop, and many interesting exhibits.

ON THE TRAIL

Climb the steps etched with John Muir's words northbound and then turn left and follow the signs, meandering west until you reach the Deadhorse Creek Trail. No one can seem to figure out whether Deadhorse is one or two words; park signs have it as two, while park maps have it as one. Either way, it's a beautiful place, so don't let the image the name evokes of what likely happened at this creek many moons ago make you wary.

Head northbound on the Deadhorse Creek Trail as it climbs through lush meadows teeming with fragrant wildflowers of every color of the rainbow and hoary marmots who nosh on whatever they can grab in their dexterous paws. Dribbling creeks dance with life as migratory and resident songbirds flit from tree to tree as if to say "Follow us, Follow us!" As the mostly paved path turns steeper and your inner motor starts firing on all cylinders, remember the old saying that "when the going gets tough, the tough get going," and think of the views you'll find as you climb higher and higher.

In 0.7 mile, arrive at a signed junction with the Moraine Trail to the left, which is definitely worth a look. As far as trails in the busy Paradise area are concerned, the Moraine Trail is one that sees few footprints, even on crowded summer weekends. Duck into the evergreens and begin to descend on an easy-to-follow pathway that reaches a sign noting the end of the maintained trail almost as quickly as the trail starts. You are still in the trees, so keep going. Even though the trail is not maintained, it is still easy enough to follow as you drop deeper and deeper toward the toe of Nisqually Glacier. Keep your eyes open for wildlife here, especially on less crowded weekdays. Deer and the occasional black bear wander here for solitude,

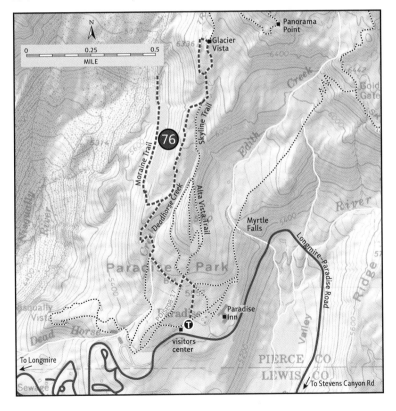

Paradise lives up to its name with gobsmacking views.

just like you. The pathway eventually peters out about 0.5 mile from leaving the Deadhorse Creek Trail but gives you a fine look over the glacial moraine, letting you imagine how big it once was. Use extreme caution at the viewpoints and watch your footing as the stones are tiny, slick, and somewhat precarious near the edge.

Retrace your steps back to the Deadhorse Creek Trail, and go left (northbound), passing a few viewpoints as you meander along the trail. In 0.5 mile from the junction with the Moraine Trail, the Deadhorse ends and delivers you to the Skyline Trail. You can turn right and head back to Paradise or get one last little bang for your buck and turn left and follow the Skyline Trail a short distance to a junction with a spur trail pointing the way to Glacier Vista, a wow-inspiring viewpoint sure to take your breath away.

Follow the spur trail past Glacier Vista until it hooks back into the Skyline Trail, then turn right and enjoy the downhill all the way back to the visitors center.

77 Myrtle Falls and Golden Gate Loop

RATING/ DIFFICULTY	LOOP	ELEV GAIN/ HIGH POINT	SEASON
★★★★★/4	4.1 miles	1210 feet/ 6400 feet	July–Oct

Maps: Green Trails Mount Rainier Wonderland No. 269SX, Mount Rainier East No. 270; **Contact:** Mount Rainier National Park, Longmire Wilderness Information Center, Henry M. Jackson Visitors Center; **Permit:** Mount Rainier National Park Pass or America the Beautiful Pass; **Notes:** Watch for sudden

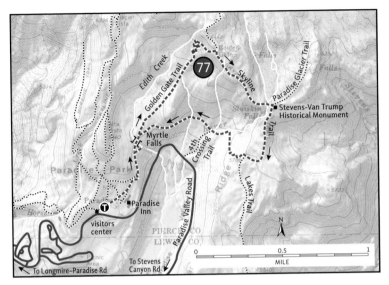

changing weather. Arrive early as parking can be challenging, especially on weekends. Stock and pets prohibited; **GPS: N 46 47.102 W 121 44.498**

![icons] *If your time at Paradise is limited and you can take only one trail, this is a perfect choice. This loop samples the best that Paradise has to offer, including seasonal meadows bursting with wildflowers, an iconic park waterfall, alpine and subalpine landscapes, and an interesting mountain monument.*

GETTING THERE

From Ashford, drive 6.3 miles to the Nisqually Entrance of Mount Rainier National Park. Enter the park through the entrance booth and proceed 18 miles, passing the Longmire area, and bear left at Stevens Canyon Road to remain on Longmire–Paradise Road. Park at one of the few parking lots or on the side

of the one-way road east of the Paradise Inn. During busy summer months, arrive early as parking gets full. The Henry M. Jackson Visitors Center has restrooms, a picnic area, a snack bar, a gift shop, and many interesting exhibits.

ON THE TRAIL

Hop up the steps north of the visitors center inscribed with the words of John Muir or follow the spur path north of the Paradise Inn and turn right (east) on the Skyline Trail.

Amble along the paved trail through some of the most breathtaking landscapes on this planet. Wildflowers in every color of the spectrum greet your feet and your camera. Look for alpine aster, broadleaf arnica, bird's beak lousewort, fanleaf cinquefoil, magenta paintbrush, pasqueflower, heather, and the list goes on and on. Autumn brings a whole different look and feel, with deep shades of burgundy that contrast with apple-green meadows. Hoary marmots with little fear of humans graze along the sides of the trail while golden-mantled ground squirrels zip about, causing big smiles and snapping cameras.

In 0.5 mile, arrive at a signed junction with the Myrtle Falls Trail just before the wooden bridge over Edith Creek. The women behind the names of the creek and falls must have been an intriguing pair since mountain guide Jules Stampfler felt twitterpated enough to deem them worthy of landscapes.

Myrtle Falls is almost as legendary as Mount Rainier, and the classic picture of the falls with the mountain, verdant meadows, and the wooden bridge in the background has appeared on countless postcards and souvenirs over the years. Follow the trail as it steeply descends roughly 50 feet to the viewpoint. Be sure to stop and get your shot, but take your turn; during the high season this place is like Walmart on Black Friday, and people don't seem to care if their elbow is in your shot. But don't despair, eventually they scoot and all will be well in the kingdom. Those with wee ones or with limited mobility will be happy to reach Myrtle Falls, earn their gold star, and head back the way they came, while others will want to continue.

Back on the Skyline Trail, continue east, cross the classic wooden bridge, and swoon your little heart out at the mountain behind the playful stream and colorful wildflowers. You might start purring if you aren't careful. In 0.1 mile past Myrtle Falls, arrive at a well-signed junction with the Golden Gate Trail. Yes, that challenging series of switchbacks in the meadows is where you are going, but don't fret with sweat yet, it's not as bad as it looks. The trail soothes you with nearby bouncing creeklets and hilarious marmots spread out like pancakes on nearby sun-warmed rocks. Again, the flowers will melt you.

In 0.9 mile from turning off the Skyline Trail, find yourself at the top of the slope, once again joining the Skyline Trail; the Golden Gate Trail is a breathtaking shortcut! Here you have options. You can go left (north) and wander higher on the ridge, or turn right (south) and begin descending, completing the loop. True alpine scenery greets you with barren hillsides, glacial deposits, and little swamps teeming with seasonal flowers, such as Lewis's monkeyflower, varietal mosses, and mountain daisy.

The Golden Gate got its name from Paul H. Sceva, the president and general manager of Rainier National Park Company, the primary

A well-defined pathway leads you ever higher on the Golden Gate Trail.

concessionaire for the park from 1916–49. In his colorful writings he said it was a gateway because "the trail on terra ferma [sic] ended and you stepped onto the Paradise Glacier." Those looking for the glacier are out of luck as today's trail stays on terra firma (firm land), but thankfully still wanders through plenty of interesting things to see.

In 0.6 mile from the top of the Golden Gate and Skyline trails, arrive at the signed Paradise Glacier Trail heading off to the left (northeast). Make a note to come back and check that out another day, or scoot up it if time and energy are in your favor (Hike 79); for now, keep on grooving!

Boom! Before you know what hit you, your eyeballs are fixed on the historic Stevens–Van Trump stone-and-concrete monument bench. In 1921, the Mountaineers and Mazamas hiking clubs constructed this masterpiece in honor of the first men to reach the summit of Mount Rainier. Hazard Stevens and P. B. (no, not peanut butter but Philemon Beecher) Van Trump made their summit bid in 1870, much to the dismay of their Native American guide, Sluiskin. Native American folklore held that the summit of Mount Rainier contained a lake of fire, so when Sluiskin reached this spot, he would not go any farther. In fact, he was so concerned for the safety of the climbing party that he pleaded with them not to go, claiming that if they went they'd be punished by demons. When they returned, he was distrustful of them, assuming they were ghosts or evil souls. When he finally realized they were the same men as before, he praised them greatly, shouting, "Skookum tillicum! Skookum tillicum!" meaning "strong men with brave hearts."

With your mind wandering back in time, continue on your way and ooh and aah over the masses of wildflowers and the jagged peaks of the Tatoosh Range in the distance. Continue following the Skyline Trail, passing both the Lakes Trail and the 4th Crossing Trail, until a small ascent puts you back where you started. All of this grandeur and an ice-cream cone from the visitors center might just make for the most perfect day on the planet!

78 Nisqually Vista Loop

RATING/ DIFFICULTY	LOOP	ELEV GAIN/ HIGH POINT	SEASON
★★★/1	1.2 miles	240 feet/ 5405 feet	July–Oct

Maps: Green Trails Mount Rainier Wonderland No. 269SX, Mount Rainier East No. 270; **Contact:** Mount Rainier National Park, Longmire Wilderness Information Center, Henry M. Jackson Visitors Center; **Permit:** Mount Rainier National Park Pass or America the Beautiful Pass; **Notes:** Watch for sudden changing weather. Steep cliffs are tempting for photos but extremely hazardous, so stay on trails. Arrive early as parking can be challenging, especially on weekends. Stock and pets prohibited; **GPS:** N 46 47.102 W 121 44.498

 Paradise has some hard hiking, especially for those with limited mobility or wee ones toddling hand in hand with their folks. Thankfully, the Nisqually Vista Trail is much easier than most in this area and is paved, although it does have its share of ups and downs. Additionally, viewpoints provide opportunities to learn about the Nisqually Glacier and get a front-row view of its deep valley below the trail.

A young buck checks out some hikers as autumn sets in along the Nisqually Vista Loop.

GETTING THERE

From Ashford, drive 6.3 miles to the Nisqually Entrance of Mount Rainier National Park. Enter the park through the entrance booth and proceed 18 miles, passing the Longmire area, and bear left at Stevens Canyon Road to remain on Longmire–Paradise Road. Park at one of the few parking lots or on the side of the one-way road east of the Paradise Inn. During busy summer months, arrive early as parking gets full. The Henry M. Jackson Visitors Center has restrooms, a picnic area, a snack bar, a gift shop, and many interesting exhibits.

ON THE TRAIL

Several trails lead to Nisqually Vista. The first way to reach it is by walking to the northwest of the first parking lot you come to when approaching the Paradise area. If that makes your head and your compass spin and/or you want a more scenic route, head outside the Henry M. Jackson Visitors Center and locate the big, beautiful stone staircase etched with the poetic verses of John Muir. After ascending his prose, turn left and follow the trail as it passes several trail junctions until, at last, all signs point to the Nisqually Vista Trail.

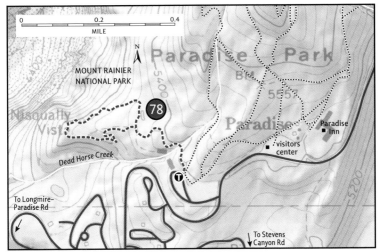

Go in either direction on the loop, taking the time to stop and smell the sun on the warm subalpine firs and watch for the deer that frolic in these open meadows and sample a smorgasbord of every plant in sight. The loop includes a small pond that attracts a variety of songbirds, such as golden-crowned kinglets that sometimes serenade you with a soundtrack of peeps and chirps.

When wildflowers are at their prime, there is almost no place easier to reach to take pictures of fragrant, rainbow carpets of flowers, such as lupine, Sitka valerian, arnica, beargrass, bistort, aster, and the list goes on and on. Swoon in the summer, but if you can't make it then, don't despair! In the fall, huckleberry bushes on this loop turn a brilliant burgundy while other perennials seem to try to one-up them with shades of gold and amber.

Several viewpoints provide interpretive signs and lookouts with opportunities to view the deep deposits of glacial debris below the trail. Rainier itself shows up on clear days, providing good photo opportunities of the volcano looming in the background while you pose with your hiking buddies. You can bypass the lookouts with old-growth trees trying to be the star of the show but on second thought, why not take a picture of them? It makes them feel wanted!

When you've looped the loop, wander back the way you came or let your feet trot off onto another trail and see more of Paradise, true to its name.

79 Paradise Glacier

RATING/ DIFFICULTY	ROUNDTRIP	ELEV GAIN/ HIGH POINT	SEASON
★★★★/3	5.6 miles	1030 feet/ 6400 feet	mid-July– Oct

Maps: Green Trails Mount Rainier Wonderland No. 269SX, Mount Rainier East No. 270; **Contact:** Mount Rainier National Park, Longmire Wilderness Information Center, Henry M. Jackson Visitors Center; **Permit:**

Mount Rainier National Park Pass or America the Beautiful Pass; **Notes:** Watch for sudden changing weather. Permanent snowfields may contain weak snow bridges and failing ice caves, so be safe and avoid all hazards. Arrive early as parking can be challenging, especially on weekends. Stock and pets prohibited; **GPS:** N 46 47.102 W 121 44.498

A few decades ago, the highlight of this trail was the most extensive system of glacial ice caves in the world, but sadly, due to glacial recession, they are no longer here. Should you still go? Yes! The trail to the site of the former caves is scenic and the panoramic views and Mount Rainier vistas are still worthy and impressive. Kids will love throwing snowballs on the permanent snowfields while adults can enjoy a peaceful picnic perched on rocks near the moraine.

GETTING THERE

From Ashford, drive 6.3 miles to the Nisqually Entrance of Mount Rainier National Park. Enter the park through the entrance booth and proceed 18 miles, passing the Longmire area, and bear left at Stevens Canyon Road to remain on Longmire–Paradise Road. Park at one of the few parking lots or on the side of the one-way road east of the Paradise Inn. During busy summer months, arrive early as parking gets full. The Henry M. Jackson Visitors Center has restrooms, a picnic area, a snack bar, a gift shop, and many interesting exhibits.

The journey is as impressive as the destination on the Paradise Glacier Trail.

ON THE TRAIL

You can hop on the trail either from the Jackson Visitors Center, the Paradise Inn, or the 4th Crossing Trail (just off Paradise Valley Road). Most folks park at Paradise and follow the Skyline Trail to the northeast, passing the not-to-be-missed spur to the photo op of Myrtle Falls in 0.5 mile. Just beyond the trail spur to Myrtle Falls, cross Edith Creek, with splendid Rainier views, and continue past the

Golden Gate Trail junction. Everywhere you look it's a feast for the eyes, with green meadows, brilliant summer wildflowers, red-in-autumn berry bushes, and, always, Mount Rainier towering above.

The trail descends a ravine and meets up with the 4th Crossing Trail and a couple of dribbling creeks before getting its climb on again and switchbacking up to pass a junction with the Lakes Trail (Hike 58), 1.4 miles from

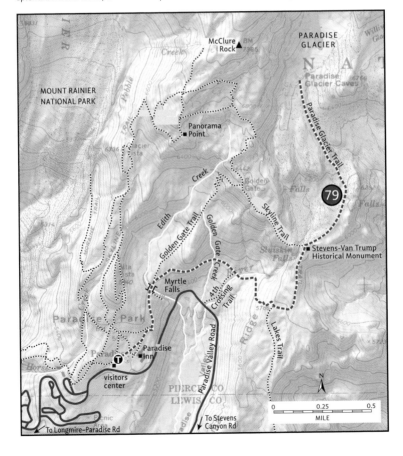

where you started. Make a note to come back and check out this beautiful hike another time; it's well worth your bootprints!

Views of the jagged Tatoosh Range to your right are magnificent and continue to be so behind you as you turn north to climb higher and higher. Stop and look back every so often for gorgeous vistas.

In 1.8 miles from Paradise, arrive at the historic Stevens–Van Trump stone-and-concrete monument bench. In 1921, the Mountaineers and Mazamas hiking clubs constructed this bench as a tribute to the first men to reach the summit of Mount Rainier. Hazard Stevens and P. B. (no, not peanut butter but Philemon Beecher) Van Trump hired a Native American guide named Sluiskin to help them find the best approach for their summit bid in 1870. In this very spot, Sluiskin stopped dead in his tracks and refused to go any farther. He begged the men not to continue as folklore held that the summit contained a lake of fire and anyone who attempted the climb would be punished by demons. Ignoring his pleas, the men headed off onto Paradise Glacier and up to the top. When they returned, Sluiskin couldn't believe his eyes and at first thought they were ghosts. When he came to realize that they were the same men as before, he shouted "Skookum tillicum! Skookum tillicum!" meaning "strong men with brave hearts."

With history swirling in your head, reach the signed junction with the Paradise Glacier Trail just beyond the monument, turn right, and begin your gentle ascent. Hoary marmots scramble about nibbling on clumps of vegetation and preparing for winter hibernation while a small tarn to the right reflects the ice-cream-cone summit of Mount Rainier.

Follow the glacial moraine for 2.5 miles to a sign noting the end of the maintained trail.

Snowy footprints, or in late summer, a stony but easily discernible path, lead beyond the sign for another 0.3 mile. Stevens Creek is to the right and the shoulders of McClure Rock are to the left. Bust out your salty-sweet snacks and enjoy reveling in the beauty that is the high country before heading back.

EXTENDING YOUR HIKE

If time permits, make a loop! Follow the Paradise Glacier Trail back to the Skyline Trail and continue northwest. Take the Golden Gate Trail back to Paradise or stay on the Skyline as it rounds Mount Rainier's southern flanks, reaching Panorama Point and eventually making it back to Paradise the long way.

80 Skyline Trail and Panorama Point

RATING/ DIFFICULTY	LOOP	ELEV GAIN/ HIGH POINT	SEASON
★★★★★/4	5.6 miles	1700 feet/ 7075 feet	mid-July– Oct

Maps: Green Trails Mount Rainier Wonderland No. 269SX, Mount Rainier East No. 270; **Contact:** Mount Rainier National Park, Longmire Wilderness Information Center, Henry M. Jackson Visitors Center; **Permit:** Mount Rainier National Park Pass or America the Beautiful Pass; **Notes:** Watch for sudden changing weather. Snow can linger well into Aug in heavy snow years, so get trail updates at visitors center. Arrive early as parking can be challenging, especially on weekends. Stock and pets prohibited; **GPS:** N 46 47.102 W 121 44.498

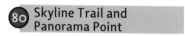 *The Skyline Trail is at the very heart of the majestic views, rainbow wildflowers, and awe-inspiring magnificence*

of Mount Rainier National Park. Hiking it may spoil you for almost any future endeavor! You'll have to work hard to earn your views, as this puppy climbs and climbs, but as much as your lungs will cry out for more air, your heart will swell with richness as you take in the panoramic brilliance all around you. Bring your trekking poles to save your knees on the descent, and when you are done, you'll have a perma-grin that will last all year.

GETTING THERE

From Ashford, drive 6.3 miles to the Nisqually Entrance of Mount Rainier National Park. Enter the park through the entrance booth and proceed 18 miles, passing the Longmire area, and bear left at Stevens Canyon Road to remain on Longmire–Paradise Road. Park at one of the few parking lots or on the side of the one-way road east of the Paradise Inn. During busy summer months, arrive early as parking gets full. The Henry M. Jackson Visitors Center has restrooms, a picnic area, a snack bar, a gift shop, and many interesting exhibits.

ON THE TRAIL

The trail starts out, as so many do, by following the steps etched with the beautiful prose of John Muir north of the Henry M. Jackson Visitors Center. Follow the signs for the Skyline Trail or Panorama Point at each junction and keep huffing and puffing northbound. Just when you think you might suck all the air out of the vicinity, views force you to stop and pull out the camera. This place is world renowned for seasonal wildflowers, such as western anemone (look for a white seed pod), Sitka valerian (white and fragrant), lupine (purple), paintbush (magenta or pink), and more, that put on a luxuriant show in these lofty heights. Hoary marmots alert each other to your presence by whistling a single loud note that will jolt you into next Tuesday if you get blindsided. "Climb Every Mountain" plays in your head and you are tempted to spin in circles . . . if only you could stop wheezing!

In 1.8 miles, reach famed Panorama Point. While the view is pleasant, I can't say it knocks your socks off completely; there are better vistas (see what I mean about getting spoiled?). Don't get me wrong, though, you'd melt into a puddle with the sights were it not for so many other ones you've already seen! It does offer some interpretive signs, panoramas of the Tatoosh Range, and a privy, which, when your bladder is screaming, is a welcome sight.

If time and gumption permit, the Skyline Trail is a must-do when visiting Paradise.

The official Skyline Trail, also occasionally called the low Skyline Trail, is almost always closed and is roped off during summer months as it poses a hazard due to steep, icy snowfields. Instead, keep climbing to better views, safer passages, and what some now refer to as the high Skyline.

At 2.1 miles arrive at a trail junction with the Pebble Creek Trail. This trail leads you up and away to the soaring heights of the Muir Snowfield and Camp Muir (Hike 75), the base camp for those taking the technical route to the summit via the Disappointment Cleaver Route. The Disappointment Cleaver Route, or the DC Route, as the cool kids call it, is the most popular and most-climbed route to the summit. Guide services and privateers alike rope up for the technical climb involved to reach the highest point in Washington State. All of those folks carrying

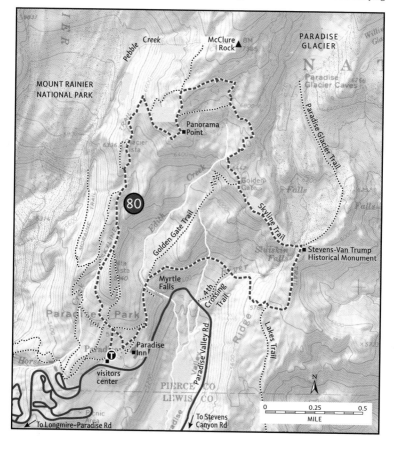

big packs, ice axes, and helmets are headed there to show the mountain who's boss. Bid them adieu and keep rolling onward along the high Skyline Trail, reaching a slightly more relaxed grade.

You're in high alpine country, dotted with giant boulders and clumps of vegetation struggling in the short growing season. Golden-mantled ground squirrels beg you for food occasionally, batting their eyelashes and twitching their noses in hopes that you'll drop a nut from your gorp. Tell them it's illegal and resist their chubby cheeks. Downhill you go now!

In 3.2 miles from where you started, arrive at the Golden Gate Trail junction. If you are craving ice cream at the snack bar and simply can't resist, this trail is a shortcut back to the visitors center. If you have more willpower, pop a chunk of chocolate in your mouth and see if you can convince yourself to follow the whole Skyline!

At 3.8 miles, arrive at a turn for the Paradise Glacier Trail (Hike 79) and tell yourself to come back and hike it when you have more time and gumption. Or, if the world is your oyster, do it now!

Onward you go, to the historic Stevens–Van Trump stone-and-concrete monument bench. In 1921, the Mountaineers and Mazamas hiking clubs constructed this masterpiece in honor of the first men to reach the summit of Mount Rainier. Hazard Stevens and P. B (no, not peanut butter, but rather Philemon Beecher) Van Trump made their summit bid in 1870. Their Native American mountain guide, Sluiskin, reached this spot with them and refused to go any farther, citing Native American folklore that held that the mountain contained a lake of fire and that demons would punish them if they continued. When they carried on, he was distraught. When they returned, Sluiskin could hardly believe his eyes and at first thought they were ghosts. Once he realized that they were still human, he praised them, shouting "Skookum tillicum! Skookum tillicum!" meaning "strong men with brave hearts."

With history bouncing around in your brain and the Tatoosh Range staring you in the eyes, make your way south, reaching a junction with the Lakes Trail 4.2 miles from where you started. Continue on the Skyline Trail, descending to a junction with the 4th Crossing Trail and then climbing a small rise to pass the junctions with the Golden Gate and Myrtle Falls trails until, finally, your feet lead you back to the John Muir steps and the busy bustle of folks enjoying the visitors center. What a day!

Appendix I: Permits and Land Management Agencies

Mount Rainier National Park

55210 238th Avenue East
Ashford, WA 98304
360-569-2211
www.nps.gov/mora

VISITORS CENTERS

Longmire Museum
360-569-6575

Henry M. Jackson Memorial Visitors Center at Paradise
360-569-6571

Ohanapecosh Visitors Center
360-569-6581

Sunrise Visitors Center
360-663-2425

WILDERNESS AND CLIMBING INFORMATION CENTERS

Longmire Wilderness Information Center
360-569-6650

White River
360-569-6670

Carbon River Ranger Station
360-829-9639

Paradise Climbing Information Center (Guide House)
360-569-6641

FOREST SERVICE OFFICES

Gifford Pinchot National Forest
1501 E. Evergreen Boulevard
Vancouver, WA 98661
360-891-5000
www.fs.usda.gov/giffordpinchot

Cowlitz Valley Ranger District
10024 US Highway 12
PO Box 670
Randle, WA 98377
360-497-1103
www.fs.usda.gov/recarea/giffordpinchot
/recreation/recarea/?recid=31180

Mount Baker–Snoqualmie National Forest
2930 Wetmore Avenue, Suite 3A
Everett, WA, 98201
425-783-6000
800-627-0062
www.fs.usda.gov/main/mbs/home

Enumclaw office
450 Roosevelt Avenue E.
Enumclaw, WA 98022
360-825-6585
www.fs.usda.gov/detail
/mbs/about-forest
/offices/?cid=stelprdb5238242

Silver Creek Visitors Center
69211 SR 410
Enumclaw, WA 98022
360-663-2284
www.fs.usda.gov/detail
/mbs/about-forest
/offices/?cid=stelprdb5302867

Snoqualmie Ranger District
902 SE North Bend Way, Bldg 1
North Bend, WA 98045
425-888-1421
www.fs.usda.gov/detail
/mbs/about-forest
/offices/?cid=fsbdev7_001660

Okanogan–Wenatchee National Forest Headquarters
215 Melody Lane
Wenatchee, WA 98801
509-664-9200
www.fs.usda.gov/okawen/

Naches Ranger District
10237 Highway 12
Naches, WA 98937
509-486-2186
www.fs.usda.gov/recarea/okawen
/recarea/?recid=57121

WASHINGTON STATE PARKS

Washington State Parks & Recreation Commission
https://parks.state.wa.us/

Other Information

CAMPING AND LODGING

Frontcountry campground reservations
www.recreation.gov

In-Park Lodging Reservations
www.mtrainierguestservices.com

PASSES

America the Beautiful/Interagency Pass
www.nps.gov/planyourvisit/passes.htm

Northwest Forest Pass
www.fs.usda.gov/main/r6
/passes-permits/recreation

Washington State Discover Pass
https://discoverpass.wa.gov

SIGHTSEEING TOURS/OUTFITTERS

Crystal Mountain Resort Gondola/ Summit House
www.crystalmountainresort.com
/summer/summer-activities
/mt-rainier-gondola/
www.crystalmountainresort.com
/plan-your-trip/where-to-eat
/summit-house/

Discover Nature
www.tourmtrainier.com
Customized Tours
www.toursofseattle.com

Evergreen Escapes
www.evergreenescapes.com
/mt-rainier-day-trip-seattle-hike
-snowshoe

Tours Northwest
www.toursnorthwest.com/tour
/mt-rainier/

WILDFLOWER GUIDE
www.nps.gov/mora/learn/nature
/wildflowers.htm

Appendix II: Conservation and Trail Organizations

Back Country Horsemen of Washington
PO Box 1132
Ellensburg, WA 98926
www.bchw.org

Mount Rainier National Park Associates
www.mrnpa.org

The Mountaineers
7700 Sand Point Way NE
Seattle, WA 98115
206-521-6001
www.mountaineers.org

Northwest Youth Corps
2621 Augusta Street
Eugene, OR 97403
541-349-5055
www.nwyouthcorps.org

Pacific Crest Trail Association
1331 Garden Highway
Sacramento, CA 95833
916-285-1846
www.pcta.org

Sierra Club
Washington State Chapter
2101 Webster Street, Suite 1300
Oakland, CA 94612
415-977-5500
www.sierraclub.org/washington

Student Conservation Association
SCA Northwest
1265 South Main Street, Suite 210
Seattle, WA 98144
206-324-5055
www.thesca.org

Washington Conservation Corps
300 Desmond Drive SE
Lacey, WA 98503
360-407-6000
www.ecy.wa.gov

Washington's National Park Fund
1904 Third Avenue, Suite 400
Seattle, WA 98101
206-623-2063
www.wnpf.org

Washington Trails Association
702 2nd Avenue, Suite 300
Seattle, WA 98104
206-625-1367
www.wta.org

Appendix III: Recommended Reading

Asars, Tami. *Hiking the Wonderland Trail.* Seattle: Mountaineers Books, 2012.

Eisenberg, Micky and Gene Yore. *Guide to 100 Peaks in Mount Rainier National Park,* Version 5.0. Seattle: Mountaineers Books, 2014.

Gauthier, Mike. *Mount Rainier: A Climbing Guide,* 3rd ed. Seattle: Mountaineers Books, 2017.

Harlin, John III and James Martin. *Mount Rainier: Notes & Images from Our Iconic Mountain.* Seattle: Mountaineers Books, 2012.

Loewen, Bree. *Found: A Life in Search and Rescue.* Seattle: Mountaineers Books, 2017.

———. *Pickets and Dead Men: Seasons on Rainier.* Seattle: Mountaineers Books, 2009.

Molenaar, Dee. *The Challenge of Rainier: A Record of the Explorations and Ascents, Triumphs and Tragedies on the Northwest's Greatest Mountain,* 4th ed. Seattle: Mountaineers Books, 2011.

Schmoe, Floyd. *A Year in Paradise,* 2nd ed. Seattle: Mountaineers Books, 1999.

Whittaker, Jim. *A Life on the Edge.* Seattle: Mountaineers Books, 2013.

Whittaker, Leif. *My Old Man and the Mountain.* Seattle: Mountaineers Books, 2016.

Whittaker, Lou. Lou Whittaker: *Memoirs of a Mountain Guide.* Seattle: Mountaineers Books, 1994.

Index

About the Author

Tami Asars is an outdoor writer and nature photographer living in the Cascade foothills of Washington State with her husband, Vilnis, and her rough collie, Scout. She is the author of *Hiking the Wonderland Trail* (Mountaineers Books, 2012), *Day Hiking Mount Adams and Goat Rocks* (Mountaineers Books, 2014), *Hiking the Pacific Crest Trail: Washington* (Mountaineers Books, 2016), and is a contributor and columnist for a host of outdoor publications and online hiking resources. She is almost as passionate about nature photography as she is about hiking, and her photos have appeared in a variety of periodicals, including *City Dog, Washington Trails, Washington Magazine*, and in the city of North Bend, Washington's branding campaign.

As a former employee of REI (Recreational Equipment Inc), she taught classes for nearly nine years on outdoor pursuits like the where-tos and how-tos of backpacking, hiking, and long-distance trails. She has also served as a professional guide, teaching and showing folks of all skill levels the wonders of backpacking in the Pacific Northwest. When she's not in her office tapping at her keyboard, you can find her on one of the many trails in Washington State, from the rugged coastline of Olympic National Park to the dense green forests of the Cascade Mountains, where she's explored almost every nook and cranny. For more information or to drop her a line, please visit www.tamiasars.com.

1% for Trails—Outdoor Nonprofits in Partnership

Where would we be without trails? Not very far into the wilderness.

That's why Mountaineers Books designates 1 percent of the sales of select guidebooks in our *Day Hiking* series toward volunteer trail maintenance. Since launching this program, we've contributed more than $22,000 toward improving trails.

For this book, our 1 percent of sales is going to **Washington Trails Association** (WTA). WTA hosts more than 750 work parties throughout Washington's Cascades and Olympics each year, with volunteers clearing downed logs after spring snowmelt, cutting away brush, retreading worn stretches of trail, and building bridges and turnpikes. Their efforts are essential to the land managers who maintain thousands of acres on shoestring budgets.

Mountaineers Books donates many books to nonprofit recreation and conservation organizations. Our 1% for Trails campaign is one more way we can help fellow nonprofit organizations as we work together to get more people outside, to both enjoy and protect our wild public lands.

If you'd like to support Mountaineers Books and our nonprofit partnership programs, please visit our website to learn more or email mbooks@mountaineersbooks.org.